SAP

- A Map of The Minefield

by
Stephen Birchall

authorHOUSE™

1663 LIBERTY DRIVE, SUITE 200
BLOOMINGTON, INDIANA 47403
(800) 839-8640
WWW.AUTHORHOUSE.COM

First published by AuthorHouse 08/02/05

ISBN: 1-4208-7387-3 (sc)

Printed in the United States of America
Bloomington, Indiana

This book is printed on acid-free paper.

Contents

Why should you buy this book

Who is the author?

Writing a book like this, especially because it relates to something as hotly debated as SAP R/3, will always raise questions such as, "Who does the author think he is?" "Everyone thinks they are an SAP expert why should I believe anything I read in this book?", "Out of so many books that have been written on the subject of SAP, why should I buy this one?" etc., etc. Well, to be honest, these are really good questions and ones that I too would ask if I was considering buying a book on SAP.

To help explain why I think it is worth your time reading this book I have to explain who I am and what my background is, especially relating to the world of computer systems. Hopefully this will enable you to make a judgement call as to whether it is worth buying this book or not. This section will detail my credentials and this is probably the hardest section of the whole book by far. I don't like talking about myself but I have to explain my experience in full and I am not the type of person who finds it easy to "sing my own praises". However I cannot expect you to spend your valuable time reading a book written by someone who claims to know SAP "reasonably well" so I will be open and honest.

I am 51 years old, born in Liverpool and after 11 years of switching from one job to another and running a few small businesses I decided to move into the world of I.T. I trained to become a Systems Analyst and in 1980 I joined a small software company in Windsor facing the Queen's residence, Windsor Castle (this was quite a big change from the streets of Liverpool). I was placed as (so I thought) a Junior Systems Analyst on a major project working on the Logistics elements of a system that was

1

going to be "built from scratch" (no SAP then). I later found out that I was actually taken on to replace a senior System Analyst who was deemed to be unable to do the job, this was a definite case of being "thrown in at the deep end. It was to be a COBOL, CICS, DL1 system covering all areas of the business including Sales, Purchasing, stock and Finance (as an SAP implementation would). I was very fortunate to start with a project like this because I was able to experience the building of an integrated system, function by function and program by program. Every function, every screen, every key stroke had to be designed from scratch.

What made the task easier was the fact that the business people on the project, particularly the senior managers, members of the Board and the decision makers, were really sure of what they wanted and they were very experienced in their business and the processes involved. Another benefit was that it was my first I.T. project and so I had no preconceived idea of what a system like this should do, this enabled me to design the system from a non-I.T. perspective while at the same time being fully aware of the I.T. restraints and design concepts so I was able to start from a blank sheet of paper and see the requirements from a business users viewpoint and I was therefore able to design a solution that was based on what the users actually needed, not just the easiest technical solution to implement. It meant that I had to rely on the strongest and most useful skill of all, plain old common sense. It also meant that I listened to the users very closely and tried to figure out exactly what they needed, not just what they were asking for. I had to rely on the fact that they knew their business and they did not let me down. This resulted in a system that was built by the users with help from the I.T. department and not the other way around (This is also the best approach for an SAP implementation).

The resulting system was (in their words) a great success and my several years there were very educational and helped me establish a really workable approach to systems design..

I had already turned "contractor" during that time, I had complained about being used as a senior systems analyst and yet being paid as a junior and for some reason they suggested that I leave my "permanent" job and become a contractor with them. They said that they could not give me the extra salary but they could pay me a contract rate of a senior analyst. That was a strange week, I went home on Friday night and came back to the same job, same desk and same software house but I was earning twice as much.

After this project I went to work for several other companies as contract Systems Analyst. In all of these I also found that the same approach worked perfectly, understand the situation from a business perspective first then interpret this from a technical viewpoint and definitely not the other way around. I was an analyst after all and so did not have to be technical or skilled in a certain programming language or operating system etc. I was meant to be a link between the two areas, the business and the technical programmers etc.

I continued to work as a contractor until the late '80s when the recession hit. The contract work dried up. So in 1989 I switched back to "permanent" work and was given a position of a Team Leader in the I.T. department for a major German chemical company. A few months after joining I was told that they were going to implement a new system called SAP and I was asked to be the project leader. After a bit of digging around (the internet was not really an option in 1989) I found out what SAP was. The idea seemed so right and logical (common sense raises its head again) and very much in line with the approach that I had used so far. Another thing that seemed to make a great deal of sense was the fact that it was basically a "packaged solution". Why go to one company and design a system from scratch and then go to another similar company and ask the same questions all over again and build a very similar system again. Why not write a system that was flexible enough to fit most businesses and tweak it each time instead of re-writing it from scratch. I was sold on the idea and said yes the very next day.

The first thing they did was to send us on every SAP course that there was available. I spent 7 weeks in their Weybridge training centre being "SAP'd". The first course was fantastic, we had a really good instructor, she knew the system inside out, was a great trainer, a clear speaker, very intelligent, well educated (and very kind on the eyes). The second course couldn't have been more different, the trainer knew SAP reasonably well but couldn't teach and "froze" every few minutes, it was hell and SAP UK had to replace her at short notice. I was beginning to think that perhaps the move to SAP was a mistake after all. Anyway the replacement was OK and we struggled through the second week. From that point on we had an excellent trainer for the remainder of the 7 weeks and all was well. It didn't take long to see just how good the SAP system was and this was the old R2 mainframe version, which, looking back was still in the early stages of development.

The project was a "Big bang" implementation of all of the basic modules, including the Plant Maintenance module (which was quite rare in 1990).

The Project manager was appointed but he had no I.T. experience and so in addition to being the Project leader for the Logistics functionality I was able to be heavily involved in the overall project management and established the approach that we were going to take for the implementation.

The project went well, despite the "Help" from a consultant from one of the big five consultancies who hadn't yet grasped that SAP was very different from the "scratch built" systems. She was treating it as a technical project and was missing out on the huge advantages of a packaged solution that could be designed by the business instead of the I.T. department. I managed to influence the approach that was adopted an the project went very well and was on time and within budget. The users were happy and the board were happy.

Following the implementation things went quiet and so I started looking around for another project. At this time the SAP market was becoming very busy and so it was not long before I found an interesting challenge. It was a Lead Consultant role focussed on material management and MRP (Material Requirements Planning) for a large confectionery company. The project was actually supposed to be just a roll out of an existing implementation but it turned out to be far more than that.

I was asked to estimate the time needed for this "rollout" and I put the figure at just under a year, this was not well received initially because the rollouts so far, to France and Germany had taken around 3 to 4 months each. I explained the logic behind my estimate. They had decided to implement the system in their plant in Holland first. They had decided that this site was small enough to make the project manageable and the site used all of the elements of the business including Sales, Purchasing, Production, Finance etc. The French and German plants were a similar size to the Holland plant and so the rollouts were relatively straightforward. But the UK plant was bigger than all of the other plants put together and the business processes were different. In the other European plants one user would carry out several tasks but in the UK in many processes there were several users involved in one task. This meant that the system had to be changed quite significantly and so I was going to take a lot longer.

The project included a need to use full MRP functionality to manage their stock and procurement processes and I had heard it said that SAP's

MRP was not that great and so I was a little unsure as to how this would work out. The rumours were unfounded, the SAP functionality relating to MRP was very powerful and very flexible but it did suffer from a common SAP problem, the power and the flexibility resulted in complexity. There were no manuals that really covered how to get the best out of MRP in SAP, there were some that would help with how to use individual configuration options etc. but nothing really helped explain the concept and high level design options.

It was an enjoyable project, the company's approach to SAP was perfect, they wanted the absolute maximum from the system but they wanted it without modifying the standard SAP software. We could use every bit of configuration we wanted but using non-standard transactions etc. was not an option. This is where I started to discover just how big the benefits of using standard SAP are and these are covered in detail in later sections.

It was such a success that the resulting UK implementation was rolled back out into the rest of the European plants.

My next project could not have been different to the previous two, it was a case of going from one extreme to the other. The company involved was a small division of a large chemical company that specialised in personal / grooming products. It was also my first R/3 project and I had been told by an ex colleague that it was "just like" R/2 but based on the PC Server concept with a better user interface. In reality the differences weren't major but they were big enough to mean a new learning curve to negotiate.

The client needed someone with experience to guide their own staff, who were relatively new to the SAP world. Unfortunately the company had already implemented SAP and had missed the whole concept. The users had asked to retain their legacy systems and not have them replaced by SAP and this meant that all of the input and output of SAP was carried out via legacy screens. Effectively SAP was running in the background and the results of an MRP run were being fed back to the legacy systems. This resulted in interfaces everywhere and it meant that they had the worst of both approaches, all of the complexity of a powerful SAP system without the benefit of the integration and flexibility in addition to all of the problems of running lots of interfaces. I did what I could to help the project and turned down an offer of an extension, I would rather be out of work than have to keep explaining to the users that the SAP system was not the cause of all of their problems, especially because I could obviously not criticise the approach that they had adopted.

The next contract was pivotal in my career but little did I know what I was getting into when I had the first call from the agency. I was in my final week at the previous contract and even though the SAP market was still quite busy I was getting worried that I might have to spend some time "between contracts". The agency rang, it was Martin Rush (Then of Montreal Associates and now a Director of the Square One agency, which is one of the best SAP agencies in today's marketplace), he sounded as if he knew the SAP basic functionality, which was quite rare for an agency. This was the Thursday with one day left on my old contract. He said that he had "another project to start on Monday morning", "Great" I said, "where do I go?", "At the SAP UK training centre in Weybridge, you are on a 5 day MM course". I thought that sounded strange, clients do not normally pay for you to attend training courses. I queried it with Martin, the response was, "Oh sorry Steve, you are not attending the course, you are DELIVERING it!". Oh well, I like a challenge and in reality I had been trying to teach people just how good the SAP system was in all of the projects I had been on so far and so I thought that I would give it a go. I asked about how I was going to prepare for the course and I was told that they were not open over the weekend but I could get in at 7:30 am on the Monday morning. The course was due to start at 10am and so this would give me a couple of hours to prepare for a 5 day course. I didn't even know the basics of how to operate the student / teacher switching of the screens and which systems to use, how the data for the exercises was managed etc.. This was definitely going to be a case of "sink or swim" but this would not be the first time and so I said yes.

The staff at the training centre were great, they did all they could to help me and so 10 am came and so did the nerves, but I got through the first day, which was mainly an overview of SAP and so I managed that without any problem. This then gave me the evening to prepare for the next day and so on until the Friday. I felt it went reasonably well, I remembered the 7 weeks training I had received and I just tried to deliver the kind of course that I would have wanted to have myself. When the evaluations were collected they were all fine and I was asked to deliver another course the following week and so on. In the end I was there for over three years teaching every single day apart from Christmas and holidays. At the end of the very first week I was so drained that I thought that I would be burnt-out by the end of 4 weeks or so, but after I had hit that "wall" I was able to continue and I thoroughly enjoyed my time there. I felt it was a bit like being a Rolls Royce salesman, the product was is so good that it sells itself and you did not have to hide anything from the "customers". I was able to show how good the system was without fear of meeting any of the attendees later on in my career and having them say that I lied or exaggerated the benefits, and so far I have met up with many ex attendees and every time it has been a pleasant event, no negative comments or accusations of my having painted a rosy view of SAP.

During my last year or so as a trainer at SAP they launched the SAP Academies and the Certification exams. I was asked to deliver the MM academy, all 5 weeks of it. Basically this was me talking about SAP all day Monday to Friday for 5 weeks and that was just focussed on MM. It does indicate just how much there is to learn about the SAP functionality, 5 weeks for one module and we didn't even get down to the finest detail of the functions. Delivering the academy helped me as much as it helped the students, it forced me into all of the corners of the system that I had not yet had to use. Subjects such as Supplier evaluation and FIFO / LIFO stock accounting used to be "black holes" to me, I had never had to use them, but thanks to the academy I had to get to know these remote areas of the system well enough to be able to teach them.

After teaching the first academy I thought that it would be a good idea to sit the certification exam myself. I was shocked when I saw the questions, they were more vague than I imagined and I was convinced that some of them were virtually impossible to get right. I managed to pass the exam with reasonable marks but I expressed my concerns to the staff at the training centre about the questions and they managed to get hold of a full set of the questions and answers for me. I read through each one and found that, in my view, far too many of the questions were impossible to get right, especially if you knew the subject well. There will always be some questions that are not perfect and some that may even be a little confusing but many of the exam questions were quite simply wrong. It looked like some of this could have been due to using multiple translations, the questions were often written in English and then translated into German and then back into the appropriate language for the examining country. In one example the exam question contained the phrase "When a receipt occurs stock is <u>reduced</u>" the wording should have stated "When an ISSUE occurs stock is reduced" and so anyone answering this question correctly would have actually have there answer marked as wrong. Errors like this are a fact of life and so when they were pointed out to SAP they investigated and corrected most of them immediately, but they disputed some of the others. After a lot of "email tennis" the remainder were corrected and even though some questions could be said to be still vague, the exam was now fair. Several months later I was invited to a meeting at the SAP HQ in Germany to discuss the exam and I was asked to write some more questions. It was more difficult than I imagined and so I felt a bit guilty about complaining so strongly about the original questions, but I managed to write some additional questions that are used in the certification exam.

Following this I delivered the whole 5 weeks of the MM academy a further eight times single-handed then a couple more that were shared with some new trainers who were going to take over after I left (I had been doing it for long enough and I needed a change).

My next contract was still with SAP UK but this time in their training offices acting as a curriculum manager helping with the courses and Academies, while they tried to recruit someone for the role. I helped manage the curriculum for a couple of months and during this time helped with the set up of the ABAP academy and the BW (Business Warehouse, also known as BIW Business Information Warehouse) academy. I sat in on the very first BW academy out of interest and managed to pass the certification exam. BW did however look as if it was not quite good enough to challenge any alternative BIW systems, but as with most of SAP's new software, it quickly caught up and now is good enough to be considered alongside the best, especially if used in conjunction with a solid SAP R/3 implementation.

Also during my time at SAP UK I was asked by a client to fill the role of SAP Integration manager for a Japanese printer manufacturer. I started working on the project three quarters of the way through the implementation and each of the main modules were nearing the first testing stages, but unfortunately there had been no real integration up to this point. The FI team had developed a chart of accounts that was totally different to the one that the MM team had been working to and this meant that when I had discovered this they had to start again and build a new chart of accounts. Other problems became apparent in the integration points between SD and MM This enabled me to see at first hand what happens if the integration aspects are not considered at the start of the implementation.

My next contract was for a home computer manufacturer (I nearly used the term "PC" but they don't like their machines to be called "PCs", perhaps you can guess who I am talking about?) and they wanted me to help them to develop a totally new approach to end-user SAP training. I developed a CD based solution that had a built in examination and management tools. I also developed the high-level training course materials for the total functionality that they were using and completed the task on time. I also helped the other consultants with some issues that they were having trouble resolving.

At this point the SAP job market was in its heyday and I managed to secure a very well paid contract as a lead SAP trainer for a large pharmaceutical company. I developed training courses for the MM, PP and WM modules. I then went on to delivery the courses and was selected as the only trainer to go to Singapore to deliver the training there. This was quite a challenge because they wanted me to deliver 4 weeks of training in one week. But the users in Singapore were very good and the task turned out to be not as bad as I had feared.

The company then opened a Competency centre and I was asked to act as SAP training manager. This was yet another challenge but for a different reason. Having a contractor as a manager in charge of "permanent" employees takes a lot of diplomacy and tact. It was made so much easier by the team of trainers I was responsible for, they were very professional and co-operative and they did not really think of me as a contractor. Part of the role involved sitting in on most of the high level meetings to represent the SAP training department and I was able to help establish the major processes that would be used throughout the competency centre. I also advised the Competency Centre manager on how to get the most out of SAP. I developed a training course that would explain what was so different about SAP and how to gain the best ROI (Return On Investment) possible. This project helped me understand how a competency centre operates and how valuable they are in the right circumstances.

My next contract was a return to consulting rather than training, I was to help a Japanese home electronics manufacturer with an upgrade from release 3.1 to release 4.6. Would I be repeating myself if I said that this was a challenge? Seriously though, this project was an eye-opener and made me change one of my long-held assumptions. The company had modified almost all of the SAP transactions and reports. I had seen a highly modified system before, but this time it was so highly modified that I was convinced that this could only spell trouble, especially when carrying out a significant upgrade. Almost every report and transaction was prefixed with a "Y" to indicate a modified function. I often joked that you didn't log on to SAP, you logged onto YSAP, which was a good question, why (Y?) SAP if you are going to rewrite everything?

I had heard so many times and from so many reliable sources that a highly modified SAP system would mean a nightmare task when a release upgrade was required. I could see how this would cause problems but what I hadn't taken into account was the amount of support that SAP now provide when upgrading. In the early days it was different, you were on your own and many organisations found that they were virtually unable to upgrade because of the extent of the modifications and the work involved upgrading the modifications.

The upgrade was well managed and went without any major problems. It took longer than a normal upgrade because of all of the modifications that had to be tested to see if they still worked but this was not an issue. This does not mean that I would ever recommend modifying the SAP code etc. but it does mean that I would not use the problems with future upgrades as a reason for not doing so. I have many other reasons for not modifying the system and these are covered in later sections.

The second project at this company involved an implementation using the Logistics Execution (LE) functionality within SAP at their Barcelona site. Logistics execution was a function that was a relatively recent addition to the SAP functionality and it includes very useful functions that assist with managing shipments and receiving of large quantities of orders, ideal for dealing with container loads etc.

It was at this point in time that the SAP job market started to slow and it was no longer a case of, if you can spell SAP you can get a contract. Towards the end of this contract I was getting several phone calls a day from Agencies and so felt confident that there was a lot of work around. After the contract finished, the phone calls continued but no genuine work appeared. This is something that you get used to as an SAP contractor, lots of phone calls from agencies with lots of opportunities but when you are genuinely looking, those opportunities seldom result in an interview.

After a few weeks I was told of an interesting opportunity, a company were taking an SAP implementation partner to court because they felt that the implementation had been a complete failure. The legal representatives of the partner wanted an SAP expert witness and so they were looking for someone with enough experience to be classed as an expert in the eyes of the court. I attended the interview and was offered the contract. It was £800 a day, working from home, it seemed almost too good to be true. Then on the day I was due to start I was informed that the case had been settled out of court and so I wasn't needed, I have always wondered if the interview process and hard questioning that was part of it had given them so much information that they already had a good impression as to how strong a case they had.

Because the job market was still depressed I had another short gap between contracts but was offered a few short-term projects, basically as a trouble shooter. It was interesting work and I was able to work on more varied SAP systems. The work covered 4 different companies who were all having problems in specific areas within SAP. I was able to offer alternative solutions that addressed the issue. In each case though, all that was wrong was that they had chosen the wrong option from the several available within SAP. The inbuilt flexibility that comes with SAP is often a double edged sword, it gives you several options which is very useful but that also means that you run the risk of choosing one that is not ideal.

Following these projects I went for an interview for a heavy building materials company as an Integration manager. I was not successful but the manager that interviewed me could see that I had a lot to offer and "engineered" a position for me. This was a fantastic project, they had implemented SAP already and were looking at additional phases that included more functionality. They had used a couple of different SAP partners and had built up a good internal SAP team of their own. I was able to advise them to take on the next project internally instead of using an SAP partner, I was convinced that they already had the appropriate skills in-house. This was a Plant Maintenance implementation and with a small team of one excellent PM consultant and good MM and FI consultants along with a small team of business users, headed by a very knowledgeable and enthusiastic Plant manager. The project went very well and the users were very happy with the resulting system. The low-cost high-quality implementation was mainly successful because we used standard SAP without modification. The business was switched-on enough to understand why we suggested that we should change some of their processes to match SAP's processes. It was during this project that I first got to know the Workflow module, this is a module that provides excellent functionality but can also cause major problems. Workflow is discussed in a later section.

During my time at this company I had the pleasure of spending a lot of time with the I.S. director Denis Sharp, explaining how to get the most out of SAP and talking about the company structure, which for this organisation was very complex. Denis was fantastic, he wanted to know everything I knew, he basically drained me of all of my knowledge churned it around and acted. It was very pleasant to work with a director that wanted to listen. He changed the approach to SAP to one where

SAP was the first option considered and only when SAP could not cover a particular process would other options be considered. The following implementations were carried out using internal staff and kept as close to standard SAP as possible and the results proved this to be the correct approach. The company went through a major reshuffle and my contract ended on schedule after two years.

The SAP job market was still quite depressed (although it was still a lot better than other areas of IT) and so I had another small gap between contracts. I went to Norway and then to Denmark to teach for SAP at their training centres for a few weeks. It was very enjoyable returning to the classroom after a few years. I managed a 6.7 average instructor score (out of 7) and so it was very tempting to consider going back into training, but I wanted to keep having a major influence on the way that SAP was being implemented and so I looked for more consulting/management roles. It is virtually impossible to get into an organisation at the top level as a contractor, for obvious reasons, and so it was a case of taking whatever came along and making the most of it.

The next project was yet another challenge (surprise, surprise), a large manufacturing organisation were changing the structure of their Company. They were switching the operation of their business from the UK to Switzerland (for tax reasons) and although on the face of this it was not a major change it did have a lot of complexities associated with the fact that they would now be acting as an "agent" in many of the standard SAP functions. The "parent" company would actually own all stock but that stock would still be stored in the original Plants (linked to another company) and all sales were now just a case of selling the products that belong to the parent company for a commission and so the cost of the items were no longer a factor. It was all fully legal and above-board and it saved the business a fortune in taxes. Other organisations have also switched to this "commissionaire" model and they have also achieved huge tax savings.

The main challenge was the go-live date, the company had been using an offshore company to carry out the changes to SAP and this was not working, they had reached a stage where they had decided that they would not achieve the go-live date unless they radically changed their approach. They contacted an agency (Square One) and asked for a team of four highly experienced people, 1 MM consultant, 1 SD, 1 FI and 1CO. I was brought in to do the MM work and the SD guy was someone I had taught on an academy several years ago, I instantly remembered him, he was a real larger than life character who was a really nice guy and so it was good to meet him again after all of this time. It was a bit embarrassing at first because he had been telling everyone that I was some kind of Guru when it comes to SAP. But it was nice to know that my course had worked for him.

The go-live date was so close that it was clear that we would have to come up with something special to achieve it. I suggested an approach that meant that we would have to adopt a one-off implementation methodology to the project. If we spent the normal amount of time getting to know the "As Is" in detail we would not have enough time left to complete the "To Be" design. So I suggested that we use our experience to go straight to the "To Be" design and spend more time in the testing stage repairing anything we had missed or misunderstood. My logic was that it would be a lot easier to fix something that was wrong than to try to get it right on paper before we even started, as long as we understood the major concepts and functions first. This approach would have been far too risky in normal circumstances but we had the experience to pull it off and in any case there was little else we could do if we were to achieve the deadline.

We worked the long hours and weekends necessary and the implementation went in on time and with no major issues. The users were happy and the project manager (who I grew to respect because of his "can do" attitude) was very pleased. Not only had we pulled it off but we had proved that, in this case, the offshore approach was not one that was suitable. The Project Manager has since said that they would now look to bringing in highly experienced consultants for any future projects rather than cheaper off-shore consultants, because in reality it really should reduce costs (it is cheaper to get it right first time than to have to constantly correct something).

After this project I was went to a major British Energy organisation to fill-in for an SD / MM consultant for a month while they worked on another project). I worked in the (3rd line) support team until the consultant became free again. Workflow was used here too and the problems experienced were the same as those I had seen elsewhere. While it worked, it worked very well, but if there were any unusual circumstances then it failed and was tricky to set up to cover all eventualities.

I also advised the company on the approach to the use of a Global Material Master database. I suggested a way forward that would be user-friendly and yet give the required control, all based on standard SAP, mainly using the classification functionality to manage the catalogue.

My next project was working for SAP UK at a client site that was having problems. They had implemented SAP but they were still having problems caused by not having the right amount of stock in the right place at the right time. Initially I was surprised to hear this because I could not imagine how a reasonable SAP implementation could have this problem. The reasons became obvious in the first hour I was there. They had, for what must have appeared to be legitimate reasons at the time, decided to keep their legacy systems and to use interfaces to and from SAP. Not only was this partly responsible for the trouble, but it made the solution a lot trickier than it should have been. It was not the first time I had seen an SAP implementation like this and I can understand how some organisations find themselves in this position. They know their legacy systems, warts and all, and they don't want to spend lots of time, effort and money retraining their users. But the reason that projects like this are implemented is that the consultants on the project should be explaining the problems that this approach brings and strongly advising them to reconsider. This is where a good consultant will not just give the business what they <u>ask for</u>, they must give the business what they <u>need</u>. It is vital for the consultant to stand firm if the business is asking for something that is not sensible. But this takes a very experienced and strong-minded consultant who really knows how to get the best out of the SAP system.

I was able to solve the specific problems they were having with some additional ABAP reports and a new transaction, but the full solution was to switch to standard SAP and that was not feasible. However, the project went ahead on time and the users were given the help they needed.

My last project was, for a change, not a huge challenge but it did give me the opportunity to be creative. The company want to be able to manage the stock levels in their service engineer's vans. I proposed a solution that uses MRP and I designed a one screen management transaction that enabled the suggested replenishments to be managed easily when the engineer calls in to place their replenishment order.

A separate part of the project was a move of a warehouse from its original site into an existing production facility. Not the most complex change but while changing the process I was able to improve it by streamlining the transactions and interfaces used.

I was then asked to deliver a 5 day Logistics course for SAP Denmark and managed to achieve a score of 6.8 out of 7.

I am now about to start another contract as a Lead SAP consultant.

This is a summary of my experience so far and I hope that it has confirmed my credentials, justifying your time reading this book.

Who should read this book and why?

This book will benefit anyone involved, or considering becoming involved, in the SAP "world" at any level, in any way. Everyone should get something out of this book if they have an interest in SAP R/3.

It covers the high level concept of SAP and why it is different from other options available. It explains the pit falls to watch out for.

It does not preach or instruct, it discusses and explains and uses real experience to back up the common sense reasoning.

Specifically it can help if you are any of the following

- A member of the board of directors of a company, however large or small, that is considering an SAP implementation, or have already had an SAP implementation and would like to know if it could have gone better (or maybe the answer is already obvious).
- An I.S. or I.T. director who has been tasked with implementing SAP or who is responsible for an existing SAP implementation and would like to know why the R.O.I. was not as expected, why the business is not impressed or why he has to retain so many SAP consultants / programmers.
- A Project manager who is about to manage or is managing an SAP implementation and feels as if he knows less than his team about SAP, or the project is not being well received by the business, or the timescales are slipping.
- A Competency Centre Manager who would like to know more about SAP and how to reduce the unresolved issues list.
- A Senior Business manager who is about to be "SAPped" and is would like to know how to make sure that his business benefits from the implementation, or has been "SAPped" and wants to know if it has gone wrong (it may be obvious)
- A project team member from the business who has been seconded to this "thing called SAP" and is unsure of where to start, or what SAP is.
- A training manager who wants to know how to train something as complicated as SAP without confusing everyone, or how to deliver so a large volume of training in the last few weeks before

go-live.
- Someone who is considering a career in SAP and is wondering if they have the skills and if it is still a lucrative market.
- A recruitment agency that would like to get a bigger slice of the SAP market or would like to be able to understand SAP better so that they can discuss it in more detail with potential clients and or consultants.

Why I believe I have enough experience to write the book

I have used my 10 years of implementing systems before SAP came along, followed by my 12 years of implementing SAP systems and my 3 years of teaching SAP consultants how to implement SAP to get me to a stage where I feel that I now know enough about SAP to write this book.

I have been involved in a large number of SAP implementations (ranging from the best possible implementations of SAP to the worst) and I have played a significant part in over 15 SAP installations. I have seen users that literally hate their SAP system but I have also seen users that think it is the best thing that happened to their department / business. I have seen implementations that went live within a few months and I have seen implementations that have taken years.

Not only have I seen these things but I have also investigated the causes and identified the do's and don'ts. This book tries to help guide people through the minefield that is SAP R3.

I am a huge fan of the SAP system based on my first-hand experience and I will do all I can to help others see what it is capable of. The thing that frustrates me most is the fact that it costs less to get it right than it does to get it wrong, it is all a case of understanding what is so different about implementing SAP and this book will help people to understand this and benefit from it.

I have seen implementations that went live within a few months but I have also seen implementations that have taken years. Not only have I seen these things but I have also investigated the causes and identified the causes of most of the major problems.

An overview of SAP R/3

What is SAP R3?

This is a high level explanation of what SAP is, it is not a technical description and it will not go into the minute detail of every aspect of the SAP Functionality. It focuses on what SAP is and what makes it different from other systems.

If you already know SAP then it may help to confirm or correct assumptions that have been made and clarify some of the confusing terminology and complex functionality

If you do not know SAP then this will give you a good understanding of what it is that makes it so different from anything else you may have seen.

Whatever happens it should enable you to get more from the SAP system

What is SAP?

SAP is NOT the name of the system, it is the name of the company that sells the software that they have designed and enhanced over the years. The actual name of the system is SAP R/3, or simply R/3. The 3 relates to the three tiers of the hardware platform that it runs on, the Client, Server and workstation. The original system R/2 had a two tier hardware platform, the mainframe and terminal. So the number is not necessarily incremental, there is a possibility that we could see an R/1 if SAP decided to sell a PC based solution for small businesses, this is something that SAP may well consider in the future. Even small businesses could use the SAP functionality, however the size and complexity may need to be reduced, but the basic processes in the SAP R/3 system is the same as those used by a small business. They procure items, they sell items and they have to manage financial accounts. Some even manufacture in a small way and could use Material Requirements Planning (MRP). As far as I am aware SAP have not yet announced a PC based, single-user version of SAP R/3 (called R/1 perhaps?), but it would not surprise me if they did in the future.

As for R/4, R/5 etc., well I suppose that anything is possible but I am not sure if there would ever be such a platform, unless you class hand-held devices such as PDA's and Palmtops as an extra tier because they download to a PC and then a Server and then a client? I am not technical enough to speculate on what a 4 tier platform would be, I am not that sure even of what a 3 tier platform is but it really is not that important unless you are involved in the technical side of the system..

One thing that does confuse a lot of people is when you start talking about Releases or versions of the software, release 3 and release 4 etc. Some people think that the R/3 relates to the release of the software, it does not. So you have release 3 of R/3 and release 4 of R/3 and recently release 5 of R/3.

As for the SAP initials, you will hear lots of different explanations of what the initials SAP stand for, many of them humorous.

Special **A**nd **P**rivileged
Satan's **A**ccounting **P**ackage
Sack **A**nother **P**rogrammer
Slow **A**nd **P**ainful
(In Germany it is even said to stand for the Hourglass (**S**andhur) **A**ctivation **P**rogram, a very unfortunate and equally unjustified play on words.)

The humour is rarely based on fact and in particular the **S**low **A**nd **P**ainful puns do not reflect reality. Of all of the implementations I have been involved in there was only one company that were complaining about occasionally poor response times and this was traced to a hardware problem not related to the SAP system. In my experience the system is, if anything a lot quicker than you would expect. The design has been built around a need for quick response times. There is no point in building

18

an "all-singing, all-dancing" computer system if it takes minutes to get a simple response instead of seconds.

My own favourite play on words for the meaning of SAP is –

a **S**ystem that is **A**lmost **P**erfect. This is actually a very fair and reasonably accurate statement. I do get the impression that the developers of the SAP system wanted to make sure that they processes worked without error (big or small) and maintained the data precisely and if any compromise was ever considered then it might mean a compromise on a small cosmetic element. This can mean that the very first thing that people see when they log on to SAP for the first time can be something that may have a small cosmetic aberration that does not detract from the use of the system, but when you know how much the SAP system costs you start to wonder if it is likely to be worth it if they haven't bothered to fix the tiniest of errors. I can only say to you that if you have not yet seen SAP, or if you are a new user, please remember that the system is huge and consists of many thousands of screens and programs and so there may well be one or two minor cosmetic aberrations that they have not yet been informed of, or if they have been informed, they may wait until the next release to apply the fix. So I would ask that you focus on the functionality, the data integrity and the seamless integration first before you complain too much. It really is a system that is almost perfect. (The perfect system, like the perfect human is something that we will probably never see).

The SAP initials actually stand for (after translation from German)

Systems
Applications
Products
in data processing

They obviously didn't include the "in data processing" in the initials or we would all be using SAPIDP instead. We have enough trouble determining if we are supposed to say S- A- P or sap. I personally use both and quite often in the same sentence it really doesn't seem to matter.

Some facts and figures about SAP (the company)

SAP was originally founded in 1972 by some ex IBM consultants who decided that it was a waste of time reinventing the wheel every time you begin a new implementation, why not start from a solid base and configure this to suit the particular business. They developed a "packaged solution" that would be suitable for the majority of businesses and ensured that it was configurable to ensure a better fit to the individual processes within an organisation.

The following details are basically correct at the time of writing and they are just a guide to give you an impression of just how big the SAP "world" is.

- There have been an amazing 91,500 installations worldwide, a staggering figure which ever way that you look at it. That is 91,500 different implementations all based on the same software but each being used in a different way.
- They employ in the region of 32,000 staff across 50 different countries.
- There are 12 MILLION Users of SAP
- SAP is the world's largest inter-enterprise software company and the world's third-largest independent software supplier overall

(Source, SAP's own website www.sap.com – 12 June 2005)

What is so special about SAP?

There are many things that make SAP R/3 special but the one element that really makes it stand out is the robust and complex integration of its many modules. Data flows seamlessly from one part of the SAP system to another and although SAP has been broken down into modules the system really is just one integrated pool of functions. At first I really believed that SAP was a collection of modules stitched very closely together and I believed that this was what would be classed as integration. But the more you get to know the system and the more digging you do, you realise that this is not the real integration within SAP. The real integration is within each transaction, each report and even each screen. This makes the level of integration much more at the micro or even macro level. The so called integration between modules does not really exist, there is no "super highway" connecting one module to another and there really is no join to find. In fact the modules are more of a logical break than anything else and that makes the implementation and training etc. more manageable. In addition to this a consultant could not possibly cover the whole of the SAP functionality, there is simply too much to take in. So the modules are important but please do try to think of the system as being one system with different functions that may or may not fall into modular divisions. In fact, thinking of the system as truly modular has caused some implementations to fail or to provide poor, or worse still, negative Return On Investment (ROI). I personally have been asked to implement one module or sometimes two. "Let's start with FI and then we will bring in the other modules as we progress" is a common request. "We just want to implement PM, or PP, or SD etc." is another. The problem is that you CAN actually do this if you want to but this causes one MAJOR problem. I have just stated that one of the major benefits of SAP is the integration and how this is actually a complex and comprehensive integration. The integration of a system this complex is a tremendous achievement and the connections are everywhere and they are complete and sound. So if you choose to just implement one module, or perhaps two, you have to consider the fact that you will now have broken many of these connections and so you will lose the benefits that they were designed to bring and the functionality is still there to maintain those integration paths and has not been removed. This means that the resulting system is still as complicated as it would have been had you not broken these connections and yet you will not have the benefit of that complexity. This is certainly not "the end of the world" but it does mean that the users will now be saying "The system is too complicated for what we want to do", or "why do I have to enter this data, we don't use it anywhere?" etc.

Let's take a genuine example of this, I was recently asked to implement the Plant Maintenance (PM) module for an organisation. They just wanted to replace their existing plant maintenance system and did not want to go "full SAP" just yet. Firstly let me say that this is certainly feasible and can be done in SAP with reasonably good results, but however it is done, it will always be a compromise. I put the case for not just implementing PM and explained that two other modules had significant integration with PM and should also be considered, Materials Management (MM) and Finance (FI). I was not suggesting a full implementation of the two other modules but I was proposing to maintain the integration aspects and break as few links as possible. This would mean implementing elements of MM and elements of FI. This would bring several benefits for the small amount of extra effort involved. If this was not done the client would have to have a high number of interfaces to and from SAP PM. They would have had to interface all costs, stock receipts, issues (to maintain accurate stock figures for PM), Purchase orders and other means of procurement, etc. and create elements in SAP that would mirror the same elements in the legacy systems that handled the stock and financial reporting. The interfaces could not be made too complex or they would be more likely to fail or contain errors etc. and so they would only contain basic information.

The resulting solution would be an SAP PM system that would have stock figures that were not current (they would only be accurate immediately after he interface). It would not be able to provide a true breakdown of the cost of maintenance because some of the costs were being stored on another system. They could not use genuine lead times for the ordering of parts because this data was stored on another system, and so on.

The Legacy system would also have been compromised because the users would no longer be able to drill down to the detail from a high level posting, unless they kept switching from their legacy system to SAP.

By implementing the Purchase order and stock functions from MM and the finance functionality they would have a PM system that did have online accurate data that could take advantage of the power of the SAP functionality and it would be a huge improvement on the "old" system, mostly because of the full integration between the various functions involved. In addition to this the future full implementation that was planned would be less complicated and the risks reduced dramatically (Mainly because the main integration points would have already been handled).

So please do think of SAP R/3 as one system that has several logical areas, rather than separate systems that have been integrated.

A quick word on the subject of "big-bang", I prefer the option of implementing all of the main modules at the same time, this does not mean that I suggest it as the only option for every implementation, it is just that in my experience it is a scary but more successful option. There are many factors that affect the decision and so each case should be judged individually, but I always start from the "big bang" approach and identify reasons not to, rather than start of with the individual module approach and seeing if we could manage a "big bang" implementation. It is not a big difference but the change in emphasis is often enough to result in the right choice. So I suggest implementing all of the major modules in one step if you have the team and the business users that can survive this approach and if you have nerves of steel.

Another major advantage of an SAP implementation is the fact that the main processes are already designed and working (and proven to be so by the other SAP implementations), so you don't have to dig to get every detail of every field and key function. An example of this is a simple goods receipt function. If you were building this function from scratch you would have to interview all of the relevant users and departmental managers to find out what they wanted the system to do when a goods receipt is posted. Do they want to print a document? What information does it have on it? What types of stock figures do they want to keep? What value should the receipt be recorded at? What accounts should be updated by the receipt? What happens to the Purchase order when the receipt takes place, especially if it was a short delivery etc? Not only would you have to design the process you would also have to design each program, each screen and each printout and then test them all and retest and so on. This is quite a heavy task and just to get to a working system. By implementing SAP the basic design work is already complete and using "best Practice" and so should be suitable for most businesses without major modification.

Because SAP already has the best practice functionality built in you can concentrate on more important questions such as, what problems should the new system be solving, how can we streamline the whole process, what extra information do we want out of the new system, etc.. In addition to this the SAP processes have been designed by experts and developed over time and so they are likely to be better than any process that you could design in the short space of time available in an implementation. In all, the fact that you are taking a working system and configuring it to your company means that you are saving a lot of time and effort and are likely to achieve a much better result.

The time that the project team spend with the main users also becomes more productive and less of a chore. Instead of trying to interview a user to find out exactly what they want, then put the suggestion on paper and expect the user to commit to that exact design on paper, after a very short amount of time. With an SAP system you can now show them a fully working system (basically you have a working system straight away when the SAP system is first loaded). You can show the actual screens and demonstrate the real processes and the user will find it easier to relate to this and see every field that will be available, instead of waiting until the system has been built before they see it and finding out that it is too late to change anything that has been missed or misunderstood due to the short time left before the implementation takes place.

This really does result in the users being able to understand the changes and enables them to play a much bigger part in the project, they feel much more involved in the project. It also makes the project team's task much more enjoyable and productive.

Another advantage is the huge customer base that SAP has, this provides enough incentive (and income) to promote a very large research and development effort. This ensures that the system will continue to improve and keep track of developments in business as well as developments in the I.T. world. I am not sure of it is still true (or ever was) but I was once told that SAP were spending as much on Research and Development as their competitors were earning in revenue and having seen their HQ and the several R & D buildings I have no doubt that it was true.

For example, if there should be a change in the way that a business is run due to legal or taxation changes then SAP will provide solutions to this and ensure that the system can cope with these changes. An example of this is the European currency changes caused by the introduction of the Euro. Imagine the chaos this would cause if you had to change your existing systems from one base currency to another, it is far more complicated than it sounds. The whole exchange rate calculation function needs to be amended, all Sales orders, Purchase orders, contracts, invoices, financial postings, etc. etc. suddenly need to be changed to reflect the new currency. In addition to this you have to be able to handle the fact that some of your customers and Suppliers will be changing to the Euro at different times. In all this would be a nightmare process for any business to cope with. But SAP developed, tested and documented a set of programs and system changes to cope with exactly this and set up training courses to explain the process (I have delivered part of this course personally and it was well received). The course not only explained the program changes it also suggested how many "dummy runs" should take place and when and how to implement the changes with minimal disruption to the business.

It is at times like this that businesses are glad that they decided to implement SAP, especially those that have implemented all of the main modules and those that have not over-modified the system, because the SAP supplied code would work without hassle and would be the only process required. Some organisations that had retained their legacy systems had to make changes to those systems as well as their SAP system and worse still had to change many of the interfaces too.

So if your government decide to "play around" with the taxation laws etc. SAP will be working alongside you (if not ahead of you) to make sure the change is as painless as possible.

Some organisations have to use systems that are acceptable to governing bodies such as the U.S. Food and Drug Administration (the FDA) etc. One such organisation that I was involved in was a major pharmaceutical company, their existing systems were not acceptable to the FDA and so they had no choice but to change to a system that was acceptable to the FDA. SAP was one of the systems that would be acceptable and so they decided to implement it to ensure that they could continue trading. In this case it was not because of cost savings, or streamlining processes etc. it was merely to move to an acceptable system. During the project it was very clear that the FDA were a very rigid professional body who would make sure that businesses in this kind of an industry ran with the end user's safety in mind throughout. Each process had to be documented and agreed by the compliance and validation department, every user had to be fully trained on every transaction that they were to use, with no exceptions, every document had to match rigid guidelines. So for a complete system to be accepted by the FDA it had to be exceptional. SAP provided a fully auditable trail for all processes, fully controlled change management of such things as recipes etc., full batch management and where used trails, in fact everything that the FDA demanded. So if it good enough for this situation then it may well be good enough for your business.

Earlier I used the term "a System that is Almost Perfect", the main area where you need perfection is in the core data storage and retrieval. This must not become corrupt and there must be no broken links in the audit trail. The whole SAP system is built on solid, accurate, timely and auditable data. In my 15 years of dealing with SAP systems I have only ever come across one example where a document record appeared to go missing. This was one single document out of many millions that had been processed and it was caused by a catastrophic hardware problem. Even though the document was lost, the system did not crash, it did not leave a "black hole" that would cause reports and enquiries to fail and most importantly we were able to rebuild the data due to the standard SAP audit trail.

So if you want to know if SAP R/3 is a proven system then rest easy, it has been proven over and over again in thousands of implementations around the world and by various independent authorities.

SAP are constantly improving and updating R/3, changes in Law, Accounting etc. are built into the releases to enable the business to keep at least one step ahead of anything that is likely to affect the basic business processes. These releases will also contain fixes for errors that have been corrected since the last release and often include new functions, often quite useful ones too. These releases happen quite often, sometimes a little too often, but at least you have the option of delaying the upgrade until you are ready, but SAP will eventually have a cut-off date, after which they state that they will no longer support older versions. Many organisations "skip" a few releases especially if they are in the middle of a major project. This is not normally an issue but if you are doing this then it is a good idea to at least try to keep reasonably up to date with the "Hot packs". These are collections of fixes that SAP have bundled together and it if you are not up to date with the hot packs then you may find you have some extra work to do if you want to apply a later fix that is causing problems for you. So check with your BASIS team to see how far behind you are and you don't have to be absolutely up to date but you should be close enough. Implementing hot packs is not as major a task as a release change but thorough testing is a must. Most organisations set aside a quiet weekend to implement a series of hot packs together and treat it as a mini project.

Occasionally SAP will issue a major release, such as from release 2 to Release 3, release 3 to release 4 and so on. These are major changes and should be treated as a full project and it was always a good idea to wait for a while so that the early "teething problems" had been corrected first. Moving to an A or B release was always a bit scary, but some businesses felt that it was essential to go to the new release as soon as possible. A prime example of this is a company that is about to implement SAP for the very first time. It would not be sensible to implement the release that was just about to be upgraded because it is difficult enough for the business to come to terms with the major change caused by the implementation, without having to change the system again within a year to go to the new release.

An upgrade often includes extra functions that may be very relevant to your business processes, but they have to be implemented into the business as well as into the system and so a lot of planning has to take place. This means that you can either just upgrade and keep the existing processes or you can plan a project that will take advantage of the new functionality, especially if you currently have "workarounds" that can be removed because the new functionality addresses this area.

Fortunately SAP has now switched to a different approach to releases. The major change is that releases will, more or less, be module specific. This means that releases should now be less traumatic (they will only affect part of your business) and you will have more flexibility about what you want to upgrade and when. This doesn't mean that if you have found an error in the system (it does happen, after all it is a System that is <u>Almost Perfect</u>) that you have to wait until the next release to have it corrected.

SAP provides a support mechanism called OSS (Operational Support System). This is used when you have a problem with the system that does not appear to be caused by your modifications or ABAP programs. You would firstly ensure that the problem is not caused by the way you have configured the system or by a modification. If you then felt that it must be a basic error with the SAP software you log onto OSS and post your problem. This is then directed to the appropriate specialist in SAP and they will communicate with you to solve the problem. Although the process occasionally takes longer than it should, SAP do act very professionally and will try to solve the problem as quickly as possible. If this is a major problem such as a complete system crash (I have never personally ever heard of this happening) then you will get the correct help and as quickly as you could expect this to happen. If the problem is an SAP error you will be given details of how to solve this and in most cases the code that you will need to correct the problem.

Is SAP the ideal system for your business?

An ideal system for an organisation would be one that helped to operate the business efficiently and accurately. It would provide information that would help make the correct business decisions. It would be reliable and auditable and it should be a benefit to all levels of the organisation from the head of the business to the end users in every department. It should also be flexible, current and maintainable. It should provide a healthy ROI and it should be able to be maintained at sensible cost. It should be able to turn the huge volume of data that we retain into information that we can use.

Is SAP R/3 the ideal system for a business? The answer depends more on how you implement the system than anything else. This can obviously be said about most systems but it is particularly relevant to SAP R/3.

To understand how important the implementation is please read the section devoted to this later in the book, but consider the following. I think of a new SAP system as being the best quality oil paints, the best quality artists paint brushes and the best quality canvass. Give this to someone who can paint and you may get the Mona Lisa, give it to someone who cannot paint and you will get a complete mess and worse still you will have ruined the paint, the brushes and the canvas.

SAP R/3 is very similar to this and there are some people who have understood how to get the most out of SAP R/3 (the artists) and there are others who haven't yet understood that it requires a different approach and try a "Paint by Numbers" approach, with a quality that matches.

The end result of an SAP implementation is directly connected to how well the decision makers understand the concepts of SAP at the very beginning, even before the decision to use SAP is made. The problem with this is the business has no experience of SAP yet and so do not know which direction to take. This is one of the main reasons that I decided to write this book, if the business knew at the outset exactly what this thing called SAP is and how to get the most out of it, then the implementation is much more likely to be a success and for no extra cost (probably at significant cost savings in fact).

But firstly, lets consider how we would get our "ideal system" if we were to start from a blank sheet of paper.

- What if - we had an IT department consisting of thousands of business system experts.
- What if - we took 30 years to develop and enhance a system for the business processes that we should be using
- What if - we had millions of users all testing the system in a "live" environment, for the last 30 years
- What if - we could make sure it works by getting the majority of the biggest organisations in the world to use it before we do.
- What if - we had a Research and Development Department, with a huge budget, whose sole purpose was to improve the system and ensure that it can react to any changes in financial methods or legal requirements , before those requirements hit us
- What if - we could make the system completely integrated so that we are able to drill down through to the minute detail or up to the highest level of aggregation
- What if - we made that system so flexible that it wouldn't require a new system or new implementation even if we sold off any part of the business that we own or bought in every business we wanted to, or both
- What if – we could build a system that could be used by all of our core departments, instead of separate systems for each one.
- What if – we could have it right now without having to build it from scratch
- What if – we could get other organisations across the world to use the same system so that it would be easier to do business together.

It would be quite a system, but this is exactly what an SAP system is, it is all of the above and more.

Has SAP R/3 changed the way that systems are implemented?

It most definitely has and this makes it extremely important to understand this and use this to our advantage.

One of the major contributing factors in problem / failed SAP implementations is the approach taken to the implementation. Many implementations suffer because they rely on outdated approaches. These approaches evolved over time and provided all of the safety that a project needed. The problem is that many of them are built on implementation approaches that were based on "scratch built" systems that understandably need a high level of documentation, because everything was being designed for the first time and therefore needed to be captured in full detail. These implementations were lead by the I.T. department because every piece of data and every screen and even every keystroke had to be designed in a way that it would work technically. A business user would not have been able to contribute to the database design or the program that displayed the screens etc. This meant that the I.T. department was the expert and the business users assisted in the project.

An SAP implementation approach should be built around the fact that the databases and the technical programming has already been completed and all that is left is to understand the business and ensure that the required processes are configured correctly. This means that the main difference is that in an SAP implementation, the Business should lead the implementation with the help of the I.T. department and very definitely not the other way around. Get this right at the very beginning and you have immediately removed one of the main causes of failure. This subject is covered in more detail in later sections.

But we want a "Tailor made" system not one that is "Off the peg"

SAP R/3 is anything but an "off the peg system", it is far more of a "tailor made" system than the old approach where a system was built specifically for a business.

To explain my logic we can have a look at a typical visit to a high-class tailor;

The first thing that happens is that you talk to the tailor about what you want in broad terms.

The tailor may then show you some design options such as lapel shape, jacket length, number of buttons etc.

You get to see samples of the cloth.

When all of the decisions have been made you are given the details on an order form.

Some time later you are told that the suit is ready for a first fitting

You try on the suit. It may be covered in chalk lines and it may have pins holding it together but you can get an idea of how it will look and feel and the tailor will be able to make fine adjustments.

You return later for a final fitting and one or two minor adjustments may be needed

You then return to collect the suit. The tailor will make sure that you are happy with the finished product.

How does this relate to an SAP implementation and why is it closer to a "tailor made" system than an "off the peg" system. If we look at the above steps individually and compare them.

The first thing that happens is that you talk to the tailor about what you want in broad terms.

You would not discuss how many sleeves you would need, or would you have to decide what a suit actually is. You may talk about the options of a three-piece suit etc, but basically the tailor already knows the range of options available.

In an SAP implementation this would be the stage where you are deciding which modules of SAP you might implement and when.

The tailor may then show you some design options such as lapel shape, jacket length, number of buttons etc.

You would not need to design how a lapel was made or how material can be cut and stitched (other than to ascertain the quality of the stitching etc.)

In an SAP implementation this would be where the business users would get to see the already working transactions and reports etc. and discuss the alternative transactions and the high-level configuration options available. The project team would then

You get to see samples of the cloth.

The tailor shows you the various cloths available and may also mention any special options that can be produced if you need something that is not in the range of samples.

In a SAP implementation this would be where the project team may configure some examples of the transactions to be used and to discuss any other options that could be configured.

When all of the decisions have been made you are given the details on an order form.

The tailor wants to be sure that you both know what is required and the order is the agreement to continue with the making of the suit.

In a SAP implementation this is where the project team will document the agreed design for the user to sign off.

Some time later you are told that the suit is ready for a first fitting

The tailor will cut the cloth and loosely build the suit to a stage where it can be sampled in a first fitting.

In a SAP implementation this would be the build phase where the configuration occurs and a system is built for the business users to test.

You try on the suit.

It may be covered in chalk lines and it may have pins holding it together but you can get an idea of how it will look and feel and the tailor will be able to make fine adjustments.

This would be the User Acceptance testing. The users get to try the system, it may still have some temporary configuration and the master data is mostly samples, but it allows the users to check to see if their business processes will work after the implementation.

You return later for a final fitting and one or two minor adjustments may be needed

You expect the suit to be virtually complete but there may be one or two minor corrections needed. This is where the suit should fit and look as you expected it.

This would be the training sessions where the users see exactly how the system will work. It may highlight one or two issues but in general the system should work correctly.

You then return to collect the suit.

The tailor will make sure that you are happy with the finished product.

This would be the "go live" and the project team would be there to help with the initial use of the system.

So if this is a "tailor made" system then what is an "off the peg" system?

The pre-SAP implementations where the system is built from scratch are classic examples of "off the peg" systems, even though they were thought of as "tailor made".

To illustrate this we can consider a process similar to that above but this time for an "off the peg" system.

The I.T. department interview the business users and ask them what they want, this is normally done in a series of short one to one meetings.

The result of these meetings is a paper design involving flowcharts and brief descriptions of the proposed solution. The users cannot really be expected to know from paper designs if the solution will work or if there are any gaps in the design.

The user waits until the system has been built to a stage where it can be tested. This is normally several months after the previous step and there is not always a great deal of interaction with the designers during this time.

The user finally gets to see the solution shortly before the go-live date. Seeing the system in operation it is very likely that the user will now be able to identify gaps and areas of the design that will not work. However, it has taken many months to build the system so far and major changes and gaps will result in many more months of work and the go live date is then threatened. This can sometimes result in the I.T. department resisting changes and corrections due to the small amount of time left. The end result is often a compromise at best, or more normally, a system that does not really bring any benefits for the users and / or business.

So when considering if SAP R/3 has changed the way that systems should be implemented, it is important to consider the implementation as "tailor made" and give the business a much bigger involvement in the project. After all, the expertise that is needed for an implementation of SAP is Business knowledge, supported by SAP functional knowledge. Technical knowledge is now less important because the system is designed and built and we just need to know how to configure it, not how to build it and configuration decisions are definitely driven from business requirements.

Is SAP the best system available?

Having read to this point I am sure that you would think that I am an SAP salesman rather than an SAP consultant. I am a strong supporter of the SAP system but I do not (unfortunately) get any commission or benefits from my support. So when it comes to answering this question you would expect my response to be a resounding YES! Well it is not that simple and even though I have been very supportive of the system I do know that it is not perfect (System that is Almost Perfect).

My honest answer to the question "Is SAP the best system available?" is yes AND no. If you look at the individual modules, then the answer may occasionally be NO. SAP may not have the best functionality on the market for an individual module. This is becoming less so as SAP increase and improve the functions within each module. But not so long ago I would have said that the SAP Plant Maintenance Module and the HR module were nowhere near the best available. They have improved these modules now and so this situation is changing but even if this was not the case you have to look at the bigger picture.

If we were to say, for example, that SAP PM and HR modules were still not the best available then I would not let that change the decision to choose SAP R/3. This is because the integration with the other modules more than makes up for any shortcomings and the fact that SAP are constantly improving their system means that they will, without doubt catch up their competitors and overtake them within a very short space of time. This has already happened with the PM module and is almost true of the HR module too.

So for individual modules the answer may sometimes be No but if you look at the system as a whole then the answer (in my experience) is a very definite YES. The benefits of integration are huge, no interfaces to fail, real time updating, full traceability, no barriers to drill down paths (unless you want them), cross modular reporting etc. etc. These benefits far outweigh any minor shortcomings.

So if you are evaluating SAP against other options please bear in mind the complete picture and not just individual functions within the modules.

Why the "Horror stories"?

One thing that surprised me early on in my SAP career was how many horror stories I had personally heard about, failed SAP implementations, people removing their SAP systems, people saying that it has resulted in their business making huge losses etc. These were genuine stories and there were lots of them, but if the horror stories were so bad then why were there so many organisations switching to SAP? It just didn't make sense. I could understand that bad news travels faster and louder than good news but even taking this into account it really did appear that the SAP system was a very risky option.

I had heard about one project where the whole project team had been removed because the implementation was delayed and was costing a lot more than it should have. I had even heard that the replacement project team were also removed at a later stage. This was scary and if I was asked to make the decision to implement SAP or another option, then I would have had to think long and hard. But this was totally against my own personal experience. I was a fan of the SAP approach from a very early stage. My 11 years of implementing systems had taught me that so much time is wasted designing solutions from scratch. Asking the same questions and designing the same base system each time was not only a waste of time, but there were also huge risks involved, it was so easy to either miss something completely or misunderstand something. So the concept of buying a system that was based on best practice and was already working was one that I could see was the way to go.

I really could not understand how the other projects had gone so wrong, the system was complete, it was fully integrated, it was based on best practice and it was flexible enough to suit most businesses. But now, several years of implementing SAP into many organisations has not only made me a bigger fan of the SAP approach but I also now can see why some projects go so badly wrong.

The main reasons are all covered in the section "How to get it right" within this section you will find lots of reasons why a project can go wrong. If I had to point to two main reasons for SAP implementation problems it would be that the following was not understood;

It is vital to understand that an SAP implementation is very different from other implementations and these differences must be understood if the project is to be a success.

It is a project that should be lead by the business with the support of strong SAP consultants, but the business need to understand SAP as early as possible in the project and certainly before any major decisions are made.

Is SAP suitable for the small to medium size business?

Many people think of SAP as being a huge system that is only suitable for major organisations and until recent years they would have been absolutely correct. SAP R/3 implementations often cost in the region of tens or hundreds of millions of pounds to implement. Most of this cost however related more to the business re-engineering tasks and large modifications to the standard system. Another large portion of the costs was due to the large numbers of users involved. But in a small to medium business (SAP define this as being businesses with 10 to several hundred employees and often refer to them as the "Fortune 500,000").

SAP (the company) realised that the major organisations would soon all have implemented SAP or would have already decided no to and so this would result in their customer base shrinking instead of growing. So they needed to find a new market for their systems and the next level down was a market that was huge and relatively untapped, so this would be their target for a new and growing customer base.

To meet the needs of this new customer base they had to change the way that their systems would be implemented, the cost needed to be reduced dramatically. One way would be to produce a different version of their software specifically designed for SMBs (Small to Medium Businesses), but this would involve starting most of the work from scratch and trying to sell an unproven system to very shrewd and cost conscious organisations. Their original system (SAP R/3) was already developed to the extreme and was a powerful, flexible system that had been proven to be a success and so why change it? The best way to enable SMBs to afford an SAP solution was to use the original R/3 system and associated processes virtually unchanged but with a radically different approach to the way in which it is implemented.

This was not that difficult to achieve, after all R/3 was built around "best Practice" and so the processes were all coherent and still applied to SMBs as much as they did to the major organisations that were the original customer base. The beauty of this approach was that to gain major reductions in the cost of implementation the system needed to be implemented without modifications and as standard as possible and this is exactly the message that I have been trying to get across in this book. Regardless of the size of the organisation, to have a good implementation of SAP you need to try to keep the system as standard as possible. This means that if an SMB was to implement SAP in as short a time as possible and with the minimum cost, then they have to keep the system standard. This means that they win both ways, not only are costs reduced considerably but the resulting system is anything but a compromise, it will probably be better than many of the SAP implementations that have cost many millions of pounds. To gain a better understanding of my point you need to read the sections in this book that discuss the use and advantages of "standard SAP".

But a completely standard SAP implementation is not going to suit all kinds of businesses, there are some genuine reasons why some organisations need to use SAP in different ways. For example and firm of Architects would have different requirements to a small manufacturer of children's toys. So how can this be handled? Well SAP have the answer to this too, they have lots of partner organisations that provide pre-configured solutions that are specific to different types of businesses. This way you can buy an off-the-shelf SAP system that matches the requirements of your business.

The end result is that you will have all of the power and flexibility of the SAP system but at a tiny fraction of the cost and with minimal disruption to our business.

The strangest thing of all is that by using this method, SAP have now opened up a huge new customer base and at the same time the SMBs now have the ability to use the SAP system, everyone wins!

So if you are an SMB and you want to have, what in my mind is, the best possible ERP system, then contact SAP and they will put you in touch with the appropriate partner. They will explain how they can provide you with al of this power at a sensible cost and yet you still get a system that matches your specific requirements and one that is "tailored" to your company.

Alternatively you can go to the author's website www.helpsap.com and register your interest in SAP's SMB solution and we can get the right partner to contact you to discus the options available.

How to get it right

There is no simple formula for how to get an SAP implementation right but there are several things that can make it go wrong and it is vital that you are aware of these. You can think of it as a map of the "minefield" that is SAP R/3.

Don't think of SAP as just a computer system,

It is far more than this, it is more of a business change than most people realise. To get the most out of SAP you need to consider it as a business solution as well as a business system. You need to even consider changing the business to suit the system in some cases, however hard this is to believe, it really will bring major benefits.

Don't think of SAP R/3 as merely a packaged solution that you just install and use.

It is actually possible to do this though, you could just install it and with the minimum of configuration be using it within weeks. But then what would be the point of doing this, the ROI would be quite healthy because the project costs would be minimal, but there would be no real longer-term business benefits. This approach has been adopted by some small businesses and it has worked for them, but this approach would not be recommended for any of the medium to large businesses.

Don't underestimate the time and effort required

Budget for extra time to investigate the options before major decisions are made.

It is far better to spend a little bit more time understanding how it operates before you jump in and go. This is particularly important in the early stages of the project because some of the earliest decisions you will have to make may well take place long before you know the full consequences of getting it wrong. This is made more difficult by the fact that SAP is so flexible that you can decide on an approach that will work, only to find out later on that another approach works better and it may be too late to change. For example one of the first things to decide is the organisation structure that will be configured. The organisation structure is the way that you map your business onto SAP. Questions will include, how many company codes do you need, how many Plants, how do they link together etc. You may not even know what a Plant is at this stage and yet you may have to decide, or be involved in the decision of how many you are going to need in your SAP system. (There is a guide to this in the section "Plant or storage location").

You may well suggest that you pay SAP consultants to manage questions like this for you, but the SAP consultant may knows the SAP system and this question relates to your business, and you (or someone from the business) need to be able to contribute to this process. I have included some guidance for these decisions in later sections, it is vitally important that the base design of the main structures like these are made with an understanding of the consequences of getting it wrong. What makes this worse is the fact that you can get it wrong and not realise it for a very long time or possibly never know that it is wrong. Getting it wrong may mean that everything appears to be working but some of the functionality in SAP may not be providing you with what you expected or it may be not appear as functionally rich as you would have expected and you may just assume (incorrectly, like many others do) that this is because SAP R/3 is simply not as good a system as you expected.

When building the original base design take some time to consider any future rollouts and other divisions of your organisation that may be implemented later. When the other parts of your business are added, you may find that the organisation structure that you have built means that they do not fit a closely as they should. This rarely results in a complete redesign of the structure (mainly because the task would be so costly) but it often results in poor functionality because a compromise is often the only feasible solution.

This is why I believe that it is so important to take more time than planned in the early stages and get the critical decisions right first time.

But there are other stages in the project where it is vital to consider spending more time than planned.

One of these stages that is normally given insufficient time are the long and emotive discussions that there will be concerning Master data. This is one area that in my experience is always underestimated. Not only do you need to establish how you are going to load the master data (and believe me, you can normally calculate how long this will take and double it) but you also have to decide how you are going to rationalise your master data before it is loaded into SAP. Most organisations start by stating that they will not load redundant or duplicated master records into SAP. While this is exactly what you should be aiming for, few actually achieve this because of the time involved. I class master data as being firmly on the critical path and I prefer to start addressing this from the very first few days of the project. Even if you are not planning to rationalise the data before it is loaded, just look at how many materials, customers, vendors etc. you have and then consider how much "massaging" of the data will be required to get it ready to be loaded into SAP. Add even more time if you are taking that data from several sources (Legacy finance systems that are separate to your legacy purchasing / sales systems etc.).

Then there will be the many debates relating to how the data will be maintained after it has been loaded to SAP, will it be centrally maintained and therefore controlled closely but involve long lead-times for changes and additions or will it be maintained locally and easier to maintain but with less control than is required, possibly the best option a combination of the two? This debate alone will take several meetings to gain an agreed approach. If you budget for extra time in the early stages of the project then you will not only save time later on in the project but the resulting implementation is far more likely to be seen as a success.

Don't underestimate the power and complexity of an SAP system

Many projects have suffered from underestimating the power and complexity of the SAP system, which is not surprising because it does take many years to get to a level where you genuinely understand how much of an issue this is. If you have been involved in SAP implementations that haven't really pushed the boundaries of the functionality available then you may be wondering why I am saying that it is so complicated. If you have been involved in SAP implementations where the system has been heavily modified then you may also wonder why, because it didn't appear to do what you wanted it too. Whatever the reasons for this contributing to the problems of an SAP implementation, it is important to grasp just how and why this is a mistake worth highlighting..

To help illustrate this lets try an analogy;

I believe that we can compare SAP to a Formula one racecar (or Indy car etc.).

It is built to be one of the fastest cars in the world. It is extremely powerful and there are many ways to set it up to suit the track and conditions and so this results in a high degree of complexity. If you or I were to jump into a formula one racecar without understanding just how complicated it was then I would imagine that not only could we not start it but we could not even fit into it or reach the controls. You just don't jump into a racecar like this without a lot of preparation. You have to configure the seating and controls before you can even attempt to drive it. But while we are struggling with this our friends in their road car could be driving around the circuit quite quickly and we would still be in the pit lane. So we need to find out how to start it, having done this what happens, we stall it because we are not used to the method of pulling away in a car such as this, then when we can pull away without stalling we drive at around 30 miles an hour, because it feels so different to anything else we have driven that it is very scary. Then we gradually increase speed and spin a few times (hopefully don't crash into anything) and our friends in their road cars are still speeding past in their road cars. So you start to wonder why it is not a quick car after all of that money it has cost. It is not a pleasant experience and you might just think it will never perform. But you persevere and eventually you start to understand what you have and how to use it. You soon start to pass your friends in their easy to drive cars over and over again and finally you are the fastest car on the track by far. It is only then that you start to realise that this really is one of the fastest cars on the road and why.

If you consider the SAP R/3 system to be a formula one racecar (which you may still doubt if you have not seen it fly like I have), then you wouldn't expect to jump in and race it straight away and yet this is what happens with most SAP implementations, the decision is made to choose SAP and the next thing that happens is you are asked to make important decisions long before you understand what it is that you are involved in..

Implement it using a methodology that has been specifically designed for an SAP implementation.

There are some methodologies that have been designed specifically for SAP and these are fine. SAP's has its own methodology called ASAP and I have found this to be a bit more effort than necessary and some of the resulting documentation can have no direct use, but its basic approach to the phases of an implementation is excellent. This does allow the project to focus more on the business and is ideal for those project teams that have the right balance of business and I.T. members.

Let the business lead the project with strong support from I.T.

This is more of a change of emphasis than a radical change in the way that projects are run, but the system functions more or less out of the box and so the task of the project is to ensure that the system fulfils the business requirements and it is only the business team members on the project that will know the true requirements of the system. But what if the users don't know what the system is capable of, they might not ask the right questions of the I.T. department? But with the support of Strong SAP consultants this is not an issue. The consultants will know the options available in SAP and they will also know how to get the most out of the system but I have seen systems that have been built around an I.T. department view of what a business needs and they simply do not match the real world of business. The users know their business better than anyone else and they will know if an idea, however clever, will work in reality. So let the business people design the business solutions and get the SAP consultants to make sure that the resulting implementation takes advantage of the options available in SAP.

It is also sensible to give the business members the feeling that it is their solution, this will ensure that the result is one that they feel responsible for and it is more likely to be seen in a positive light, whatever the outcome.

Don't lose sight of the ROI

There are organisations that really don't use the ROI figures as a measure of the success of an SAP implementation. The pharmaceutical company that implemented SAP so that their system was accepted as compliant with the FDA regulations were not driven by ROI, they simply had to implement the system regardless of this measure. There are other organisations that will only approve a system implementation if the ROI is projected to be achieved in an agreed time period, but then do little to prove this after the event because it is too late to do anything if it didn't achieve this target. There are even a few, although I have not actually seen one yet, that not only set this target but also actually measure the resulting cost savings to see if this target was achieved.

However, of the many implementations I have seen, I do get the impression that the vast majority not only don't know if they achieved the target ROI, but also don't even want to investigate if they have achieved it or not, mainly because they know the result would show that they did not achieve it or worse still they are in a negative ROI situation where costs are still spiralling but the benefits have yet to be realised.

Whichever of the above applies in your case the most important thing to remember is that it is the WAY that SAP is implemented that will affect the ROI and not just the mere fact that it has been implemented.

The main thing to do is to decide the type of implementation you actually want;

- Do you want just to replace your existing systems with an SAP solution based on the "as is"? or do you intend to just implement one or two modules for now? Then a good ROI will be very difficult to achieve. (Worse still, if you plan to keep many of your Legacy systems and interface to and from SAP).
- Do you aim to replace all of you major systems with SAP R/3 but may have to modify the system substantially? Then your ROI will probably be a positive one but it may take many years to achieve this.
- Do you want to replace all of your existing systems, use SAP as a basis for improved processes and aim to keep the system reasonably standard? Then you can probably expect quite a healthy ROI and achieve the target quicker than you had hoped.

Change the business to match the system?

This is one of the most difficult concepts to swallow, the possible need to change the business to suit the system. This went against all I had learned in the previous 10 years. If you went to the board of directors to tell them that they have to change the business to suit the system then, you would be out of there as quick as you could say "SAP".

How do you justify this statement to yourself, let alone the business? Well you don't without a really good reason and that reason is "Best Practice".

Regardless of the type of business you are in, the basic business functions are very similar, if not identical. For example, if you buy something part of that process includes a purchase order of some kind and a delivery later and pay for the goods. Why then are there so many ways of doing this correctly? There must be a common process for this that encompasses all of the requirements of such a process. A Purchase Order is needed as an agreement between the two parties and the contents of a PO are pretty basic, who are you buying it from, what are you buying, how many and at what price and when and where do you want them delivered. If you include some flexible texts and basic terms and conditions then this would suit the vats majority of businesses. Why then should you have to develop this process each time, for each business? You may wish to have the layout, font, paper size etc. different in your business but the basic process remains the same.

The justification to change the business to match the system only works if the system really is based on best practice and if that same system is powerful enough and flexible enough to be up to the job. The processes within SAP, even in the late '80s, were good enough to be classed as "best practice" and they have improved dramatically since.

This means that when the SAP functionality does not do exactly what the business wants, we must ask the question "If SAP doesn't do it, then perhaps it isn't necessary" or "if SAP doesn't do it then how are other companies who use SAP doing it?". The worst thing we can do is to just "write something" or modify the SAP system just because it doesn't operate in the way we currently do.

This is one of my basic "golden rules" and it is one that has stood me in good stead in my 15 years of implementing SAP. I am not saying for one minute, that the SAP system is perfect or that if the SAP system doesn't do what the business needs, then change the business. What I am saying is that the question must be asked and it must be asked with vigour. The consequences of changing the SAP system just to match the business as it is now (other than by accepted configuration) are not to be taken lightly and the consequences are covered in later sections.

Try not to keep your legacy systems just because your users are used to them and understand them.

This happens far to often, to differing extents. Keeping some of the legacy systems because there is no way that SAP can provide the functionality (after rigorous checks that this is true) is one thing. Keeping the legacy systems just because the users are familiar with them and don't want to change is another altogether. If it was left to most users there would be very few Legacy systems replaced with anything, however bad they were, the phrase "better the devil you know " is overused in this situation. There are a few people that welcome change with open arms, there are some people who actively fight against change, many people don't like it and most people fear it to some extent. So if you use this fear of change to keep the legacy systems then I would suggest that you do not even consider an SAP implementation.

I have been involved in two implementations that have retained most of their legacy systems and effectively just run SAP in the background and interface everything to and from it, using it like some kind of engine. The worst example of the two just used the MRP functionality in SAP and the legacy systems fired requirements and stock movements to SAP and received suggested order quantities in return. This was the worst SAP implementation I have ever seen. The users still had their legacy screens and reports and so they didn't mind, but ask them if it was an improvement and the answer was a resounding, "Well, it is a bit better". Match that against the cost of the implementation and the added complexity of a fully integrated system, with no benefit of that integration and the extra risk and complexity of all of those interfaces. It was not a pleasant sight.

This was very early on in my SAP career and so I thought that this was an exception that I would never come across again. I was wrong, very recently I was asked to help an organisation that had implemented SAP, they were having problems with their supply chain, they were not matching the delivery dates that they had promised their customers and yet this was one of the main problems that the SAP system was supposed to resolve. This organisation had also kept their legacy systems and saw SAP as just another of their many systems rather than a complete change of approach. This resulted in lots of interfaces and lots of problems, so many problems that they had to devise a plan to somehow stabilise the system before their busiest sales period. This meant a freeze on all developments other than the stabilisation changes. At the end of this project they would, at best, have stabilised the situation, improvements and ROI were way off in the horizon. So imagine the response you would get from these organisations if you asked them what they thought of SAP R/3? It wouldn't be very complimentary and yet the problems were caused by the way that they implemented the system not by any shortcomings of the system itself. These were two extremes but cases like this do explain why there are so many horror stories and yet the SAP system is such a good one.

Don't try to keep the design too simple.

Many organisations fall into the trap of trying to keep the implementation too simple. To aim for simplicity in itself is not wrong, but when it comes to mapping the business onto SAP (i.e. the organisation structure etc.) many businesses make the mistake of keeping this far too simple. For instance, they decide to have one company code instead of several, they decide to have a handful of Plants instead of scores of them etc. often backing this up with the statement that this will save them a tremendous amount of master data. My response is that it is more important to get the structure right than to limit the amount of master data. How many times do you maintain master data, at best occasionally? But how many times do you have a receipt, an issue, a transfer a sale, an invoice etc. etc., thousands of times every day. So which is more critical? I would argue that it is better to have more master data to maintain than to lose functionality and block off options, as is the case with an incorrect organisation structure. Master data maintenance programs can be written if the volume dictates it.

It is entirely understandable that people will try to keep things simple and it is an approach that I adopt myself in most things I do, but the organisation structure is meant to represent the reality of the business organisation as closely as possible. By simplifying the structure you will be removing many options and a lot of functionality that you will need to be able to use either now or in the future.

If the business structure is actually quite complex, then the organisation structure on SAP should reflect that complexity. I have been involved with many organisations that have complained that SAP is unable to handle some really basic functions correctly. The second I hear this complaint I point them to the organisation structure that they have configured in SAP. After investigation this always proves to be the cause of the problem.

If SAP R/3 cannot handle a really basic function or if it does not handle it without workarounds or messy processes, then most organisations would suffer from the same problem and it would be a very poor system.

SAP would not just ignore a basic problem such as this and it would have been corrected years ago. So I hope that you will agree that SAP R/3 will at the very least do all of the basic everyday functions reasonably well. If this is the case and the business is saying things like "This SAP system is pretty useless it doesn't even do ......" then it is a very clear indication that something is wrong with this individual implementation and the first place to look is the organisation structure.

So to sum up spend as much time as you can on mapping the organisation structure to the business as accurately as possible, even if this means a larger amount of master data than you expected. Master data can be managed, lack of functionality is far more difficult to handle.

To modify or not to modify, that is the question

This is an easy one for me, quite simply do not modify the SAP system in any way at all, under any circumstances. Use the configuration options to the full and get as much out of the system as you can but don't modify it, ever. This is my approach and it has served me well so far, but the emphasis is on the word approach. I always start from this approach and stick to it under all circumstances, that is until the "real world" bites. There will always be genuine exceptions to a rule such as this and it would be stupid of me to blindly adopt a strategy that was unbreakable, because in the real world there are generally exceptions to every rule. Modifying SAP standard code, transactions, screens etc. will certainly give you problems at some stage and for various reasons. These may well be small manageable problems and so they can be justified, or they could be major problems that would be difficult to resolve and often lead to a compromise of some sort.

So if you start out with the approach that modifications will not be allowed and only break that rule when a genuine case can be supported, this will result in fewer modifications than if you start out with the approach that modifications are an acceptable part of an SAP implementation.

In my career so far I don't think I have ever seen a system without a modification but the degree of modification has varied tremendously. At the top end of the modification scale was a company where it seemed like the majority of the standard system was modified, at the bottom end of that scale the modifications were minor and only affected the system cosmetically. I had held the belief that one of the major reasons for not modifying the system was because it would be very difficult to move to a new release due to the changes that had been made to the standard SAP code etc. This is a comment that you will hear time and time again and from all perspectives. It sounds sensible and in my early SAP career I believed it to be 100% true. In fact as part of my first SAP implementation I decided to visit some businesses that were already using SAP to try to learn from their mistakes. One business we visited made it very clear, "Do not modify the standard SAP system, we did and we are now stuck with an old release because we cannot move to the latest version of SAP without losing all of our modifications". Enough said, not only did I understand the reasoning but I had also now seen at first-hand the consequences and so I was convinced that this was an unbreakable rule. That was until I joined the project where they had carried out a huge number of modifications. Strangely enough part of my role here was to help with an upgrade from 3.1 to 4.6, a big step even if the system had not been modified. So at last this was a chance to change the theory into practise and I was expecting a nightmare scenario. Much to my amazement, the project went very smoothly, it went in on time and without any major issues. Most of the modifications were completely unaffected by the move and those that were affected were easy to identify and easy to apply. In all there was little more work involved that there would have been if there were no modifications. This was thanks to two main reasons, firstly the project team that modified the code initially had fully documented the changes including why it was modified., secondly SAP now provide excellent help when an upgrade is attempted, they highlight the areas that have changed and those that remain unaffected. In some cases the modifications were no longer needed because the later release now contained functionality that enabled us to use the standard SAP solution instead.

So have I now changed my mind about how strongly to resist modifications? The answer is not one iota. The reason behind the approach has changed but the consequences of modifying the SAP code are still as serious as ever. The full justification is contained in the section "Standard SAP?" but in short, you have a system that has been developed by hundreds of experts over many years and every fine detail is integrated with many other areas within the system so what is actually happening is that we are breaking the connections and building new ones from scratch in a matter of days. This will never be as solid, as integrated and as flexible as the standard code and it is like trying to replace a jet planes control instruments with that of a car, you may be able to make it work in some ways but you will definitely not be able to make it a seamless join.

Avoid a "Best of Breed" approach

Many organisations choose the "best of breed" approach and this is understandable, they want the best functionality in each of the areas of the business, but if you mix SAP and best of breed together then be prepared for hidden costs and an SAP system that would be rightly criticised for not providing the expected benefits.

In a recent implementation, I joined after they had implemented SAP in an initial phase. They were then looking for a system that would handle their delivery processes because their business was quite unique. Most companies think that their business is unique and that they need a system especially designed for them but when you analyse their processes they are seldom that different from other businesses, especially in the core modules such as SD, MM, FI etc. In this implementation however, they had a valid point. They delivered concrete and this had many features that made it unique. In another business if you had to deliver 3 loads to a customer and the third load was delayed you would annoy the customer but it wouldn't be a major disaster. In this case though, if you have delivered and poured two loads of concrete and the third was delayed, not only could you not pour it on top of already setting concrete (it would cause a "join" and this would be a weak spot and totally out of the question), but you would also have to dig out or break up the concrete deposited by the first two loads and this was often impossible let alone costly. Try doing this in the centre section of a new bridge or on the top floor of a skyscraper. So to be honest they did have a case, they were unique. There were systems on the market that were designed especially for this purpose and even though they were far from ideal the company were quite correctly considering implementing them. This would have meant an interface to and from SAP, which in itself is not difficult and this is the problem. SAP is a system that can be easily interfaced to and from. The data is stored and managed in such a way that it is very easy to build a simple program to create a file or update data from in incoming file from an interface. So it is an option that people use very frequently. But the more interfaces you have the more integration you are losing. In this case the proposal was to enter the Sales order into SAP and then handle the delivery within the other specialist system. The interface would be quite simple, the customer details and the material required could be interfaced to the other system and the details of the delivery could be interfaced back. On the face of it a suitable solution, but the affect on SAP was that a lot of the in built integration paths had now been broken and many of the standard functions that prove to be so useful would not be useable. Even something as simple as the document flow that SAP provides to give you the list of documents related to an order, and the ability to drill down the path and see each document in detail, is now lost. To check a sales order to see if it has been delivered yet, when it was delivered and by whom, now means using two systems. Master data now has to exist in two systems (customer and material master data) and this always causes problems, one is updated and the other isn't and so they are both different, or if they are both kept in line then this is a waste of time and effort due to the duplication. The SAP system is still as complicated as it was before but now we have interfaces as well. The end result is a compromise.

When you implement SAP R/3 you should decide there and then how committed you will be to retaining the system as the only one you use wherever possible, in order to take advantage of the integration and flexibility that it offers. If you want a successful implementation you really should see SAP as the main system within your organisation and you should be committed to using it for all solutions unless it is technically impossible or completely unfeasible to do anything else. If your commitment is not that strong or you see SAP as being just another system amongst the others you have, then you will not get the ROI you expect and you will join several other companies who think that SAP is disappointing.

If you have to decide whether to use SAP or another system, then my suggested approach is as follows;

Firstly make absolutely sure that you cannot use SAP processes for this requirement, it may be possible to get very close to the requirement using clever configuration. If this is not possible, then still consider using SAP but by copying and amending one or more transactions, if this is not possible then consider triggering all of the required functionality from within SAP, so that SAP holds all of the required data in its standard databases. This could be done by writing new transactions and storing the data in new SAP tables, basically this would be designing the functionality using SAP tools. Finally, if this is not possible then the only option left is to built one or more interfaces to and from SAP to the new system, but this must be the last option considered.

This approach will ensure that you are retaining as many of the benefits of SAP as possible and any problems caused by using interfaces will be reduced to an absolute minimum.

Should you re-engineer the business at the same time as you implement SAP

This is a tricky one, you will be making a mistake if you re-engineer the business at the same time as you implement SAP and you will also be making a mistake if you DON'T re-engineer the business at the same time as you implement SAP. It is all depends on the degree of re-engineering and the basic approach that is adopted.

If you try to carry out re-engineering of the business at the same time then you will probably get a really good implementation that will have both streamlined the processes you use and produced some serious cost savings. The downside is that your project may take twice as long as you planned.

If you do not try to carry out re-engineering of the business at the same time then the project will not be delayed by the effort required but the benefits will be significantly lower.

To re-engineer a business fully you would start with a blank sheet of paper and start building your processes from scratch. This a long and bumpy path to follow, prepare for a lot of heated debates and even more duplication of effort as ideas are discussed, rejected, re-proposed and then rejected again. Even the smallest and least important process will be dissected and reassembled (often in its original guise).

There is however a real alternative that gets the amount of re-engineering just right. Instead of starting with a blank sheet of paper you start from the standard SAP functions. These are tried and tested and are considered (by many) to be genuinely best practice. This option goes hand in hand with my earlier justification for changing the business to match the system. This approach limits the debate to a more manageable level. It also removes the need for detailed "as is" documentation because you will be starting from square one and so this saves some time that can be used for producing better "to be" documentation. The end result is a limited but extremely useful re-engineering exercise that also helps to make the implementation less complex (because the "to be" will reflect the SAP processes a lot more closely). The debates / design meetings become more constructive because it is easier to discus an option that to produce one out of thin air. Another benefit from this is that it gets the business users more involved in the SAP functionality and at an earlier stage.

Use the best SAP consultants you can afford

(I suppose that I would say that wouldn't I?)

But it is very true, it really is false economy to use less-experienced consultants just because they are cheaper. I am also not saying that just because a consultant is not expensive that they are not as good as a more expensive one, all that I am saying is try to get the best available resource first and then consider costs. If you ask an agency to send you the CVs of consultants that will charge no more than X or if you set the maximum fee before you start looking then this may cost a lot more in the long term. I genuinely feel that after 15 years of SAP implementations I am only now at a level where I can honestly say that I know enough about SAP to build the best system possible for a client. Of course after 3 to 5 years of SAP experience I knew enough to do a really good job but there were still many areas that I had not delved into in enough depth to fully understand them and the options that were available.

I can back this up with personal experience gained during my spell as a trainer for SAP UK. I had already been implementing SAP for many years before I started working as a trainer and so I was able to use experience and theory to get the message across. But the thing that surprised me most of all was the number of times when I had just explained a function in SAP and someone said "But my consultant told me that you couldn't do that in SAP", or words to that effect. In fact many consultants with several years of experience just do not know certain areas of the module they specialise in.

Consider the following. If a consultant works as a project team member in a major SAP implementation then the chances are that they will not be the only consultant on that project dealing with the module that they specialise in. This means that they may be tasked to look after (for example) the purchasing elements in MM and possibly some other functions such as Invoice verification, vendor master etc. They will not be expected to manage the entire MM module by themselves. So they can be working for years on a project and still get no experience of certain functions, especially the less popular ones such as "External services management" or "Supplier evaluation" etc. This may be the case on their next project too, the next client wants them because they are experienced in the Purchasing side of MM and so they play a similar role in the next project. Even when they are given a broader scope to deal with, the client may not intend to use some of the SAP functionality available. This can often lead to there being gaps in the consultant's knowledge. The risk is that when they are working on another project they cannot always be aware of options that may be available and so the client is often told (without meaning to lie) that the function is not possible in SAP or not advised. Put yourself in the shoes of the consultant being paid a healthy rate for his / her experience and being asked about functionality that resides in their specialist module that they know nothing about. It is not a pleasant position to be in and there is no real way of dealing with this other than saying I don't know, if it is a specific question, or I am not aware of a solution if it is a less direct question.

So please do try to have one highly experienced consultant for each of the modules you are implementing, lesser experienced consultants can then be used to support this consultant if necessary. One top consultant with one junior consultant as support is far better than three average consultants and probably costs less even in the short term. In addition to this I am always in favour of smaller project teams because this results in a more focussed solution and a better view of the overall design. Too many consultants can result in nobody having an overall view of the design and this is essential in a truly integrated system. I will discuss the ideal project team size and structure in another section.

Keep the number of new ABAP programs to an absolute minimum

I have already stated that it is best not to modify the system but this is different. ABAP is SAP's own programming language (and a very good one at that). This sometimes leads people into thinking that SAP provide this to allow you to write your own reports and transactions and this is basically true but this does not mean that ABAP programs do not come with problems that are often well hidden.

I have covered this subject in more detail in the section on "Standard SAP" but the basic points are as follows.

SAP provide ABAP to assist you where you need to get something extra from the system, perhaps there is an additional report that an organisation such as yours MUST have and it is not built into SAP as standard. ABAP is also needed for interfaces into and out of SAP. Even though I avoid interfaces wherever possible it is very rare indeed to have an SAP implementation without an interface of some kind (EDI is a classic example). ABAP is also used for one-off data loads and conversions etc. So there are many uses of ABAP.

Some organisations see ABAP as an everyday tool that can be used whenever something is needed and the standard SAP option does not provide it in the format that the business wants it in. This is not a good approach, this results in a system that is as modified as if you had changed the standard SAP code.

The best approach to ABAP is to use it as a last resort and not a first option (for reasons discussed elsewhere). Do not write a new ABAP simply because the standard SAP ABAP is not quite good enough or if it is nearly OK but there are a few fields that we would like to add or we would like to see the data presented in a different format. If this is the situation and you must have it corrected then copy the existing ABAP and make as small a change to it as possible. This is not just because of the effect of any later upgrade, it is more due to the fact that the standard SAP has often been developed over a long time and uses data from many sources. To re-write the program from scratch or to change it significantly will mean that the programmer will have to understand thoroughly not only where the data comes from but a lot about exactly what the data means and what alternative data sources are available and when they should be used.

Let's take a simple stock report as an example. The business users have asked for a new report that shows the stock figures in a different format than the standard program and with some extra data taken from another table within SAP. One of the fields to be displayed is the "Stock in Transit" quantity, in other words the quantity of stock that has been issued but not yet received. There is a field on the material master record entitled "stock in transit" and the programmer has been told to use this, or they have decided themselves that this is the source of the data. Unfortunately in reality there are several "stock in transit" fields and so the chances are that the data displayed on the report may well be correct in some circumstances and yet incorrect in others. There are "stock in transit" fields at the Plant level as well as the Storage location level. Which one is required? It depends on many factors. The problem is made worse by the fact that there are several fields that hold "stock in transit" quantities even within a storage location and within a plant. This is because there are separate fields that hold the quantity depending on where the stock is being transferred from and to, there is a "stock in transit" field for storage location to storage location transfers, there is a separate one for stock in transit for Plant to Plant transfers, there is another one for those transfers that a plant to plant but are crossing from one company code to another etc. etc. This one small piece of information is just an example that shows that writing a simple ABAP program is rarely that simple. At best the program will take a lot longer than planned because of the need to determine the exact source of the relevant data, at worse the data will be taken from the wrong source and give a meaningless report. This is more common than you would think and errors like this slip through the testing "net" quite often. In the above example if the Stock in transit should have come from the Storage location instead of the Plant then when the test is carried out it may appear to be correct because there is only one storage location at the plant and so the figures match, then later on in the project, perhaps many months after the original "go-live" has passed, another storage location is added and suddenly the program is now producing the wrong results. Believe me errors like this are plentiful and are in a strict ratio to the degree of ABAP changes that have been implemented.

Get the training right

It is often said that a system is only as good as the training you have given to the end-users and this is very true, particularly of an SAP system.

I have already spent a lot of time pointing out how different an SAP implementation is, but this also applies to how different the training should be. There is a separate section that covers training but I will cover the most important issues here first.

If you are implementing the smallest and simplest of systems then you still need to give the end-users appropriate training at the correct time. If you train them too early, then they will forget most of it and lose their confidence when they have to use it for the first time. If you train too late in the project then there is rarely enough time to do it properly. Another problem is how much training to give, too much and it becomes confusing, too little and it doesn't really help much. But even if you do the training at exactly the right time and give the correct amount of training this will still not work. It is a bit like (forgive the nostalgia here and nostalgia isn't what it used to be) when I went from a typewriter to my first ever word processor. It was very, very scary. Give me a typewriter and, using 2 fingers and 10 sheets of paper, I could probably produce a one sheet document that looked reasonably good enough. It was slow and painful but I could see what I was doing and felt that I had control. When I moved to a word processor I simply could not handle it, I hated it and I demanded my typewriter back. I felt like I had lost all control of the machine, I didn't understand the concepts let alone the functions available. I had read the manual but it was a waste of time, I didn't understand anything. But I eventually decided to persevere and I started to use it. It was three times as slow as my typewriter at first because I had to think before I hit each key. Eventually I started to get used to it and found things like a spelling checker and cut and paste functions. After some time had passed I eventually was starting to get used to it and actually began to like it. I was not wasting any paper and not having to type the whole thing each time I made a mistake. Before long I was using automatic page numbering and table of contents functions etc. etc. If someone offered me my typewriter back then I would have told them that no way would I go back to it. A big turnaround in my appreciation of the new way of doing things but no amount of training would have made that turnaround painless.

My approach to training people to use SAP is fairly radical when compared to the more standard options but I really believe that it is the only way to reduce the pain of the transition.

Firstly, I point out to the users that it will feel scary at first and I even use the typewriter / word processor analogy to explain this. I feel it really is important to manage people's expectations. If they feel scared and think that it is just them, then they will take a long time for that user to build any confidence in the system at all. If they have been told that it will take a while to get used to the new system and that they will know what to expect and it may make it a little easier to accept. This in itself is not that radical, it is just good practice. Where my approach can be said to be radical is in the amount of training I prefer to give and the type of training I encourage.

Most approaches rely on giving the most classroom training that can be achieved in the time available, my aim is to give the least classroom training possible. My reasoning for this is that SAP is as I have already pointed out quite a complex system and if you try to teach it in depth then you run the real risk of confusing the users and alienating them at the very time you want to try to get them to be very positive about the change that comes with an SAP system. My training is focussed on the process that they will have to follow rather than teaching them the screens details and which keys to press and when. If there was a simple linear path through the screens then that would be fine I could teach them that they press button A then enter XXX then press button B then enter the qty etc. etc. But the vast majority of SAP transactions are just not like that, they provide many functions within each screen and there are many options available to use. To teach all of the appropriate combinations would not only take too long but it would cause most users to have a nervous breakdown. There have been many genuine examples where people have attended their End-user training and left the company within days, quoting the belief that they cannot cope with the degree of change. In a less severe response many people convince themselves that they will never be able to take it all in and so they switch off altogether. This is yet another source of some of the horror stories, imagine what the people who are going through this kind of training would say to some one who announces that their organisation have just decided to implement SAP R/3?

So If I don't believe in training the end users to use all of the functions that they need to know about, then how will they ever learn how to use them? My basic approach involves firstly explaining to the users in a classroom environment what SAP is (briefly), how it will feel, what happens after the training course and then we go through a business process that they are involved in. I don't just show them the screens that they will be using I go through the main parts of the whole process so that they can see what has happened before their part in the process and what happens after they have done their part. This helps them understand how it all fits together and also shows the integration and the importance of them getting their bit right. I then show them how to complete the transaction that they will be using, but just using basic examples of a normal example. I show them what error messages they may get and what to do if they get one, I show them where to get help when they need it and that is it. I give them one or two very simple exercises but I like to keep these to a minimum because they rarely relate to the "real world" and so the users can't really relate what they are seeing in the classroom to what they will be doing "on the job".

I try to keep the sessions as short as possible and for most users this is one day, possibly two. For more senior staff this can obviously expand to longer sessions but even these are to be kept to a minimum.

I am not pretending for one minute that these users are now able to operate the system, but they now know more about what it involves and they have seen the end-to-end process. All of this is carried out as close to "go-live" as possible and because the training sessions are much shorter than with other approaches this is easier to achieve.

The real training starts on the first day that they start using the system for real, after the system is made live. I tell the users that the first time that they need to use SAP they must ask for someone to guide them through, either face to face or over the phone if this is not feasible. I make sure that they are told that we genuinely want them to do this and that we actually prefer them to do this rather than having them struggle. As they use each function for the first time they are actually doing it for real and so they can relate so much easier to what is happening. This "hand-holding" is the best way for them to learn, it does take a lot of planning and effort from the implementation teams but the effort pays off over and over again. The fact that the team of hand-holders consists of many of the project team members means that when errors are discovered (as they always are in the early days of a new implementation) they already have a personal link to the user involved and may even be hand-holding with the user at the time the error occurs and therefore able to see exactly what happened.

In all I believe this approach is worth considering, it takes a lot of planning and some extra resource post go-live but in my experience the length of time that heavy support is required is dramatically reduced and the overall perception of the system is massively more positive.

Carry out a full Post Implementation review (PIR)

Many organisations will do this but there are some that don't and with an SAP implementation this really is a must.

As I have pointed out already, many decisions will have to be made by the business users long before they understand SAP and certainly before the understand the consequences of their decisions. So it is vital to ascertain if the project did actually implement the system that was promised. This is not a check on the project management, the I.T. community or even the business users, it is merely looking at how close to the initial design scope and aims, the delivered system actually is. This is not designed to be a finger-pointing exercise, it is meant to establish of more work is needed just to get the system to a stage where it performs as the business planned. The scope of the project may have drifted more than is desirable (most projects experience some scope creep, but this should not be excessive). Most of the scope creep is often due to the originally defined scope being vague or inaccurate or unachievable, but when dealing with a system as flexible and as functionally rich as SAP it is very easy to fall into the trap of just providing bigger (and no doubt better) solutions, that are in effect a lot more than was requested. This scope creep is not normally a problem if the implementation has gone well and a healthy ROI has been achieved, but it is a definite problem if the implementation has not gone well and some of the basic functions have problems whereas other areas of the system now have "bells and whistles".

The PIR should therefore indicate those areas that need to be addressed to bring the solution up to the desired standard. Mini projects can then be launched to address those issues and a final review at the end to ensure that the project has now achieved a fully working implementation.

My own approach to the PIR is slightly different (I guess that this does not surprise you if you have read to this point). I would launch the PIR at a much later stage than normal. This is because in the early stages the users will still be struggling to get to grips with the new processes and the complexity of the SAP implementation. I would almost guarantee that if you launched the PIR three months after go live, then the feedback from most of the users would be very negative indeed, most would be asking for their old systems back and several would be saying that the new system simply does not work. This may be the case but even the most successful of all SAP implementations would get this really bad press at this stage. Hold the same PIR after six months instead of three and the results are likely to be more positive, wait for nine months and you will probably get the best picture, in fact waiting for as long as nine months would probably introduce a new and surprising problem. The users will probably be saying that the system is fine and they now want more. (This is all based on the assumption that the implementation was at the very least a reasonably good one).

This doesn't mean that I am suggesting waiting for nine months before you address any problems. The normal support process should continue (albeit gradually reducing over time) and issues and system problems should be addressed as and when they arise. But this must be done in such a way that only genuine system errors and major showstoppers are addressed. Changing the design because "it doesn't seem to be working" should be resisted quite strongly (within reason) until people are more familiar with the system and it can be ascertained that the problems are not being caused by people not following the agreed processes (either by choice or by mistake).

The PIR can include suggested improvements but these should be just collected and logged rather than investigated in any depth, unless they are so obviously required immediately. There should be a further stage after the PIR to examine the possibility of small changes that will make big improvements, a kind of fine-tuning. This could be scheduled for one year after go-live, to ensure that the system is now stable and fully implemented according to the PIR and that the users now feel comfortable enough with the SAP system and are now knowledgeable enough to know how to get more out of the system. So few organisations actually try to fine-tune their SAP system and this may be because they only plan as far as the PIR and the project is then seen to be complete and it would be difficult to fund an extra project. But if you really want to get the benefits out of the SAP implementation you really cannot just implement and stop. It takes commitment and it certainly will cost money, but the benefits of a fine-tuning stage will far outweigh the costs and the effort involved. Another reason that this fine-tuning does not take place is down to the belief that implementing SAP gives you the cost benefits anyway and so there is no need for such a stage. This may be true and is definitely tied into how good the implementation was, but even the best SAP implementation will gain huge benefits if it is fine-tuned after it has settled down. If you realise at the very beginning that this step may well be necessary then it can be included in the original plan.

Hopefully this section of the book will help you to get the most out of the SAP implementation. It should also help you to understand why it will take a lot of time and effort to produce the benefits but they can be spectacular if you are aware of the do's and don'ts of a good SAP implementation. It may also help to manage your expectations and give you some idea of what to expect, especially because most of the time it will feel that it is not going well, even when it couldn't be going better. Hopefully you can use this section as a map that will help to guide you through the minefield that is a new SAP implementation

The hidden advantages of standard SAP

Why have I written a separate section devoted to the benefits of using standard (i.e. unmodified) SAP? To be perfectly honest, most people involved in SAP in one way or another would say "I already know that standard SAP has many advantages, I only use non-standard SAP when it is necessary, we can't be more standard?" Well to be honest I would agree that most people know that standard SAP is a good approach but I am equally sure that many people don't actually realise just how costly non-standard SAP systems really are, or in fact what is actually meant by "standard SAP". So I am sure that this section will be of use to you even if you think that I am just "preaching to the converted".

So what do I actually mean when I use the term "Standard SAP"? To answer this question it would help if we look at the two extremes.

Firstly the extreme of the <u>absolutely</u> standard SAP implementation.

This would be an implementation where the system has had basic configuration to "personalise" the system to the business, the organization structure has been configured and other items such as number ranges built and activated, but no new or changed ABAP programs (other than SAP supplied) and no significant interfaces are used. This type of implementation is quite rare but far from impossible.

Secondly the extreme of the completely non standard SAP implementation.

This is an implementation where there are large numbers of ABAP developments and lots of modifications to the standard SAP programs, screens and reports etc. This is not quite as rare as the first extreme but (fortunately) still quite rare.

There are many different reasons why people argue that non-standard SAP is not a major problem. You will often here statements such as the following;

> "But ABAP is Standard SAP, surely SAP provide it because they know that you are going to need to use it".
> "Everyone adds lots of new ABAPs?"
> "Everyone produces in-house built reports"
> "We haven't modified SAP"
> "Everyone has interfaces"
> "Many people who use non-standard SAP manage to upgrade to later releases without major problems."

However, if we look at each comment in more detail

"But ABAP is Standard SAP, surely SAP provide it because they know that you are going to need to use it".

This is a fair point, why would SAP provide you with a powerful programming language if you weren't supposed to use it? Of course it is there to use if you need it but it doesn't mean that there are no negatives involved.

ABAP is there to be used sparingly and only when you absolutely have to use it. If you start using ABAP without thinking about the consequences then you will soon find that you have a system that is becoming more and more dependent on a team of ABAP programmers for support, (increasing costs) and with the true integration benefits of SAP being gradually eroded.

I am not saying that you must not write any ABAP reports, I am just saying only use ABAP it if it can be completely justified and part of the justification must be that there it is something that the business MUST have, not just "would like" and there is no way that the same results (within reason) can be obtained from standard SAP.

"Everyone adds lots of new ABAPs?"

This is not strictly true. I would agree that it would be virtually impossible to have a reasonable SAP implementation without having to write or change any ABAP code, but there are lots of implementations that have managed to keep this to an absolute minimum and it is no coincidence that these implementations are more likely to see SAP R/3 as being a success story.

"Everyone has in-house built reports"

This is a fair comment, it would be very rare for the standard SAP supplied reports to be sufficient to match every requirement for every kind of business that has implemented SAP. It does not follow though that ABAP reports cannot cause problems just because they do not update anything. In my earlier example I demonstrated that a simple ABAP report could easily use incorrect data and cause problems mainly because the SAP functionality is so rich and the integration so detailed that it is rarely a case of just collecting data from a field, often there are several fields involved and it can take a high degree of SAP knowledge to ensure that the correct data is collected in the correct manner.

"We haven't modified SAP"

Many companies strongly believe that they have a standard SAP system with no modifications when in fact this is not true. For example, if you have retained one or more significant legacy systems, then you are likely to have some degree of modification. Data will now be stored across two or more systems and to update and retrieve this data will require custom built programs. If they are just straightforward interfaces then this is not really a modification but few organisations running SAP and legacy systems can do it without modifying SAP in some way. Transactions have to retrieve and update data in another system and this is not a standard SAP option (apart from one or two very rare situations such as those involving RFC and/or EDI).

"Everyone has interfaces"

This is not absolutely correct, it is possible to run an organization on SAP without the need for interfaces and this is an aim that I would strongly encourage. Interfaces are a necessary evil and if you have been forced into using them because of a retained legacy system, you are in fact losing in two ways. You have the risk of the interface failing, being run twice, losing data or not being run at all and in addition to these risks you also now have a system that has had some of the complex integration data in SAP reduced to the number of fields on the interface.

"Many people who use non-standard SAP manage to upgrade to later releases without major problems.

As I have stated elsewhere in this book I would have strongly argued this point several years ago but I have to agree that this comment is based on fact. There are several organizations that have upgraded (often a major upgrade) even though they have a highly modified SAP system. I now longer use this as the main reason for not modifying SAP, but at the same time the upgrade is still far more costly in time and effort and contains a much higher element of risk than a less modified system.

A simple ABAP?

Using "standard SAP" has very clear and substantial benefits and most of these are known and understood by those that are experienced SAP professionals (and experienced business users too), but they are often grossly underestimated.

Many experienced consultants will often use the phrase "We could use a simple ABAP to solve that issue/problem" In fact I use this phrase quite often myself. But even small developments such as a simple ABAP report can be very costly in reality and so the long term cost needs to be fully considered before the decision to progress is made.

Let's look at a genuine example of a simple ABAP that was suggested in an organisation that I was involved in that would have resulted in significant costs that could have been avoided by using the standard SAP alternative.

A business user requested a report to be written that would show them invoices that are currently blocked due to a quantity mismatch and the report should be able to be produced by site and not by just by company code. There did not appear to be such a report available in "standard SAP" (especially as they wanted the report broken down by site because the standard SAP reports are broken down by Company code) and so a new ABAP was specified an it would not have taken long to produce, because it was a relatively simple report.

When the report was written and the user received the first copy they realised that it would be more useful if totals were added at the bottom of the page, not a problem and a small change, in theory, but the changes have to go through (quite correctly) the change request process, involving authorisation for the change, additional testing, transports and possible changes to training documents. This already starts to increase costs above the forecast and the report is not yet completed.

The user then continued to use the new report for a few weeks and liked the new information but requested an additional report similar to this one, but this time one that shows invoices that had value discrepancies instead of quantity discrepancies. Then they wanted to be able to double-click on a line (when the report was viewed on-line) and go straight to the actual document involved to see more details such as who raised it and what else was included on the invoice, etc. Then they requested another change so that the report could be selected by company code and they wanted the results to be sorted by Plant, Value, Vendor, invoice clerk etc. etc.

Before long, the report had been developed so much that the original cost estimate was a fraction of the actual cost involved. In addition to this there were errors in the calculations and displays etc. that were not spotted in the original testing and these surfaced later when the report was being used.

The report had been developed so much that it was now a major program rather than the simple report that was first proposed and the cost was now huge, but the biggest shock of all was when the user was shown the standard SAP transaction that was originally thought to not be sufficient. They discovered that this did give them all of what they now needed (and more) and the original problem that prevented them from using this standard report was not in fact a showstopper, because the standard report could be selected, sorted and totalled by site by using the Purchasing group and Plant fields combined to produce the correct breakdown, it was just that nobody had really investigated the options available in the first place. In addition to this the standard SAP function was accurate, on-line and quick and it also came with plenty of "bells and whistles" that the user didn't even think of, that proved to be very useful and of course, all of this came at ZERO cost. This was a very painful discovery and you only have to experience this once or twice and you really do understand the importance of making absolutely sure that a standard SAP function cannot be used (albeit with a workaround) before any ABAP work is undertaken. The other negative outcome was that coding and design of the in-house report was only fully understood by a handful of people in the IT department and so this information had to be retained or handed over if personnel changes were made. If the standard SAP function had been used instead, then the design, coding and use of this function would be likely to be known by other SAP consultants.

This also emphasises another rule that I like to follow and that is never simply give the user what they are asking for without first questioning the reason for their request, this enables you to ensure that there are no alternatives that the user is unaware of that may prove to be exactly what the user needs. After all you cannot expect the user to know enough about SAP to know exactly what it can do, or what to ask for, that is what the consultant is being paid for.

In this case if the users request was questioned more thoroughly we may have been able to establish the reason for their request and provide them with a solution (such as the standard SAP transaction that is very comprehensive) rather than providing them with merely what they asked for.

In the case of more substantial ABAP changes such as programs to provide alternative solutions without using the standard SAP functionality etc. then you should consider the following;

What if - you had an IT department consisting of hundreds of business system experts and you then took 30 years to develop and enhance a system for the business processes that you use in your business.

What if - you had hundreds of thousands of users all testing the system in a "live" environment, for the last 30 years?

What if - you could make sure it works by getting the majority of the biggest organisations in the world to use it before you did?

What if - you had an R & D Department, with a huge budget, whose sole purpose was to maintain and improve the system and to ensure that it can react to any changes in financial methods or legal requirements, before those requirements hit you?

What if - you could make the system completely integrated and be able to drill down through to the minute detail or up to the highest level of aggregation

What if - you made that system so flexible that it wouldn't require a new system or new implementation if you sold off any business that you own or bought in every business you wanted to, or both

And then !!!!!!

What if - you just wrote a quick ABAP?

Would it be as integrated?
Would it be as well tested?
Would it be as flexible?
Would it be as powerful?
Would it be as thorough?

Would it be advisable?

I think not.

So please consider this when making a decision to write any substantial programs to introduce additional functionality to the standard SAP system.

Best Practice

If we were to accept the fact that SAP is built around "Best Practice", (This statement can be debated at great length but lets assume that it is basically true for now) then there should therefore not be any mainstream process that is missing or just simply does not work. This includes basic reporting requirements that should be included in the standard SAP system in one form or another. If they weren't included then other organisations that are using SAP R/3 would have pointed this out to SAP at some stage already. So in effect, most organisations should be able to function without modifying the standard SAP functionality. This is why there have been full implementations of SAP that have only taken three or four months in total, they all decided to accept that SAP was built on best practise and designed their processes around the SAP functionality instead of changing SAP R/3 to match their current processes. This therefore is an indication that the basic structure of SAP is sound and should not need to be modified in any significant manner for most organisations. However, it cannot be a perfect fit for all types of businesses in all situations and so there are situations where certain organisations will find genuine gaps in functionality that may be specific to their type of business. One system cannot possibly be an exact match for all types of businesses and SAP is no exception. However, to overcome these gaps, SAP has designed "Industry-Specific" (IS) solutions for industries such as, gas and oil, utilities, retail, footwear and apparel, real estate, etc. etc.

Filling in the gaps in SAP functionality

There are a variety of businesses that will not find a suitable IS solution and so their gaps in functionality will have to be filled somehow. BUT, these "gaps" should be used to justify either not using SAP R/3 at all, or to justify ripping out functionality from SAP R/3 and replacing it with another system. The gap will only affect certain specific functions within the business and this can often be resolved by focussed developments instead. These developments may well involve modifications to SAP, but they can be achieved with minimal affect on the overall SAP system. It is for cases such as this that the rule of "no modifications" can be broken.

A genuine example of this that I personally experienced was while I was on the project for a heavy building materials company.

They like almost every business believed that they were very different to other businesses because of the products that the dealt with. One genuine example proved this to be true; Ready Mixed Concrete. This is a product unlike any other in many ways but even this product is not that different when you analyse the end-to-end process. This is where I feel that a positive attitude towards the SAP R/3 system helps to achieve what the business actually needs. It would be easy to use the fact that this product is so unusual to justify not using SAP R/3 for the related processes, or worse still not using SAP at all because it didn't match the business requirements. My approach is to try the fit first and identify exactly where the gaps occur and how big the gaps are, even though it is obvious in this case that the standard SAP system simply could not handle this type of product. This is because even the most complex and the most unusual products still share a high degree of common processes. This also includes products as unusual as utilities such as electricity, gas, water etc. even products such as Real estate, insurance, advertising can and are handles by SAP using SAP supplied Industry solutions.

So if we look at the end-to-end process involved in Ready Mixed Concrete in detail.

The ordering process,

This is generally handled by standard SAP functionality but there are one or two differences that would, on the surface, appear to require special treatment.

When the Concrete is ordered there are many factors that affect the exact "make-up" of the product. There is no simple formula for the ingredients and there are varying ratios of each ingredient to affect the properties of the resulting Concrete. This makes the ordering process more complicated but it is not something that SAP R/3 cannot handle. It has functionality for what it calls "Configurable materials" and it also has a powerful Bill Of Material (BOM) function. In addition to this complexity regarding the ingredients, there is also a very complex pricing calculation.

In reality, the SAP "to be" design for the ordering process would be very complex, matching the complexity of the end product, but it would not be classed as a gap in the functionality. If any modifications were required then I am convinced that these would be very minor and quite acceptable when compared to the huge benefits that could be achieved by retaining the power of the SAP R/3 integration.

The production process

Concrete is not produced in a factory and the raw materials are dug from the ground and this sounds very different from any other product. In fact the Concrete is produced virtually within the truck, it has such a short shelf life (a few hours) that It cannot be produced elsewhere and then loaded onto the truck as with other products. But is this as different as it appears? The batch size is obviously smaller, the production plant is the truck and the ingredients are consumed at the point of production in varying quantities according to the requested design specification of the ordered product.

So I would argue that the production process could also be mapped onto standard SAP functionality. The production process functionality within SAP R/3 is very powerful, extremely flexible and more than capable of handling the processes that would be required to produce and manage this product.

The delivery process

This is where I would accept that there are major differences in the product being delivered and even I would accept that the standard SAP R/3 system would not cover the required functionality. But this product really is very different when it comes to the delivery process and for many reasons.

The delivery time is absolutely critical. Concrete has to be delivered on time. If the delivery is late then there will be people standing around on a building site who cannot continue until the product arrives and the knock-on effect of this can be substantial. If the delivery is early and the customer is not ready then the extremely short "shelf-life" of the Concrete would be compromised.

The weather has a major effect. If it rains or if the temperature drops below freezing then this normally means that Concrete cannot be poured and so the delivery would be cancelled. If a the rain stops then the customers will expect the replacement deliveries to take place almost immediately.

The properties of the product result in special procedures. Multiple deliveries of Concrete for the same stage of the construction MUST take place without gaps or delays between each delivery (known as a "pour" in the industry). Even when dealing with "normal products" customers will often state that they want a complete delivery in one-step and that partial deliveries will not be accepted and so this can be handles in SAP quite easily. But the consequences of getting this wrong are far from "Normal". Consecutive pours of concrete into the same "mould" MUST occur within a very short space of time. If there is a gap in-between pours then this results in a weakness that simply cannot be allowed to happen. Imagine if this were to happen during the construction of a skyscraper and sections were being poured into large moulds at the very top of the construction. A vehicle breakdown, a heavy traffic jam, a driver that could not find the site (difficult when a huge skyscraper is being built but by no means impossible), these could result in a delay that would mean disaster for all involved. Not only would the customer be unable to pour the Concrete when it finally arrived, but the concrete that had already been poured would now have to be removed. This could cost the company a small fortune, let alone damage their reputation, simply because they could not get the pour done in time. So it is issues like this that make this very different from the scenarios that SAP R/3 was meant to handle.

There are special software solutions designed specifically for this exact situation and they are very impressive. Not only do they include full GPS location software to show exactly where every truck is, but they also have sensors on each truck to indicate if the pour has commenced or not. They can estimate the time of arrival and give the driver directions as with any satellite navigation system. In all this software fulfils the requirements of the Concrete company exactly.

So what happens now to my approach of "Not modifying SAP R/3 in any way and under any circumstances", "Not having legacy systems" and "Not having interfaces" etc. Would I therefore recommend that SAP was simply not suitable for this company, or would I recommend that I break the rules that I seem to indicate are unbreakable. Well I certainly wouldn't recommend the former, this really would be "throwing the baby out with the bathwater". I would have to reluctantly and very carefully break my golden rules. But as I indicated when I defined these rules, it all changes when the "real world" bites. This is a genuine example of a gap that not only does the SAP R/3 system not handle, but one that I cannot see SAP as a company spending time and money on "filling", it would just not be worth the effort for the handful of customers that would benefit. But I would have only decided to break these rules when I have exhausted all other options entirely first and this is important. In addition to this, because I value those rules so much I would make sure that the degree to which I break them is as minimal as is possible.

The solution would be to install the specialist software and have interfaces between it and SAP, but here is where I start to limit the degree of which the rules are broken. The specialist system also has the sales order process built into it and it would be , on the face of it, easier and safer to retain the specialist package as a complete system. But I would state that it is far more important to retain SAP R/3 as complete as possible. To have the sales of Concrete sit entirely on one system and the sales of all other products on SAP would result in the loss of a huge amount of standard SAP tools and reports etc. What would be the point of looking at the overall sales figures if you have to add together the results form two systems? Why store the financial data in two systems? Of course this data can be interfaced but I have already expressed my dislike of interfaces. So I would actively seek out a more radical solution, especially if the end result is the "best of both worlds".

I discovered that the specialist software had a "What if?" function and so you could feed it the details of a specific requirement or group of requirements and it would change the planned deliveries to match this requirement. This therefore meant that there appeared to be a point at which an interface from SAP could feed in the requirements of an order to the system removing the need to actually enter the order in the specialist system. This would result in the company being able to retain all of the sales functions and all of the integrated data within SAP and yet still get the benefits of the GPS navigation, delivery planning and truck manage-ment from the specialist software. This therefore meant that there was a simple interface passing minimal data (what to deliver, where and when) instead of ripping out a whole portion of SAP (the order entry and man-agement) and using the less functionally rich and less integrated solution involving the other system.

This is a genuine example of why I make so much fuss about making sure that SAP cannot do it before you decide to use other options. To me the importance of retaining the vital integration and flexibility of SAP R/3 is worth spending the time and effort of considering other design solu-tions first, before choosing to dilute the benefits of such integration and flexibility and increase the risk inherent with interfaces and large modifi-cations..

The effects of non-standard implementations after go-live

I think I can safely say that SAP R/3 is not an inexpensive system by anyone's standards, but if you agree with this statement to any extent then you would reasonably expect it to be well built and fully operational. So why then do many organisations, after spending so much money on implementing SAP R/3 and after paying substantial licence fees, think that they should be paying for large teams of programmers and analysts to develop and support the system? What is it that they are paying SAP for? These really are basic questions and few, if any companies actually ask them. It just seems to be the way of the SAP world and so people accept it.

The reason for the need to retain large SAP teams normally results from the number of modifications and ABAPs that have been built into the standard system. But why does a more standard SAP implementation result in the need for smaller teams? Surely the number of queries and issues we will get will not be dramatically increased just because we have modified the system slightly. I personally think it will be significantly increased. I have already explained how the standard functionality has been built and developed over a number of years and involving many experts and our own in-house built solutions are built over a period of months, tested over a period of weeks and normally involve a handful of experts at most. So I think this does indicate a potential for more problems and more issues.

Even if you disagree with this and the number of problems and issues are similar, the degree of modification can still mean that they will take longer to resolve and therefore result in a need for larger teams to maintain the backlog to an acceptable level. A problem within a totally standard SAP function is less likely to be caused by a program error or bug. It certainly happens, I am not saying that SAP R/3 is perfect remember (it is a System that is Almost Perfect), but the same program is being used by many other companies and has been for some time and this definitely reduces the number of errors and bugs.

If the problem is caused by an error within the standard SAP system then it is SAP's responsibility to correct this and so the problem is passed for them to resolve and any solution will be passed back to the team as a fix that is applied using the SAP supplied instructions. If the problem occurs within parts of the system that have been built or changed "in-house" then the team have to solve this themselves and it is not impossible for this to result in a significant redesign if the problem is caused by a design error.

If the problem is not caused by an error or bug then it will often be "operator error" which is easy to solve, or it may be a configuration error. To solve a configuration error the team will have to change the configuration and this is nothing like making a program change. The configuration has been designed to be changed and so the process is not as risky as a program change and more emphasis is placed on the business effects of the change than the technical effects. This means that the person with the skills that are used to identify the problem is often competent enough to make the configuration changes and so there is no need for two people to be involved in the change.

So the size of the team required is, in my view, certainly affected by the degree of modification.

Writing in-house reports in SAP R/3

In-house built reports should not be seen as outside of the rule of trying to use standard SAP wherever possible. All too often they are seen as something that we write as and when requested without really questioning the need or investigating the alternative options available. It is almost as if the user requests a report and the next step is that the consultant writes a program specification and the report is then written. There generally appears to be a lack of investigation because it is "just a report", but it is equally important to look at the standard SAP options first for a new report, as it is for a new transaction or modification.

There are several SAP options to choose from, there are standard SAP reports that are designed to meet most requirements, there are report writing tools that are designed to be used to create reports that use standard SAP data, quickly and easily and there are also the Information Systems reports, an under-utilised option that many people don't even know exists

The standard SAP reports are generally far more useful and certainly far more flexible than many people realise. By utilising options such as "Variants", selection ranges and flexible screen layouts, these reports can often fulfil user requirements without a single line of code being written.

Variants can be thought of as a method of defaulting data into the selection screen. SAP reports often have so many selection options that people find them too flexible and not very user-friendly and I can see why. Many selection screens contain more than 30 or 40 fields that can be used and it is very difficult to know which fields to fill in and what the result will be and so the user often requests a report to be written that just contains the relevant selection options and produces just the information that they need. Even if the user understands the fields that have to be entered and exactly what is to be entered against each field then it is a daunting task to do this every time the report is needed. This is where Variants help, you can enter the data that you normally select (this is often the same each time with one or two exceptions) then use the variant to save the selections for future use. Many different combinations can be saved for each report

77

and each one given a different variant name. Then when the report is required, the appropriate variant is selected and the screen appears with the data defaulted into the appropriate fields. Importantly this data does not have to be fixed, variables can be used and so certain entries can change depending on circumstances. A prime example of this is a selection field where a date is entered, you may want to enter the last day of the month as a default, or today's date, or today plus X days, weeks or months etc. and then when the report is run, the date is calculated using this variable or variables. This means that month-end reports, etc. can be scheduled to run automatically or the different versions of a report selected by choosing a variant and just executing this variant as it is (you have the option of changing any selection field if you want to, even if it has already been defaulted. You can even prevent this by locking fields from input when creating the variant to make sure that the data cannot be changed. The many options available make Variants well worth considering.

One genuine example of this was a report requested by the finance department on a project that I was involved in. They wanted what they called a PPV (Purchase Price Variance) report. This was to be used to highlight any materials that were being bought at a price that was dramatically different to the accounting price (in this case, the "standard price" in SAP terminology). There was no such standard report supplied with the system and there appeared to be nothing even similar to it. It would have been very easy to decide at this point that a new program should be written to produce this report, but in the end it was produced without a single line of code and the end result was not what the user asked for, it was far better than that, it had many useful options that the user had not even thought of asking for (yet).

How was this achieved?

Firstly, this is a genuine illustration of how it is possible to reduce the need for program changes and new programs just by using existing programs, but it is also a prime example of how the use of more experienced consultants can actually save money and at the same time produce better results.

As an experienced consultant I knew the area of purchasing very well and I understood the concepts and processing of the material master valuation price (in this case known as the Standard Price). I knew that every time a receipt was processed the system posted the stock and also the financial elements at this point. I also knew that one of these elements was a posting to the PPV account if the Purchase Order price was different to the Standard Price. So I knew that the data we needed was there. I also realised that the data was just stored as a collection of individual postings and as such not exactly what the user needed. They wanted to be able to specify the material or a range of materials and a date and to see the variances that occurred for this combination of events along with the Purchase Order number that related to the difference. They also wanted to limit the resulting report to only those postings that were above a certain value, they were not that interested in minor differences.

I knew that the data did not store the Purchase Order number that related to the difference but I also knew that it could be made to do this by changing the "sort key" on the PPV account. This would mean that we had the correct data but we needed a way of turning this data into a report. Trusting SAP R/3 as I do to be more flexible than you would expect, I started to look at the standard SAP reporting options and I discovered that the standard enquiry that SAP provide for interrogating an account (any account) looked promising. By using this transaction and the many selection options I was able to produce a report that looked like it would be worth showing to the user. Their first impression was not great, they didn't like the selection screen, it had too many fields and didn't appear to have the ones that were needed, but the resulting screen with the data was more than they asked for, not only did it give them the information that they needed but the standard functionality built into it provided a full "drill-down" function. This meant that any suspicious looking postings could be clicked on and more details were shown, including the full Purchase order with all of the relevant data and the complete material master record and all of the relevant data too. The user was very impressed but asked if we could do anything with the selection screen. I built several Variants to match the different ranges of materials that they were interested in and added variable settings so that the date ranges were all automatically defaulted. This meant that they just had to select a Variant and click on the execute button. To this day, as far as I am aware, the report is still produced in this manner and thanks to the in built flexibility of standard SAP no further changes have had to be made.

So this is a real example of how the time spent exhausting all SAP options pays off, not only in time saved not having to produce a report, but also in the in-built benefits of using an SAP provided report with all of the "bells and whistles" that come with it. "Bells and whistles" it is fair to say, that we would not have taken the time to build in to a in-house report, even if we thought them to be useful. It also hopefully demonstrates that using a more experienced consultant can be not only cost effective in the short AND long term, but the quality of the solution means that the business gets the system that they need.

Another very short example of this was when a user wanted to know the purchases that we have made for all of their Plants in a specific area, where we have had not yet had a full receipt but the delivery should have already occurred by now. This report would be useful for chasing late deliveries and also for finding Purchase Orders that had been short delivered and it looked like the Vendor was not going to deliver the remainder. Quite simply you will not find a standard SAP report that states that it does this. But if you use the Purchasing lists (ME2L etc.) they have a field entitled "Scope of list" and this contains many options that can be selected, one of which was one that only selected those Purchase Orders where the delivery was greater than zero and the Purchase Order quantity was more than the delivered quantity. This provided the user with the information needed and again by clicking on the Purchase Order number the screen would display the complete order and all of the details so that it could be investigated. There are other examples but these two hopefully help to prove the point.

So what do we do if there really isn't a standard report to suit the requirement?

Well I have to admit that this will happen, it is always surprising to see just how imaginative the business users can be when it comes to reports. There always seems to be different ways of dissecting the data and fortunately enough SAP R/3 is exceptionally good at storing the data in the correct format and with the correct amount of data. This does mean that I have yet to have to consider building any new databases to hold data required by a new report. It has always been there in a useable format somewhere in SAP. I may have created simple tables to store temporary or specialist data but this is rarely necessary.

If a report does have to be written for a specific requirement then an ABAP program is not the only option available. ABAP query and Quickviewer are available for this purpose. They are designed to be easy enough for a reasonably competent user to be able to write their own reports and enquiries without the need for a programmer. This is certainly possible but fraught with danger. All too often the resulting report works well enough but it is not normally the most efficient code and so if the report is running through many thousands of records it can soon start to affect response times. Not only that, but the less-experienced users will understandably take a long time to produce their report due to their lack of expertise. An additional problem is that you will often find many different reports that are actually just different versions of the same report because the user did not see the existing reports or did not think of using one that has already been written, often for another user in the same department. This does not mean that these tools are not useable, far from it, if they are controlled correctly they can be extremely useful and once again help to reduce the size of the SAP teams.

One option that can be used involves the rule that no user is allowed to write their own, they have to be written by the team. This ensures the correct level of control and the reduction in duplication of reports, but I have just said that these tools can help reduce the size of the teams not increase it. The difference is that the tool can be used by the consultant rather than the programmer and so the demand for ABAP work can be reduced. If the resulting report has proved to be useful then after a period of time the report can be converted to "normal" ABAP code and therefore become more efficient. This approach should result in the right balance of quick response to requirements without giving up the necessary controls to make sure that the resulting reports are not a waste of time.

Information Systems reports

The one thing that will never cease to amaze me is how few people are aware of this in-built functionality within SAP R/3. It is not just a series of reports, it is almost a Business Information Warehouse. It is part of R/3 and so the reporting is not carried out on a separate server and the reports are interrogated using standard SAP instead of by graphically powerful software, but apart from this it is a BW type of function. The data is retrieved in real time (although this can be switched to batch mode if required) and summaries of this data are stored in a format suitable to the reporting programs. The end result is very impressive and in most cases comes free and fully operational without any programming or significant configuration.

The reports are aimed more at the middle to senior management but are often useful for all levels of the business. They are effectively summary reports at the highest level that can be drilled down to get to a level just above the raw data, but you can still drill down further from within the reports and get to the source data at the lowest level possible. This approach means that the reports run very quickly and without major impact on response times because the programs are only interrogating summarised data, but with the added advantage of providing a drill down function from the summary data to the detailed data.

They do have graphic functions built in and various different graphs can be displayed at the click of a button, but the graphics capability is very basic. However there are many other options available within these reports that make them even more useful. You can add, remove and re-sequence columns within the report. You can send any results that are shown on the screen to any other SAP user via SAP mail or via external mail, you can change the sort sequences and the drill down paths, the list of possibilities is extensive. The best thing is that it happens almost invisibly and many organisations are not even aware of this extremely useful tool or that it contains this history from the go live date forwards. If I was an SAP salesman then I would show this to potential customers as part of my presentation and I am sure that this would tip the balance if anyone was deciding if SAP R/3 was worth it.

The last resort (or perhaps the last report)

If none of the above options are appropriate then the final option is to write a new ABAP. But even if this is the last option available you can still avoid some of the problems by copying an existing standard ABAP and modifying this. The reason that this is recommended is that you will then be retaining the flexible options that are built into SAP programs and the calculations necessary for some of the data can be done using the existing SAP supplied code. There is almost always a standard SAP report that is close enough to be useful, if not then you have to write one form scratch. If this is the case then if you consider the above points and are aware of the issues this may cause then at least you are unlikely to get any nasty surprises.

How to avoid modifications or keep them to a minimum

Finally, because the sections above have concentrated on the problems that you may experience if you move away from standard SAP, I thought that it would be worth including a section on how to avoid the problem in the first place and also a section on what to do if you find that it is too late and that you have an implementation that has too high a degree of non-standard SAP.

Look for a standard SAP solutions FIRST

Start from the assumption that the solution is available in standard SAP rather than assume that it isn't.

If it is something that you genuinely must have to be able to operate your business, then it is likely be in SAP, if it isn't, then are we sure that we need it?

Investigate SAP completely before considering a development or modification.

Solve the problem not the symptom and you will normally find a standard solution.

Question business requirements thoroughly to establish the real reason for the request so that a better, long term solution is provided, rather than simply what has been requested.

The business users should not be expected to know what is available in SAP without help from the consultants and so their requirements are their only view on what they need and so they may well not match the solution that SAP provides, it is therefore the job of the consultant to identify this and show the users the SAP option and explain the differences.

Some requests are for reports and functions that are not necessarily essential, but are perhaps extremely useful. These should be classed as enhancements rather than fixes and the true cost should be calculated and communicated to the business before work commences. They may wish to "spend their money" on other more important issues. All too often a project suffers from overspend or missed targets and yet the reporting functions include elements that are at best "nice to have", try to bear this in mind when dealing with the reporting requirements.

All projects should aim for a standard SAP solution in all areas wherever possible.

Projects should be using SAP as the accepted solution wall to wall unless there are special circumstances that prevent this.

The overheads from the maintenance of interfaces and developments are extremely costly in the long term, even though they appear to be sensible in the short term.

In addition to this a standard SAP approach results in a "single solution" across the organisation rather than different degrees of SAP being used in differing businesses thereby reducing the benefits of integration and making long term maintenance more difficult and therefore costly.

And finally

To simply list some additional benefits of a more standard SAP implementation that have not been discussed above;

- Replacement project / support staff would be productive more or less from day one. Because the system is totally standard any competent SAP consultant would be able to start working almost straight away without the need to understand where any modifications have been made and why.
- SAP standard help documentation and training courses would be entirely relevant and could be used without needing to be adapted.
- Recruiting end-users that have experience of SAP in previous positions are more likely to be able to start being productive earlier (unless they came from a company that were using heavily modified SAP system, in which case their SAP experience would be mostly irrelevant wherever they went)
- There would only be a need to maintain a small ABAP resource capability, which could be entirely offshore if required.
- All of the standard SAP functionality would be available because no integration links have been removed or changed.
- The vast list of standard reports would at the very least produce accurate and complete information.

A new SAP R/3 Implementation?
Some points to consider

If you are considering SAP R/3 or if you are about to implement it then there are some decisions that will affect just how successful an R3 implementation can be in addition to the subjects already covered in earlier sections of this book.

It is important to be aware of some of the main reasons for unsuccessful SAP R/3 implementations so that you can either avoid them or if this is not possible, at least understand the consequences so that you can make a judgement call.

The earlier sections covered the more important issues, particularly relating to the subject of knowing what SAP is and why it is different and therefore why it needs to be treated differently. The following subjects although appearing less important, are factors that can also lead to a failed or poor SAP R/3 implementation.

All modules in one implementation (Big bang) or Phased over time (firecracker)?

Do you implement all modules in one large project (a big bang approach) or do you implement one or two modules at first in a small way and then build the other modules into the system at a later stage (a firecracker approach, i.e. a series of slightly smaller and often less predictable bangs)? This is a question that is often asked and the answer depends on so many things that it is impossible to answer without knowing the business in detail and the budget constraints.

Let me put my cards on the table straight away, I strongly favour the big bang approach. I have been involved in several and they have been painful at times but the end result is normally far better and the long term costs far less, than a phased approach.

When considering which approach to adopt, consider the following;

SAP R/3 is a highly integrated system and even though it does give the impression that is consists of discrete modules (MM, SD, FI/CO etc.), this is not actually the case. In fact, if you visualise it as distinctly separate modules then this can often lead to a poor implementation. Thinking of it as one system ensures that you do not fall into the trap of thinking that you can "cherry pick" functionality and leave out other functionality that does not appear to be a 100% fit to your organisation. The concept of SAP R/3 being modular merely helps to break the system into manageable chunks of related functions for training and resource management reasons.

Implementing one or two modules first and then adding the rest later is certainly feasible and many organisations choose this option, but you will be breaking too many of the complex integration "points" and you will probably have to build significant interfaces to the remainder of your legacy systems that are currently handling the processes relevant to the modules that you are not implementing in the initial "phase".

Big bang approaches involve a high degree of change over a relatively short period and you can think of this as positive or negative, depending on your viewpoint.

The positive side of this is, if there is a high degree of change then it is easier to make a significant improvement in business processes at the same time as moving to a new system. It is easier to maintain a focus and to throw out old ways of thinking that are genuinely now obsolete because it will be seen to be something that the whole of the business is involved in rather than just a change in the finance or procurement departments (or wherever you are implementing the change). Because everyone will experience the change it will be more difficult for people to ignore it and "bury their heads in the sand".

The negative side of the Big Bang approach is that the resulting project may be too large to handle or the costs may not be acceptable in one "hit".

Big bang requires a lot of resources and hits the business very hard in one short sharp shock. This may be too hard for many organisations and the perceived risks to the business may be large enough to force a decision away from Big bang. The smaller and more manageable approach of implementing one or two modules first does seem more attractive because of the reduction of the risk and the lower the impact on the business, but the amount of duplicated effort during each phase, the amount of temporary interfaces and work-arounds involved and the constant feeling of the implementation dragging on often results in a more costly, less welcomed and less successful implementation in the longer term.

But for me the most important thing to consider is that SAP R/3 is basically one system and a very integrated system at that and to implement part of it will result in problems without a doubt. It is possible to manage those problems but only by compromising functionality in the short term to enable you to obtain the full benefits in the long term.

Some of the advantages and disadvantages for both options;

Big Bang
>
> Advantages
>> Retains the power of the complex and useful integration of SAP R/3
>>
>> Does not require temporary interfaces (I have already made it clear how much I dislike interfaces, I dislike temporary interfaces even more)
>>
>> The users only have to be trained once
>>
>> The degree of change helps to focus everyone on the project.
>>
>> There is only one project to manage (albeit a large one)
>>
>> The consultants are all working together at the same time and so the integration issues are easier to resolve.
>>
>> The interruption to the business occurs over a shorter period
>>
>> There is only one go-live date to miss.
>>
>> The users will experience the benefit of the integration much earlier
>
> Disadvantages
>> The degree of change could prove too much too handle
>>
>> The cost of the project hits the business in one "hit".
>>
>> The required resources may not be available all at the

same time including the members of the business who will have to assist the project as well as the I.T. resources

If the project fails then the consequences could be more severe because it will affect all areas of the business at the same time

The phased approach

Advantages

The degree of change could be more acceptable

It can be seen as a "toe in the water"

It requires fewer resources during each phase

Lessons can be learned in one phase and passed on to the next

The effect of a failure is less dramatic

The cost of the project is spread across the phases

Disadvantages

The degree of change may enable people to lose focus on the "bigger picture"

There will need to be a lot of temporary interfaces and reports etc.

At the end of each phase the users will not experience the full benefits of the SAP integration and may not be impressed by the "new system"

There will be an element of duplication of effort (it will be several smaller projects with some common tasks that will be repeated)

The end result may be a collection of unequal modules (earlier modules may have not been as well implemented as later modules and this may be apparent in differing levels of quality and poor integration.

Early modules may have made configuration settings that need to be changed by later modules, causing elements of redesign and retesting.

The final go-live date may be so far in the future as to not appear to be important.

Most organisations will not spend long debating this decision, it is normally decided by the most senior business managers / directors, but if the decision really is open for discussion and the resources are not an issue then I hope you will look at the advantages and disadvantages of both options and decide that the risk of a Big bang approach is mitigated by the major benefits it has to offer.

How to get a good ROI (Return Of Investment / Information)

At the risk of repeating myself (have I said this before?), aggressively aiming for as near a standard system as possible is the best way to get a good ROI. But you should also aggressively aim to get the most out of the SAP functionality using the configuration options available to the absolute maximum.

If you have decided that SAP R/3 will be the mainstay of your business solutions software then have a clear mission statement along the lines of "SAP is the chosen solution for the business as a whole. We will aim to extract the maximum benefits from SAP and all business processes will be carried out using only the SAP system." and make sure everyone is aware of this and how rigid this approach is to be adhered to.

Consider a "big bang" implementation as a preferred option and adopt it if it is at all possible.

Let the project be driven by the business and not the I.T. department.

Implement a rigid change control procedure that will protect the system (and therefore the business) from negative, unnecessary or ill-advised developments and configuration.

From day-one try to involve as many of the business users as possible in the project, as much as is possible, it is vital to not only obtain their full buy-in, but they also need to be kept fully aware of the project and its future effects on them and their departments.

Allow extra time in the early stages for the major decisions, especially those that relate to the organisation structure, these are the foundations upon which you will build the entire system.

Start a separate but connected project to look at all master data at the earliest possible point, even before the SAP implementation project has launched and aim for quality, rationalised data to be available before the go-live date.

Ensure that you have used the best SAP consultants available to lead each of the modules being implemented, supplement this with less-experienced resources, ideally internal staff that will stay with the system after it has gone live.

Give the users the appropriate training at the right time (see the separate section on this subject for more details) and ensure that their expectations have been managed.

Finally, I nearly forgot the most important way to ensure a good ROI, read this book!

"Roll outs"

I do not really have any major bias when it comes to the choice of whether to implement the system into all physical locations / branches of your organisation in one project or to implement in one branch and then rollout that solution to the others separately, but one thing that I am absolutely certain about is that regardless of the option chosen, you must produce a solution that will work for all branches of your organisation. By this I mean that you must do the analysis across all branches even if you are just implementing in one then rolling out to the others later. This is based on personal experience several of the projects I have been involved in.

In one example the company decided to produce a solution based on their facility in Holland. The Dutch site had all of the business elements that were going to be affected by the implementation, planning, sales, purchasing, production, warehousing etc. and because it was a relatively small site it was felt that it would be easier to manage and yet it still covered all of the required processes. I can certainly see the logic and I may have agreed with the approach at the time myself but as it transpired it was not the best decision.

I joined the company as a contractor after they had already rolled out the system from Holland to Germany and France. I was asked to lead the rollout to the UK site and my first task was to look at the solution that had been developed and rolled out already to other sites and estimate the size of the project and the time required to implement this solution in the UK. My answer was greeted with surprise and dismay. My estimate was much larger than any of the actual rollouts that had already taken place in France and Germany, in fact it was more than double. They were convinced that I had miscalculated, but I justified the figure by pointing out that the UK site was bigger than the Dutch, French and German sites added together and as a result the business processes that were used in these sites were just not appropriate for the UK. For instance in Holland the site was small enough for many of the processes to be handled by one person. In the UK the same process would not only involve more people but it would also involve different departments. This meant that many of the processes had to be redesigned so that they would work in the UK. This in itself was a major reason for the extra time, but other aspects such as the volume of people to be trained also had an impact.

This problem would not have occurred if the original design had considered the differences between Holland and the UK at the very beginning. I am not suggesting that they should have implemented the UK at the same time, but they should have validated the design before it was implemented in Holland. It is important to implement a solution that will work for all sites even when using a roll-out approach.

So if you are considering a rollout approach please carry out the analysis across all sites that will eventually use the solution regardless of the rollout process, so that any re-work is kept to a minimum during the rollout phases.

Getting the right project teams together?

The project teams I am referring to are the teams that are required to actually design, configure and build the system. Somehow you need to be able to make sure that you not only have the right number of teams but you also have the right number of resources in each team. Decisions like this are very difficult, especially if you have never been involved in an SAP project before, which is more than likely the case. One resource that I normally like to see in place as early as possible is someone that I refer to as the SAP champion, or Lead SAP consultant.

What is an SAP champion and why would you need one?

An SAP champion is someone that will advise Project Manager, the board of directors and the business managers on the high level aspects of an SAP implementation. Not only will this person help to establish the approach that is taken by the project, such as using standard SAP wherever possible, using SAP R/3 as the core solution, etc. but they will also ensure that the agreed approach is adhered to throughout. This person will work closely with the head of the project and will attend all of the steering committee meetings to help and advise the top-level management with their understanding and decision-making, relating to SAP. The champion will mostly be involved in the non-module specific design aspects of SAP but they will also be seen as the person that the SAP consultants report through to the head of the project.

This role is vital if the approach and standards used throughout the project are not going to be diluted by the many consultants involved each with their own views on which approach should be adopted. The champion will also be tasked with ensuring that the integration aspects of the system are managed and that the resulting system actually looks and feels like it is one coherent solution. It is often found that certain modules, because they are implemented by different consultants, have a completely different look and feel. It is important to ensure that this does not occur at the detriment of the overall use and control of the system.

The champion also needs to ensure that any issues raised by the teams are explained to the head of the project in a manner that will allow him/her to understand the issue and the options available. Remember that the head of the project is unlikely to know SAP R/3 to any great extent.

The SAP champion will obviously need to be a highly experienced SAP consultant but the cost of such a role will be repaid many times over in the quality of the resulting solution and therefore the healthy ROI that will be achieved. If this role is not provided then the head of the project will have to deal with each of the teams and their varying approaches to the implementation as well as handling any SAP issues that a team may wish to escalate and this would be difficult without the required SAP skills.

How many teams do we need?

The project teams are normally split into SAP Module specific teams that have the responsibility for one SAP module such as MM, SD, FI/CO etc. The first advice I can give is to consider the possibility of splitting these teams by business area instead of by SAP modules. I have already stated several times that I consider the SAP modules to be an artificial splitting of the system to make it more manageable and this will become more obvious when the project teams start to get into to the detail design. They will find functions that appear to be in the wrong module. Invoice verification is a prime example, this is included in the MM module and yet many people will see this as a financial function. There is a real danger that the MM team may therefore either assume that the FI team will deal with this, or perhaps worse still, the MM team may try to deal with this themselves without sufficient input from the FI team.

In addition to this, there are several cross-modular functions that are contained in each module and there are also some functions that are classed as central functions and so do not sit in any specific SAP module. But the main reason for splitting the teams by business area is that, the best SAP projects are those that are lead by the business, and this includes the project teams, so it also makes sense that the teams are kept in line with the business areas involved instead of the system-driven modules. In reality the split into business areas will often be extremely close to the split by SAP module, but it is rarely identical.

This approach enables you to build the right teams for your business because it helps to get the right balance. In a large organisation you may have a department that is responsible for the Inventory management side of the business and a separate department that deals with Procurement. This may lead you to have two teams whereas a modular split would only have one team, the MM team. If your organisation is set up slightly differently then you may find that you have just one department that deals with Procurement and they also cover the inventory. The end result is likely to be that you have a more appropriate number of teams and this will help the project retain the focus on the business rather than the system.

Some people would argue that after the SAP implementation, the business might well be split totally differently than it is before the project starts and so the split will be wrong. This is a fair comment but if the business changes shape because of the project then this decision will be made by the current business teams and they would know best if the split is likely to be a benefit to the organisation.

I would also strongly suggest that you also have a team that has sole responsibility for master data. They will have to integrate heavily with the other teams but master data requires a team that can focus on the many issues that relate to this element of the project. If you leave the master data decisions with the individual teams you will not get a "joined up" solution and they will not be able to devote enough time to the bigger picture that is essential with master data.

The structure within the Project Team?

The project team is the equivalent of the driver of a formula one race-car, you can get everything else absolutely right but the wrong choice of "driver" will prevent you from achieving success.

The size of the teams

There is no ideal formula for how big a project team should be, it really depends on the complexity of your business. But the number of users involved is not normally a factor in the size of the team. The project team will be designing the solution for the business processes involved, the number of times that the process is instigated or the number of users involved in that process obviously affects the design of the solution but it does not have a direct affect on the size of the team involved. The size is more affected by the complexity of the solution required. Multiply this by the degree of non-standard SAP that you plan to use and this will be a guide to the size of the teams you will need.

The team leader

The basic principle that I have used to suggest who the team leader is as follows;

The project will fail if the business tries to implement it without the help of someone who knows SAP well enough to point out the options and suggest alternative solutions. The project will also fail if the SAP consultant tries to implement it without the help of someone who knows the business well and what will and will not work from a business perspective. So the ideal structure would have the team leader position shared between the business "expert" and the SAP "expert". But in reality sharing a team lead position just does not work, the whole point of a leader is that it is someone who can make decisions clearly, this just won't happen if you are expecting two people to agree with everything every time. So what do we do then, do we flip a coin? Do we choose the person who has the best leadership skills?

I would suggest that we choose the Business expert to be the team leader, after all, if the system works well technically but doesn't work from a business perspective then it is a failure. If the system works well for the business and yet it is technically a mess then the degree of failure is less (but it is still not a success). In addition to this I have explained my reasoning for having the project lead by the business and the benefits that this brings and so this adds up to sufficient justification for my suggestion (I would hope) of the business team lead being the Team leader.

The structure of the team

There are two main elements involved, the business knowledge and the SAP knowledge. Both of these elements need to be covered as fully as possible. This applies equally, if not more so to the business element than the SAP element. The project can only be seen to be a success if it works for the business. This means that the business representative on the team must be someone that knows that area of the business extremely well and ideally someone whose business expertise is respected by the other business users in that area. It is no coincidence that the most successful projects I have seen used very high quality business users on the team and the projects that had the most problems had been given user representatives that were chosen simply because they were available and the business would not be affected by their loss to the project.

The business representatives on the team

The project teams will need one business expert per team, if you think they need more than this then I would suggest that this might just be an indication that you need more teams instead. The business expert must be someone who knows the high level business extremely well, if they also know the processes at a low level then this is a bonus. The ideal person is often someone who has started more or less at the bottom of the ladder and worked their way up to at least a managerial position. But they must understand the business well enough to make decisions either by themselves or after consultation with other users and these decisions must be reliable.

To check to see if you have the ideal person or not ask yourself the following question. Suspending reality for a moment, if you had to have a solution designed for this area of the business and the this person was unable to discuss it with any other users in the department, would the result be a disaster?. If the answer is yes then you have the wrong person. I am not for one minute suggesting that this user will need to be able to make all of the decisions themselves but there will be lots of occasions during the project where the SAP consultants will need an answer to a question very quickly and it may not be possible or justified to consult all of the appropriate users in the business. This will definitely happen and when it does the team must be confident enough that they can rely on the business expert to either answer the question themselves, if they have the knowledge, or at the very least the expert will know who to ask in the business to get a quick but accurate answer.

If you choose someone who thinks that they know far more than they do, then that is very risky, if you choose someone who knows a reasonable amount but is the type of person who needs to verify their facts first then this is not ideal but it can work, albeit more slowly. So please do try to ensure that you use a knowledgeable, respected and humble user as the expert.

This business user would have to leave their current position in their department and have their role taken by someone else, often permanently. This often results in strong resistance from the senior management when they are asked to release someone who is seen as a vital member of their team. They may find it difficult to replace them and therefore they will have to use someone who is not of a sufficient level of expertise. This is a genuine problem and one that I can sympathise with but this is a short term impact on the business and should be manageable. In addition to this the knowledge that this person has relates to the existing processes and systems and these will no longer be in use post go-live and so the expert that they are reluctant to give up would not be an expert on the new processes and system in any case and so they should really be able to release them for the project. If they do release them then the knowledge they would gain of the new system and processes would prove very valuable to the department when they return after the project. In fact the most difficult task of all when building the teams is persuading the business to give up their best people for these positions, there is almost nothing that you can do to persuade them, even though it is a short-term problem they will often state that by removing these people from the business there will be no long-term to consider, the business will fail.

If you are fortunate to be able to persuade the business to give up these people then there is another major problem to resolve. That is the problem of persuading the individuals to take up their new posts in the project. From their point of view they will be taken out of a position that they have grown into over many years and be replaced by someone else who probably hasn't yet earned that promotion. In addition to this, they feel comfortable in their current position, they are using their specific skills set that matches their role. Now you want to take them out of that environment and place them in an I.T. environment that many know little or nothing about, it is a scary proposal. Even if they are prepared to consider the position they are worried about what happens to them after the project is over? Their old position has been filled (at least temporarily) and at this stage nobody knows what the shape of the organisation will be after the project and so there can be no promises of a job of any description, post go-live, at this stage.

I have spent many hours talking to selected candidates and trying to persuade them to make this "leap of faith", it is not easy I can tell you. I have interviewed many candidates who are perfect for the position and keen to give it a try but the lack of clarity of what will happen post go-live is too frightening and so they turn down the offer. You can persuade people to do many things but if you cannot dispel their fears then you will not succeed. So please consider this before you make the first offer, try to find a way of dispelling those fears about their position after the project. In reality they will almost be indispensable, not only will they still have their business knowledge but they will also have the expert knowledge of the system. They may also have heard some of the SAP horror stories and this may be enough to make them say no, all you can do here is to use some of the reasons I have outlined earlier that explain why those horror stories, true though they are, exist. I would seriously suggest that you could lend them your copy of this book to read before they make their decision, I really think that it would help dispel some of their fears (I would of course prefer it if you bought them a copy but you might think that I am using this as a marketing ploy).

So try very hard to get the best person available and if this is not possible then please do try to compensate for this somehow, perhaps by using this person as more of a communicator or "channel" to the business, so that the SAP consultants can use this to get the correct answers from the business.

I have yet to find any reason for having more than one business representative per team but there may be reasons why you want to do this. But please do not use this to enable two people to take the position and share the job, two knowledgeable part-time users would be worse than having one less knowledgeable user. You need a decision maker and if this is spread across more than one person then you will simply not get the clarity that is needed from this position

The SAP resources on the teams.

There is one thing that I can say with confidence and that is, wherever you do make sure that you get the best possible SAP consultants you can afford. By trying to reduce costs in this area really would be increasing the risk of a poor solution just by saving money on consulting fees. You don't always get what you pay for and so it is wrong to assume that the most expensive are going to be the best, but you have to at least consider the concept that a really bad SAP consultant that has a poor CV will not get far if they try to charge the top rate and equally the chances of you getting a top consultant at a bottom rate are also very rare (but not impossible). The most important thing to consider is their attitude towards an SAP implementation and their proven experience and knowledge of the appropriate module. This applies regardless of if you have decided to choose to use individual consultants or use a consulting company. The difference is that if you have chosen to use a consulting company then make sure that you interview the actual people that will be working with you and not just their senior managers or sales team who may never actually work on the project to any real extent. It is vital to ensure that the individuals have the approach to an SAP R/3 project that is in line with your approach, hopefully adopted from the approach options I have outlined in this book.

Should we use a consulting company or contractors?

I am not going to make any specific suggestions here because I am very obviously biased (I have been an independent I.T. contractor for the last 25 years) and even though I would give you my honest and unbiased advice I would not expect you to take this on face-value and but there is no way that I am not going to offer at least some help that may be of use if you are pondering this decision.

In some organisations this will really not be a difficult decision, you may already have a very clear reason for choosing one or the other. This is fair enough and I can honestly say that you have a similar chance of success whichever option you choose and there will always be an element of luck involved. If you have already formed a clear approach to this then I am not going to persuade you to change your mind either way. If on the other hand you are prepared to consider both options and choose whatever suits your organisation best then I will try to indicate some of the pros and cons. But I will perhaps have to show that choosing to use contractors instead consulting companies is a viable option because so many people are unaware that this can work too.

If we look at what we have already said that we need, we need the best available SAP resources for the related modules. If you disagree with this basic concept then I cannot see that you will be swayed by my logic here but I will still try. So where are the best consultants going to come from? There are certainly lots of them working in consulting companies such as the "big five" and the many other excellent SAP partners. But there are also many that work in the contract market.

I have heard many contractors stating that if a consultant is any good then they will move into contracting and get more money for their skills and while there may be some truth in this but I personally have worked alongside many top-quality SAP consultants who would just not switch to contracting for many reasons and so this statement really is not true. But it is important to realise that the two options will both offer a chance to get the best.

The one reason that I personally prefer to choose consultants from the open market is because of the wider choice. If you choose a consulting company you will certainly have the opportunity to screen the proposed consultants but this will be a limited list of the consultants that they employ that are available for the period that the project will involve. So if they have better consultants they may not be available and it is quite reasonable to assume that their top consultants may be already working on projects. But you may find that they are just about to finish one project right at the time your project is about to start and so you may be lucky and get the best they have to offer. Whatever happens you will only be able to select from the consultants that are on their books. If you look to the open market you will find that you are able to choose from every available contractor from every agency. Granted the top-quality consultants here may also be busy but the sheer volume of consultants that work in the contract market far exceeds the number of consultants available on one consulting companies books.

You could of course, consider using the best of both and sourcing consultants from both options. This may cause some issues with the consulting companies if you are asking to use some of their staff on a project alongside or within teams of contractors but many of them would consider this as a workable option. But the most common approach is using one or the other and not mixing the two.

If you choose to use independent contractors then there are of course issues to consider. They would be individuals and not part of another organisation. This means that they do not have the backup of the consulting company for things such as additional training, help and guidance and replacement staff if absence due to sickness or other reasons result in the consultant not being able to continue. But how you view this depends on the importance of the benefits that a contractor lacks. The help and guidance for a contractor normally comes from ex-colleagues rather than fellow employees and as such may not be available on demand. The ex-colleague may be in meetings, on holiday or unreachable for many other reasons and so this help may well be unavailable, whereas the employee of a consulting company can generally have someone available to help whenever required. I would see this as the biggest issue regarding the use of contractors, but if you are able to find high-quality consultants then the need for this help becomes less of an issue.

Another issue to be considered is the availability of a replacement should the consultant fall ill or leave the project. Illness tends not to be a showstopper and whichever option you choose there is little benefit in bringing in a substitute consultant for a few days, the learning curve would be such that it would take a lot of time before the temporary replacement would be productive. If the consultant should leave altogether then I believe that there is a major problem whichever option you choose. If you have used a consulting company then they would certainly be able to replace this consultant very quickly and without fuss, but the question is, would the replacement be one that you would choose, or would it be just someone who was available? In addition to this the learning curve would again be a major issue, whoever replaces the consultant will need a lot of time to get up to speed before they become productive. If you were using contractors and this situation arose then finding a replacement could also be very quick and you would again be able to choose from the whole contract market rather than the employees of one company.

In a recent short-term project I was brought in with three other contractors to replace a team of consultants from a consulting company and from day-one we became a team that worked as closely as any team could and the client later commented that we acted more like a team that the people we had replaced. If you do get the right contractors with the right experience and attitude then I am convinced that you will get as good a project as you could from the best company available.

I can almost hear you thinking how biased I seem, but believe me all I want to do is to present you with some of the facts and perhaps encourage you to think of things from a different angle. Nothing I can write here will directly affect how busy I become as a contractor so please just consider my comments as my own spin on the subject. If you disagree with this or if you are part of a consulting company, don't see this as criticism, just see it as one viewpoint and you never know, some of my criticism may even help to change the way you operate the company. Perhaps if more consulting companies would be prepared to offer you resources from the contract market in addition to, or instead of their own staff then maybe this would be the best of both worlds. But until they do this I am simply suggesting that they are offering resources from a limited pool.

One option that may be suitable would be to use both kinds of resource, perhaps using the consulting company to manage parts the project and use contract staff for the actual teams. But this again would rely on the company providing someone with enough experience and knowledge as well as someone who wants to implement the SAP R/3 system the same way that you do. This is not as easy as it seems because consulting companies have methodologies and approaches that may not fit with the way you want the system to be implemented (especially if you agree with the points I have made so far in the earlier sections of this book.)

So I will leave you to ponder this subject and wish you the best of luck with your selected option, whatever that is.

How many SAP resources do I need in each team?

My suggestion may seem radical and many people will disagree with this, but I expect that you will not be quite so surprised because most of the time I seem to be questioning established methods. The thing is that it is probably the word "established" that causes me to question these methods. If something is established that means that it has normally become so over time, it also gives the impression that by being established you don't really need to question it. My approach is to take nothing for granted and base every project on the best possible approach for that individual project and not just one that has worked for other projects. In addition to this the approaches that have been established for SAP implementations are often based on approaches that have been developed before SAP came along and SAP R/3 is a system that can be strangled by outdated methodologies and approaches. It is time for fresh thinking based on experience that relates to SAP implementations and not based on very different systems altogether.

After all we keep selling Business Process Re-engineering to the business so we should not be so rigid that we do not re-engineer the processes of systems implementations.

In my experience most projects suffer more from being over-resourced than under-resourced. I have been involved in projects where it is blatantly obvious that there were too many SAP resources and I have certainly been involved where there are too few.

One of the main problems of having too few resources is that the pressure on the individuals involved can be so great that it can soon turn into genuine stress and this can be a serious consequence that must be avoided. But I firmly believe that if you ensure that the resources are low but not so low as to cause stress then this is the ideal balance.

Having too many consultants on the team will lead to duplication of effort, lack of an overall vision, gaps caused by the assumption that someone else was dealing with an issue and long-winded debates that involve far more time than is necessary. Of course it is good to discuss options and debate which is the most appropriate but the options available in SAP are not difficult to identify, especially if we have adopted a "standard SAP" approach, and the benefits of the various options should be discussed with the business and not between the consultants alone. For example, if you have 10 consultants or if you have one consultant then the discussion should be the same, the business expert should be informed of the options available and the discussion should be based on the benefits to the business.

One thing that has become obvious to me over the years is the resulting system often indicates the level of consultants that were utilised on the project. The systems that I have seen that appear to be very "regimented", very bland and that are often accused of being "not in touch with the real world" are often those that have been built by a large team of consultants. I really do feel that this removes the possibility of producing a system that feels like it was built by the business for the business. The systems that have a comfortable feel and seem to reflect a degree of common sense are often the ones built by small teams that were able establish a rapport with the business and really build something that has a coherent and "real world" feel to it. This may be a coincidence or it may somehow be relevant to the size of the organisation, but I do feel that there is more to it than that, it is almost like listening to a story that was written by many people and told by a group instead of a story that was written and read told by one person.

My preferred option is to start with the one SAP expert consultant for each module and consider expanding this if there are specific areas of SAP that may drive the need to have additional resources. An example of this could be the SD module, your expert SD consultant may specialise in the order process and in your organisation you may need to make full use of the Transportation planning functionality. Your expert SD consultant may not have sufficient experience to cover both areas and in reality there may well be very few consultants that are experts in all aspects of their specialist module. So in this case you will need more than one SD consultant. But if you are really lucky and find an SD consultant with experience in all of these areas then this would be ideal, not only would you be saving money but you would also have a more focussed implementation. If the sheer volume of work required indicates that it would be too much for this one consultant then use a junior or less experienced consultant to assist in the workload. This could be an ideal opportunity to take on a permanent resource that can grow with the project, learn from the expert and give continuity of support post go-live.

So once you have established that you have sufficient resources to cover all aspects of the system, you now need to consider the workload. This is not that easy to plan and at best it is normally down to educated guesswork. But the SAP champion should be able to help and advise on the potentially complex areas of the business that may require additional or specialist resources.

The resulting project team would consist of the following members

> One Project leader that is a business expert
> One SAP consultant that is the SAP expert for the module relevant to the team
> The possible addition of another SAP expert if this is seen to be required
> One or more "junior" SAP consultants that can assist with the workload

The number of teams required should match the number of major business departments involved in the implementation. Examples of these departments include, Finance (the accounting department, Finance controlling (The management accounts department), Procurement (possibly split into separate Procurement and Inventory teams), Sales, Delivery /

transportation planning, etc. (depending on the modules being implemented.

The business experts on each team report directly to the head of the project, the SAP resources report through the SAP champion to the head of the project.

The above suggestion is aimed at prompting discussion rather than being prescriptive, but I am sure that it will be better than starting from a blank sheet of paper and trying to decide how to build the teams without any previous experience.

Offshore resources, is it a cost saving?

I think that this is a section of the book that is going to generate a lot of disagreement and debate. If I was forced to give a basic answer to this question then that answer would be a simple and resounding no! If you have read this far and if you have understood, let alone agreed with my discussions on the quality of the resources required and the importance of the team working closely together then my answer is hardly surprising.

I have worked in at least two major projects where offshore resources have been used. In both cases an offshore ABAP team were used and in one of these an offshore consultant was also used. Were these resources less costly than the more traditional options of using in-house teams or contract resources? In both cases the answer was a definite no and cost is not the only consideration, the quality of the work and the confidence of the business in the resulting systems was not of the required level.

The hourly or daily rate was certainly lower but the amount of work produced in the same amount of time was less. This was not simply caused by the quality of the resources that were used it was also caused by simple things like the difference in time zones. The offshore companies were based in India and the time difference meant that the actual time that they were working at the same time as the UK team was approximately 4 hours a day and this was only this high because they were working later than normal in India to try to reduce the problem. This meant that if an error was discovered in testing in the morning they would only get to know about it four hours later, then if they were working on it in the second part of their working day and had a question to ask the UK team then they had to wait until the next morning before the team would see the question and reply. This then took another 4 hours before they received any answer to a query. This in itself meant that the actual time taken to achieve any results was extended significantly. The language differences did not present huge problems but there were occasions when misunderstandings (on both sides) caused delays and retesting, especially because the communication delays often resulted in many questions simply not being asked and assumptions made to reduce the communications and associated delays.

I was also sure that they were switching resources around more than they were admitting and even though there were some really good programmers in their team I did get the distinct impression that they were using some relatively new programmers on some of the work, supposedly without our knowledge. I even found that some of the replies I had to emails were totally out of character with earlier email conversations that I had with one or two of the programmers. In some cases the same questions had been asked more than once and although this is not unusual it did give me the impression that I was actually communicating with two different people one of which was pretending to be the other person. I felt that this was where they had started the process with a skilled programmer and then used lesser skilled programmers to free up their highly skilled programmers to work on other projects. I have no proof of this and I cannot be sure that it was happening but I am sure enough to raise it here as something to watch out for. There were certainly one or two very good programmers who I would have gladly recommended to any project but the overall quality was often poor.

In one case it had taken approximately four weeks for the programmer to produce a new Purchase Order layout and this should have taken 5 days possibly 8 maximum. I had provided a detailed specification and an example layout to ensure that they had the full details required so that the communication delays would be kept to a minimum. It soon became obvious that the programmer had written the code based on the layout and not read the detailed specification document. The questions that were asked and the mistakes that were made were all covered in the document in full detail.

Changing document layouts in SAP can often be a long-winded process but four weeks was totally unacceptable. On one occasion I had been told that the new layout was ready to test. I printed a document to check the new layout and for some reason it was being overprinted with an invoice layout. I checked to make sure that the paper in the printer was new and that I was not just overprinting on used paper. I then checked to make sure that the correct output type was being used etc. In fact I spent the best part of a day checking why this was happening. The next day I contacted the programmer and asked if there was anything that I had missed or misunderstood. When they heard what was happening they replied "Oh yes, that was happening when we tried to print it here too!" I was speechless I couldn't believe what I had just heard. The programmer had made the changes and told me it was ready to test even though it was overprinting the Purchase Order layout with an Invoice layout. This resulted in a day wasted while I tried to validate the set-up and data I was using. It is for reasons like this that I don't particularly think that offshore resources are a cost efficient alternative. They appear to cost less but in fact they often cost a lot more and the quality cannot really be guaranteed. Other people may have had a totally different experience and I am not for one minute saying that offshore companies are all like this, but I can only talk about my own personal experience.

The second project where I worked with offshore resources was not quite as bad but the delay in communication had a very definite impact on the elapsed time and the end quality of the work carried out. Tasks that were estimated to take two weeks (estimated by the UK team and the offshore team) were taking four weeks or more.

So please give the offshore option a try if you are being forced to try to reduce costs, but don't burn your bridges, leave yourself with an option to revert to the in-house resources, if necessary.

Documentation, what is required?

This is a subject that I have very strong opinions about and I have very definite ideas on the level of documentation that is required on an SAP project and these don't necessarily fit in with the accepted norm. I have personally experienced the whole spectrum of different approaches to project documentation in my 25 years of implementing systems. I have worked on projects where there was virtually no documentation at all, I have also worked on projects where there was so much documentation that there were documents to control the documentation. The one thing that I have learned is that the best level of documentation is where the documents produced are the absolute minimum required. Any more than this is a waste of time and money, any less than this is very, very danger-ous. Get this right and you will have a bank of documents that will actu-ally be useful and will be read. Get this wrong and you will either not have enough documentation or you will have so much that it is virtually always out of date has no real value.

Let's have a look at the extremes.

A project where there is zero documentation was a easy to work on, you could roll up your sleeves, get stuck in and build the system, you didn't have to constantly stop work to produce documentation that took ages to produce, especially if it has to be written to a precise standard. Nor did you have to re-write the same document if something changed or was added. It meant that every minute that you spent on the project was invested in the building of the system.

During testing, if we found any errors we could just fix them and not then have to correct any documentation, only to correct it again when we found other errors. It seemed to be reasonable to do this at the time. In fact, it was not supposed to be this way, we were supposed to produce the documentation but the time we had left was not sufficient to do both and so the documentation was left, until later on, possibly after the go-live, in reality though, this often means that the documentation is never produced.

We had gone live and had little or no documentation to support it and yet the system worked well and the project was felt to be successful, so where was the harm? I will tell you where the harm was, it was just waiting around the corner. After the system had been bedded down the original consultants that were brought in to build the system were no longer required and so left to move onto other projects for other businesses. Then the next time an error occurred and the support team (not originally involved in the project) had to solve the problem, they had no documentation to help understand not only what was happening but also why the system had been built in a particular way. This often resulted in the fixes that were applied causing other problems elsewhere in the system. After a short period of time the system began to become out of control and it was more and more difficult to maintain. The lack of documentation had resulted in a good system becoming almost unusable. But as I have said this was one extreme and hopefully there are not too many other organisations that have suffered from this problem.

The other extreme was an organisation where I was brought it to work for six months on a project and there was so much documentation that I felt like I had worked for two months and spent the other four months documenting the work I had done. It was a far from pleasant experience and the system was not one of the best that I have worked on to be kind to it and I firmly believe that much of this was due to the heavy workload that was necessary to produce and maintain the documentation. The problem was made worse by the fact that they even had documentation to control the documentation because there was so much of it. I have never felt so unproductive in my career as I did on this project.

Even in my first ever SAP project I was being asked (by an external consultant from one of the "Big Five") to produce far too much documentation. This is hardly surprising because I have never heard of consulting company that had been accused of producing too much documentation, it was simply a safe option. But the level of documentation required for an SAP implementation is different because of the fact that you are not developing a system from scratch, you are configuring an already developed system. Luckily enough I was able to fight off the request and common sense prevailed. The resulting implementation was a success and the documentation that was provided was of sufficient quantity and quality to be genuinely useful and well maintained. Many of the "big five" suffered initially from producing too much documentation for an SAP implementation but this was due to the fact that SAP was so new and it was seen to be safer for them to produce the level of documentation that had been required pre-SAP. These organisations have developed their approach to SAP over the years and now use methodologies designed around SAP implementations, most of them based on the ASAP (Accelerated SAP) implementation method that SAP themselves developed and this has just the right level of documentation involved..

So what is the ideal documentation for an SAP implementation?

Would you be surprised if I said that there is no ideal amount? I think not, but there is an ideal approach to documenting an SAP implementation.

Firstly, in general, the level of documentation should be kept to a minimum. This is made even more possible by the fact that the system is already documented in the many help documents and training documents etc. and also by the fact that you are not actually developing a system, you are changing (or to be more precise) configuring a system to meet your needs.

So how can we tell if we genuinely need a document?

There are some basic guidelines that should be followed and some really basic questions that need to be asked to determine if a particular document should be written or not.

Firstly you have to determine what it should contain, who will read it and when will they need it and what for?

For example, writing a fully detailed "as is" document to describe the existing processes in detail with diagrams and text is something that many people assume is essential. But let us ask the questions,

What should it contain? In this case it should show all of the existing processes, who carries them out, when, why and the links to the preceding and resultant processes. It should be a complete and accurate representation of every process. This in itself is a mammoth task and would take weeks if not months to produce.

Who will read it? This document would be useful to the people designing the "to be". But surely this may be the same people who would write the as is? So they would be producing a document to help them with the "to be" design when they could perhaps build the one document instead. I would not deny for one minute that a "to be" document is absolutely essential. It forms an overall picture of the proposed solution and is useful to the entire project team throughout the life of the project. Even if the "as is" was written by totally different people then what is the actual value of the document. I cannot deny that it does have value but does this exceed the enormous cost in time and effort that it takes to produce it? I think that it does not in many implementations. It might be argued that it is useful for checking to see if there are any gaps in the "to be" when compared to the "as is". A valid point, but is there any guarantee that the "as is" document is complete and there are no processes missing from it that may lead to those same processes being omitted from the "to be" document?

The "as is" document can sometimes introduce a false sense of security. If you produce a system that covers all of the "as is" processes does this make it a success? I think not, in reality what you will have done is to have built a system on the foundations of the old system and these foundations may well be either shaky or in many cases simply not strong enough for the power and complexity of the new solution.

So in this case I can see why an as is document could help, but the benefits do not always cover the costs and so I would rather invest the time saved in producing a better "to be" document.

Another example of a type of document that is normally seen as essential is the "Help document". This is a document that is designed to be read by the users post go-live if they need help when using a specific SAP function. Yet again it sounds very sensible, surely we have to provide help documents, the users will not remember everything that they were told during training? Some organisations even develop methods of attaching this help documentation to the SAP menus so that it can be easily accessed. It really does sound like it is an essential document, but one of the biggest problems with this type of document is that once it has been written (and that can take a lot of time and effort) it has to be maintained. If it is not kept up-to-date then it is worse than having no help document at all, because it would be inaccurate or misleading. This is especially so if the document contains a high level of detail. For instance the document may explain what is to be entered in the SAP standard field entitled "Material Group". If the document states something like, "Select the appropriate group" and more groups have been added then it need not be changed, but what is the value of a help document that doesn't actually help you to decide which entry to choose. If it lists the entries in the help document such as "select the group RAW, for all raw materials and the group A011 for all machines that we produce in-house" then this really is helpful but what happens when someone adds another group? The document is now out of date and has to be corrected. This means extra work and often results in the change never happening. So you can either have vague documents that don't require a high degree of maintenance, but don't actually help either, or you can have really useful help documents that are fine while they are up to date but they contain so much information that they are not kept up to date sufficiently to make them reliable.

This type of document fails on the question of who will use them and when. The theory is that they will be used by all of the users whenever they need help. But the reality is that even the highest quality, up to date help documents are rarely read. If you have implemented SAP already and have made your help documents available on-line then I would suggest that you to monitor their usage. The last time I carried out this exercise at an organisation that had good quality help documents that were up to date and available on-line, the usage was virtually zero. The company had been spending a large amount of time and therefore money on maintaining these documents and yet the effort was virtually wasted..

I think the main thing that I am trying to say is don't assume that documents are actually useful just because they are normally part of the standard set of documentation produced in most projects. Question each document aggressively and establish the consequences of not providing it before you go through the expense and pain of devoting a major part of the project to this task. Take into account the fact that the SAP system comes with help documentation that may be not specific enough to be ideal for your organisation, but it is free of charge, maintained by SAP and integrated (try clicking on the technical help button within the help document and then double click on the fields, especially the program name and database field names, you will be taken to a screen that shows these items in full detail). You would not spend the time to build this into SAP and yet it comes without cost in the standard SAP system.

Remember also that if the users need help with a specific function, you can always refer them to the training documents, which really are essential documents and really should be kept up to date.

The less time wasted on documents that are not going to be read, the more time available to design a better system.

Existing implementations

If you already have SAP R/3 installed then however good the implementation appears, I am convinced that you will be able to significantly improve it normally without major costs. But one of the biggest problems of all is that it is not always easy to measure the quality of the SAP implementation. It is quite possible that you may be unaware of the opportunities for improvement that exist and can be achieved, in some cases with very little cost.

The really bad implementations tend to be obvious and if you have one of these then you are probably already planning to do something about it (If this is the case, then I do hope that you are not contemplating ripping it out altogether and implementing a non SAP solution).

Regardless of your impression of the quality of your SAP system there are ways to improve it and I will address the main options later in this section.

How can you tell if the SAP Implementation is a good one or not?

This is not as easy as you would imagine. I have seen implementations where the system is seen to be a success and yet in reality the benefits that have been achieved are almost non-existent. It is also likely, let alone possible that an organisation that has recently had SAP installed see it as a failure regardless of how good it is in reality. This is a genuine characteristic of an SAP implementation. It is extremely rare for an SAP implementation to be appreciated by any level in the organisation until several months have transpired, regardless of how good that implementation is.

However, one thing is quite clear, the really bad implementations are easy to distinguish. They will have many of the following characteristic; the more they have the worse the implementation is likely to be.

- The user community will be demonstrating very clearly that it is simply not helping them, in fact, it has probably resulted in more effort with little or no benefit at all. They may feel that they are spending all of their time on the system carrying out tasks that add little or no value and they have little time left to simply do their jobs.
- The management are saying that they have no real visibility of what is happening and do not use the system as a tool to identify problems or correct them.
- The senior management and board members may be finding that costs have spiralled upwards instead of downwards and again they are not able to use the system to get a view on what the business is actually doing.
- There may be regular problems with overnight batch jobs failing or taking too long to run. Month-end processing for the finance department takes longer and is a time when stress levels have increased.
- The overall consensus of opinion is that SAP is a system that they would strongly recommend that other organisations avoid at all costs.
- The project went in late and is still not completed.
- The Post implementation review has a long list of issues.
- The support department cannot cope with the number of problems.

Implementations of SAP R/3 that are classed as successful have many of the following characteristics during the first six months or so of the new implementation.

- The users feel that some aspects of their job have been made more difficult but they can appreciate the reason for this and that the benefits may well be experienced elsewhere.
- Some of their tasks have either disappeared altogether, been made easier or at worst are no different than before.
- They are often asking if there are other options available in SAP

that they can use.

- There is a growing list of requests for enhancements.
- The managers are asking for more reports from SAP and they see SAP as the tool to use to measure the success or otherwise of their departments.
- The senior managers and board members are starting to see some financial benefits even though at first these may well be quite small. It will take a long time for the real financial benefits to be felt.
- The overnight batch runs are not a major issue, there will still be the usual failures etc. but in general there are no concerns with this.
- The overall consensus of opinion is that the new SAP system is OK but many people will reserve judgement until some time has passed.

What if the implementation of SAP was seen as a disaster, what are the options?

Firstly, if you are seriously considering removing SAP R/3 altogether then please do not do this until you have read this book. I would hope that I have been able to demonstrate that SAP R/3 is a good system but only if it is implemented correctly. If your implementation was a disaster then consider reworking the system along the lines I have recommended.

It may be possible that the bad implementation has turned the business community so far against the SAP solution that it may not be possible to correct this. I hope that this is not the situation in your organisation because this may mean that you have little support for a rework however major.

One thing that you can do before you rip out the SAP R/3 system is to locate a similar company that has implemented SAP R/3 and approach them to see if they will meet with you to discuss their system and demonstrate how successful it is. If you find a company that has got it right then you will at least be able to prove that the SAP R/3 system can work for your business, providing it is implemented correctly.

If you can't or won't do this and the user community cannot understand that the system itself was not the problem then it may be impossible to convince them of this. So if you have had a bad SAP R/3 implementation and if this has damaged the perception of SAP beyond repair then there are only two possible options. Replace SAP with something else that will not be as good and may well result in a similar disaster anyway, or mount a major campaign to explain the causes of the problem and to describe the way forward with the SAP system. Be prepared to blame the project implementation team or at the very least the Project implementation approach, if it can be proved that this was a major contributing factor, because this may well be the real cause of the disaster. Point out that the business community may not have been as involved in the project as it should have been.

Then make sure that this rework is a success. It sounds simple doesn't it? Whatever happens you need the business community to see the real benefits that SAP can bring and be prepared to get involved in this rework project to make sure that they get what they need.

How to get more from an existing SAP R/3 implementation

If you have implemented SAP R/3 and it was not a disaster but you would still like to get more benefits, then this is quite possible and with a very healthy ROI.

I have even considered setting up a small company that would offer a "Tune-up" service for organisations that are already using SAP R/3. I am confident that there are many benefits that can be had for a very small amount of effort, so much so that it would be possible to offer a free service that would spend a couple of weeks looking at a clients SAP Implementation and then proposing a series of changes that would improve the system from a cost / benefit point of view as well as making it more "user friendly". I would have proposed that no fee would be charged for the work, instead a percentage of the perceived cost savings would be invoiced at the end of the project. No gains, no fee. This is an indication of how convinced I am that you can get significant benefits from an SAP implementation without major costs. Why haven't I done this then? Well to be honest, the whole business would rely on the companies that have implemented SAP admitting that it was not a good an implementation as it could have been and in addition to this, major organisations may be suspicious of getting something for nothing. But the benefits are definitely there.

I believe that the "fine-tuning" step should be added to the project plan, there is no way that you will switch to the SAP way of working and get the right system in one "hit". SAP systems should evolve over time as the users become more aware of its capabilities and as the basic requirements are met.

But before you start to dig for more benefits it is a good idea to take a few steps back and look at the current implementation and get an honest and open view of how successful it was. I do not see a Post Implementation Review (PIR) as being the tool to use to achieve this and the PIR is the final closing of the project. If you are only just at this stage in the project then you may find it very difficult to get a true picture of how well or otherwise the system is operating. People may still be getting used to the complexity and some of the processes may still be settling down.

The best time to start is at least six months after the PIR has been successfully completed. The only exception to this would be for those organisations that are absolutely sure that they have got it wrong in such a big way as to force them to do far more than fine-tuning. In this case the work cannot start soon enough.

I would start with a collection of interviews with as many of the SAP users as possible. This must cover all levels of the organisation from the company heads to the shop-floor workers. Construct a list of questions that will ascertain if the implementation has been a positive or negative step for them. I would start with precisely that question although a negative response does not automatically indicate that action is required. It is often the case in SAP implementations that some parts of the organisation will find that their workload increases and this is not necessarily wrong. A theoretical example could be as follows,

A user has stated that the system has now given them more work to do than they had before SAP was installed. For instance they now have to enter data that someone else has been responsible for until now and they expected that a good SAP implementation would result in less for them to do, the processes were supposed to be streamlined.

This comment is very common in SAP implementations and it rarely indicates a major issue. It is often happens that pre-SAP this data was being entered by someone who had no genuine connection to that data and was merely keying it because they had been asked to. Part of changing the processes to match SAP involves ensuring that no user has to key any meaningless data or data that should really be the responsibility of another person. It is important to ensure that data is entered by someone who has a connection to that data and therefore understands the effects of it being omitted or incorrectly entered. This often means that some users will have to enter data that they never used to, but perhaps should have always keyed because it is their responsibility. In this particular example the system has been improved because the data is more likely to be accurate but for this user they appear to have more work to do.

Some other questions to be asked are as follows;

"Has the implementation of SAP improved your job function in any way?"

If you get a high proportion of people saying no then this may indicate that some more work has to be done.

"Has it had a negative effect on your job function?"

If the users often say yes then this too is worth investigating. Although I would be very surprised if at least a proportion of the people interviewed do not say yes to this, after all it is likely to be a more powerful system than they were used to and so it may feel that the extra complexity is a negative. Explore the responses to make sure that it is not simply a question of complexity rather than a negative affect.

"Has it had any effect at all on your job function?"

If a high number of people think that it has had little or no effect on them then this is not a bad thing. Many people will jump at the chance to criticise any new system and so a reasonably neutral response can be seen as a plus. This has to be balanced against the overall response from people who believe that they have been affected.

"Would you prefer to have your old system back? "

This is a dangerous question and should be worded in such a way that it is obviously not going to happen but it is a worthwhile question to ask. It is a major success if the answer is a resounding no (and it often is when SAP has been well implemented)

"Do you feel that some of the new processes add no value?"

All processes must add some value and even if do then they must also be seen to be doing so. Negative results here can sometimes be caused by a lack of knowledge of the overall picture. The user may not realise the value that is added. If there genuinely is no added value then the process must be removed or redesigned.

"Are you able to get the information you require from the SAP system and is this easily retrieved?"

SAP implementations normally provide far more options fro retrieving information than most people are aware of. If there is a negative response then this should be investigated and the users educated on how to access this information in SAP.

"Have you seen any genuine cost savings achieved as a result of the SAP implementation and if yes, what are they?"

This is not something that every user will see but many of them should be aware of some cost benefits. There should be several very positive responses to this.

"Have you seen any day-to-day costs increasing because of the SAP implementation?"

It is possible that some negative responses may be received but they should be justified and extremely rare.

"Do you know of any enhancements or additional SAP functionality that may be useful?"

If you get a good response to this it does tend to indicate that the system is not that far wrong. If there were major problems then you would find very few people who want to use more of the system or improvements instead of repairs.

"Would like to have the opportunity to talk to one of the SAP consultants regarding your use of the system?"

The users should be encouraged to do this and the SAP consultants should welcome such discussions. There may be some "quick wins" and "hints and tips" that are possible and the SAP consultant should be able to point these out. Often users will not experiment with options (Thankfully in some cases) and this can mean that they are missing shortcuts and tips that can help streamline the process. These cannot be taught in the original training sessions because the users have enough to take in during the lessons without having to take in the "bells and whistles" too. There will often be users that have useful suggestions that can be considered, they need a chance to tell someone.

"Do you have access to all of the transactions and reports that you need to use?"

In most, if not all SAP implementations the approach taken to the authorisation of access to transactions etc. is very restrictive and can be so restrictive as to ban users from certain transactions that would prove useful to them. Some organisations MUST have this level of control because of the nature of their business, but there are other organisations that do not need that level of control and yet the users are only given access to the minimum of transactions. If you do not need strict authorisation control then give the users access to everything apart from those transactions that are classed as sensitive or dangerous. This is a must more enabling approach than giving the users access to only those transactions that they are believed to need, this will definitely result in them not being able to use some non-vital but useful transactions.

"Would you use more of the appropriate functionality available in SAP if you were aware of it?"

Some users will say that they would not, this may indicate that they may be struggling with the current use of the system either because of their need for more help or it may be that they are just not coping with the extra complexity that it is already causing.

A positive answer shows that the user not only appreciates what they currently use but may also be aware that there is more available and this should be encouraged.

When you have established how successful (or otherwise) the implementation appears to have been you will have some idea of the size and cost of moving it to a point where you are getting somewhere near the maximum benefits possible.

If you have established that the project was not successful then this step is more of a damage limitation phase than a "mining for gold" phase and after you have addressed the major problems you may need to repeat this step again to gain the benefits. I would suggest that you establish the main causes (hopefully with the help of this book) and try to address them using some of the options I have suggested. I would guess that if you have major issues to address then you have probably either heavily modified the system or possibly under-utilised the SAP software and used it as part of the solution instead of it being the core of the solution.

If your project appears to have succeeded, regardless of how well it has succeeded, then this is the time to start mining for the "golden nuggets" that are hidden away in the SAP system resulting in not only providing the user community with a system that actually helps them to do their jobs easier and better, but also one that has real and quantifiable cost benefits.

I have often heard people saying that SAP is an expensive system, and if it has cost you more than you have had returned then I would totally agree with this, but if the system has returned more than it cost then not only is it an inexpensive system but it is saving money and will continue to do so. Yes it is a big financial outlay originally, there is no arguing with that, but if you have implemented it, then the costs have already been spent and so now it is time to start to profit.

To me the term ROI not only stands for return On Investment, I believe that it also stands for Return On INFORMATION. If the SAP R/3 system does anything well then it certainly stores the data in a format that can be retrieved and utilised better than any other comparable system. Basically it is good at turning data into information and this can give your business the edge over your competitors, especially of you mine that data correctly. So even if your competitors also run SAP R/3 you can still increase your edge by fine-tuning the system before they do and better than they do.

In my experience the most difficult part of fine-tuning an SAP R/3 system is trying to persuade the board / senior management to give the go-ahead to the project. They will, understandably, want to know the cost and benefits that are involved. This is normally tricky enough with a "normal" project and it is nearly impossible to estimate this for a project like this. The cost and benefits depend to some extent on how good the implementation was. So you could try telling them that the implementation was so bad that the costs would be fairly high but the benefits would be huge. But how do you tell the board that the implementation was a disaster, especially if it was your project, not easy I would guess.

You could always try to persuade them to read this book and they may then have some idea of how an SAP implementation can have so many hidden benefits that can be exploited without significant cost. But whatever method you prefer I am sure that any such project would be welcomed by the SAP users and the benefits would be clear for all to see.

The fine-tuning project.

The first thing I would do would be to put in place clear guidelines that will ensure that no further modifications are implemented and at the same time something that will closely control the growth of new ABAPs, I would then follow this with further phases that will gradually remove some of the in-house ABAPs and modifications.

It is vital that an approach is agreed and published (as well as understood and supported) that gives a clear indication of just how standard you wish your system to become. If you enforce this approach rigidly you will regain the power and the flexibility that is inbuilt in SAP R/3 and free up essential technical resources to enable you to concentrate on the genuine developments that may be necessary to produce real benefits from the system for the business. At the same time, the functionality available in standard SAP is sufficiently broad and flexible to handle the vast majority of requests and so you will still be able to continue to provide the users with the functionality they need. The end result will be a more useable, more accurate, more flexible system that has a better ROI and significantly lower running costs.

This new approach should not necessarily lead to you having to say "no" to users when they are asking for changes but you may need to investigate certain requirements more thoroughly. In fact, not only is it acceptable to question requirements fully, it is actually advisable to do this, because requests for developments are often driven by more fundamental problems. Merely providing what is requested may just be treating the symptoms rather than the cause.

The solution involves three main phases

1. Change the current culture within the I.S. department.

Produce a presentation that highlights the message that "Standard SAP" has many benefits, some of which are hidden. This presentation can be based on the various points I have raised so far. Aim for the presentation last for a half-day and present this as soon as you can organise the teams to attend. Many people in the department will already be aware of the benefits of standard SAP but you do need to set a clear approach, demonstrate the benefits and make it clear that you want to take advantage of those benefits.

You should build into your current Change Request procedure (hopefully you already have one in place) an additional step that checks the change for compliance with the "standard SAP" approach. Those changes that take you further away from standard SAP, without full justification should be questioned and probably rejected. Ideally this validation should take place at an early step in the development so as to not delay the change or require rework at a late stage.

You should also try to get the message through to the "business" (perhaps via the senior managers at one of their management meetings) so that the users understand why you may be relying more on standard SAP and therefore providing fewer developments. It is important to explain the benefits that will be achieved and that the end result will, in no way, mean less functionality. (You could use a slightly modified version of the presentation that was given to the IS staff).

This initial phase would reduce the flow of further non-standard developments (and the follow-on corrections and enhancements that they inevitably lead to) and start to bring real benefits, but would still leave you with the current non-standard developments and in-house developed reports etc., so additional steps would be required if you want to take maximum advantage of the benefits of the SAP system.

2. Commence an active shift of emphasis towards standard SAP

Aim to convert selected non-standard developments back to standard SAP. This would be a case of picking those developments that are relatively easy to switch and at the same time the benefits are seen to be large enough to justify the effort. This can be thought of as a test case (or two). This is an opportunity to prove to the IS and business people (and yourself too probably) that the benefits I have mentioned are genuinely there and can be achieved without major effort.

There are probably developments that are very close to standard SAP that could be switched with minimal effort and there are others that would require more effort. Aim for the quick wins.

Rather than trying to achieve this across the whole of your system, I would suggest that you test the approach by using a section of the business as an example and then monitoring the success (or otherwise?) of this before eventually spreading the new approach to the whole of the business. I am sure that there are departments in your organisation that have used more non-standard SAP than others, so it should be easy enough to select one of these departments or perhaps one of the processes in one of the departments as a test case. If the test case proved successful you should then examine the remainder of the business for similar situations.

I would not (in this phase) propose any major changes to the core design and use of SAP.

3. Complete the shift in emphasis towards standard SAP

The final phase will involve a more significant change than the first two phases but will result in major benefits. It will also require full commitment from the businesses to switch to a more standard SAP approach. (It is hoped though that the results seen from phases 1 and 2 will help justify the change and therefore enable you to obtain the level of commitment required.)

It would be at the end of this stage that the major cost benefits would be realised. One major benefit would be the possibility of an IS department restructure and a shift to a true Competency Centre approach to make full use of the resources at hand. This could be achieved with fewer resources now that the system is more standard. There should be no need for significant resources in the ABAP and non-SAP technical areas. Instead the support teams would need to be able to understand basic SAP and how it is used in your company rather than them having in depth knowledge of the many special programs and interfaces that require specific technical knowledge. In this environment the loss of a technical support person should have far less effect and a replacement should be easier to find and be more productive from day 1.

At the end of this phase I would envisage that the SAP implementation would be as close to standard as was sensible across all divisions within your company.

The one golden rule is to actively seek out standard SAP options before even considering modifications and ABAP solutions. Only when this has been exhausted should you reluctantly consider in-house developed solutions.

Every SAP implementation will need to have some modifications and ABAP solutions but if you keep this to a minimum you can still reap the benefits of the power and flexibility of a good SAP R/3 implementation.

The Competency Centre

Is a Competency Centre (C.C.) right for you?

This should not be a question that is affected by the size of the organisation or the size of the I.S. department. The only affect that size will have will be on the number of staff and the size of the facility that is required. All organisations, however small, can benefit from having at the very least a Competency Centre approach, if not a physical competency centre itself.

But what exactly is a Competency Centre?

Effectively it is simply a structured IT department that will contain all of the skills and personnel necessary to ensure the efficient use of computer systems throughout the organisation.

A lot of time and money will have been spent on the business including re-engineering of the business processes and taking full advantage of the benefits of a fully integrated system such as SAP R/3. The same approach should be applied to the I.T. department and the end result is a Competency Centre. It is surprising just how many organisations spend a huge amount of time and money on an SAP R/3 implementation and yet they don't apply the same approach to the I.T. department. I suppose that it is a case of "not being able to see the wood for the trees", they are so focussed on the various departments of the business that they forget to look at their own department.-They have been "selling" the benefits of re-engineering and integration and yet few of them actually think of applying the same principles to their own department and obtaining the

126

same level of benefits that the business have enjoyed (that is if the project was a success).

The switch to a Competency Centre approach enables the I.T. department to look inwards and develop a fresh approach to their processes and structures. Ideally this switch should be run as you would any other project. It needs careful planning and a total understanding of the desired end-result.

One of the biggest decisions is the timing of the switch, you could create the Competency Centre before the SAP implementation commences, you could organise it so that the actual switch coincides with the go-live date of the implementation or you can make the switch just after the go-live date. Switching before the implementation commences can be achieved but I believe that this is not the best time to do this, the shape of the resulting implementation and the degree of change that the business will experience is not yet fully understood. In addition to this the implementation team will most likely be very different to the Competency Centre team that will be required. The volume of work will be such that the teams will be much larger during the implementation than they will be post go-live and there may well be a third party supplier involved in the implementation. So I would suggest that you should aim to either switch to a C.C. approach at go-live or shortly after. Logistically it is easier to set it up after the implementation but I feel that this misses out on the momentum that has been built up during the project. There is a climate of change during the project and so I would tap into this and aim to switch at the go-live date. Switching a short time after go-live means that the intense activities caused by early problems should have subsided and so there is less "noise" but I think that the biggest problem is caused by the degree of uncertainty regarding how long it will take for the system to stabilise. If you plan to switch some time after go-live, actually choosing the date for the switch is very tricky indeed. If the implementation was anything less than perfect then you may find that there is so much focus on just managing the backlog of errors that there is little or no interest in changing the shape of the I.T. department. My preference is to switch on the go-live date, this will give you the time during the implementation to get a feel for the size and shape of the C.C. and yet there will also be time after go-live for a transition period during which the final shape and size can be defined. The biggest advantage of this approach is that the personnel that will be involved in the C.C. will have chance to be involved in the support from day one, not only will this build their hands-on experience but they will be involved in the resulting "fixes" and so will adopt more of a feeling of "ownership" of the system.

Once you have agreed the timing you will need to determine the structure and size of the department, the structure is not difficult to define, the sizing however is another question altogether.

The structure is defined by the activities to be carried out and these include the following;

Support – This can be broken down into the three main levels.

The first-level support is a team of people that have some basic knowledge of the systems used within the company. They have been trained to handle the everyday calls relating to user ids and logons, printing problems, known errors and some of the minor new issues that arise. They have responsibility for the call even if they cannot solve it themselves. They log the details of the call and any solution provided, or details of the contact in the second-level support should it need to be passed on. Call-logging software is readily available to handle the volume.

Second-level support consists of experienced consultants with specialist skills. This is normally a pool of consultants with medium experience in the SAP modules being used and any legacy systems that have been retained. They should be skilled enough to handle most of the problems that will arise but they should not be expected to be genuine experts.

The third-level team handle the issues that are too complicated for the second-level. Hopefully these will be rare occasions but whatever happens there needs to be this third-level in some form or other. Some C.C.s employ a team of experts to fill these roles and the expert consultants also act as the team leaders that manage the second-level support teams. In other C.C.s this level is not manned in-house, but contracted out to another organisation (one of the SAP partners perhaps), in some cases this level is handled by using SAP via the services they offer such as OSS or remote consultancy. The size of the implementation will help to indicate how involved this third-level support needs to be.

Training – Most C.C.s will be large enough to retain a training department of some size and this is an essential department that will help to improve the overall performance of the system. There will be staff constantly changing roles and new starters, in addition to this there will be changes and corrections to the systems as well as enhancements and new releases, so there will always be a need for training and retraining. I have covered the subject of training in a separate section but as far as this section is concerned there is one important point to make. People who know the subject but cannot teach, and people who can teach but do not know the subject, will never deliver the appropriate level of training required. Of the two, the latter can be addressed with time and experience but the former will just not work! I would recommend that you look to the users that have been involved in the implementation when building the training team. I would expect that some users have already proved that they have picked up a fair knowledge of the system and this matched with their knowledge of the business gives them the required skills as far as knowing the subject and their teaching skills should already be apparent. A strong training manager who knows SAP well and can also teach would be ideal to give the training department the vision and focus it needs.

Technical – The technical team is split into two main sections, the day to day infrastructure team dealing with PC, printer, network issues etc. and a BASIS team that is responsible for the technical side of the SAP R/3 system, including authorisations, batch jobs, archiving etc.. Many organisations outsource their BASIS support but even if this is the case there still needs to be an in-house presence that can be a channel between the C.C. and the outsourced BASIS team.

Programming – This team would be responsible for the ABAP programs (with additional skills if you have retained any legacy systems). If you have followed the guidelines in this book and kept the SAP system reasonably standard then this team need not be huge. One senior programmer that is also acting as the team lead ,plus however many other ABAP programmers that are appropriate would be an ideal structure.

Change management – This is a vital team and one that should be in place for any size of implementation. There is no point in building an excellent SAP R/3 solution only to then make changes and corrections that undermine the balance and security of the system. All changes however small must be controlled and authorised. The team should be reasonably skilled in SAP in general and they should be strong supporters of the approach to an SAP R/3 implementation as I have outlined in this book. They should ensure that no change to the system is implemented that breaks any of the rules or guidelines that have been established. Most importantly they should be involved in the early stages of any changes to ensure that standard SAP is used unless it is completely impossible to avoid non-standard solutions. They should also be ensuring that the appropriate changes to the documentation have been made to reflect the changes and also that training has been provided where appropriate. In general this team maintains the quality of the system.

User representatives – This team is a vital part of the C.C. but they are not actually part of the physical team. The strengths that they bring to the C.C. are their knowledge of the business and their ability to represent the various user departments within the business. They are normally senior managers within the departments such as Sales, procurement, finance etc. They need to be able to make decisions for their departments and also communicate details of proposed changes etc. to the business as a whole. They would be present at the C.C. on a part-time basis and their main day to day tasks would be attending the various meetings to represent the business and also to sign-off changes.

The C.C. Manager – As long as the person filling this role understands the major concepts I have outlined in this book then I don't believe that it makes a lot of difference whether this person is from within the business or from the SAP world. The main requirement is strong management skills, there will be many occasions when strong individuals in the teams will want to use different solutions or approaches and it will take a good manager to turn these heated debates into something constructive.

It is vital that all of the teams integrate fully, some organisations have poor integration between the C.C. teams and the consequences are not that obvious and so often go unnoticed.

The first-level support team are often left alone to get on with the day to day task of logging and monitoring the calls. They often solve issues internally and this is good but this also means that the second-level team don't get to see these issues and there may well be higher level solutions that will prevent the problem in the first place rather than constantly fixing it whenever it arises. In addition to this the first-level team don't get the chance to expand their knowledge and learn more about the systems that are used. By having members of the second-level team visit the first-level team regularly and perhaps even acting as first-level support occasionally, there will be a better bond between the two teams and the knowledge of both teams will be improved. Many organisations have their first-level team situated separately from the other teams, sometimes in a different part of the country and occasionally in a completely different country. There may be some real financial benefits to this approach but the lack of integration will show over time. If there is no option but to have the teams separate then so be it, but at least try to maintain as much integration as possible.

It is also important to have full integration between the teams within the second-level support. There will be a natural split caused by specialist skills (such as SAP modules etc.) but as I have already mentioned in this book the level of integration within the SAP system is very high indeed and changes within one module will often have an impact on other modules. This means that no solutions should be kept completely within one team, full use of the regular team meetings should ensure that there is full visibility of proposed changes long before they are implemented and the teams should be encouraged to get involved with changes regardless of the module that is directly affected.

The need for integration does not stop here, it is also important to integrate the training team will all of the other teams. The training team need to be involved will all changes at a very early stage, if they are going to have to demonstrate the changes to the users then they need to have a full grasp of the change, not only what it is but why it has changed and what alternatives have been considered. This should enable the trainers to fully understand the change and therefore be able to explain it fully to the end-users rather than just reeling off a scripted demonstration.

The change control team also needs to be involved in all changes, again at the earliest stage. If the change is likely to be rejected by the change control team then this should happen before too much effort has been put into the change itself. The change control team should ensure that they are not merely a "rubber stamp" they must have "teeth" and be able to challenge proposals vehemently if necessary. To do this they must know the system very well.

The User representatives will be managers that can represent their departments and prioritise any work. They should take into account the cost of the change and use this to decide if and when the change will be implemented. It must not be a case of them deciding what is good for the business without them understanding the full cost of the change. It is genuinely surprising to see how the complexity and quantity of changes is reduced when the cost benefits analysis forms part of the change control process. This is especially helpful if you are trying to retain as standard an SAP system as possible.

The day to day running of the C.C. will vary greatly depending on the size of the department but whatever the size of the department you should be prepared for more meetings than you would imagine. Too many meetings can simply waste time and people become bored and unmotivated, but unfortunately a well run C.C. will have more than it's fair share of meetings and it is vital to manage people's expectations. One of the most important benefits of integration is that problems are discovered early on in the process, but to discover these problems you have to sit in on many meetings where people will often be discussing something that you are convinced has no effect on you. If you sit in on a meeting that lasts an hour and you find that 55 minutes of that was wasted but 5 minutes of it was relevant, that doesn't mean that it was a waste of time. That 5 minutes may have made you aware of something that you would never have found out until it was too late. You have to be prepared to go through this process and you have to convince people of its value long before their first meeting. I must have spent a huge portion of my working career sitting in meetings that don't affect me and I hate the fact that so much time is lost, but I would do it all again because the time saved by this process greatly exceeds the time wasted and the end result is a system that is more robust and more acceptable. So aim for a representative of every team to attend virtually every meeting, because of this though you have to make sure that the meeting itself adds value. Getting this balance correct is vital if you are to have a successful C.C.

IS SAP right for YOU?

It is not merely a question of is SAP R/3 right for you, it is more a question of is SAP R/3, <u>when it is implemented correctly</u>, right for you and the answer to this is a very definite yes. However, if you are about to join a company that has implemented SAP R/3 badly and they either don't realise it or they do realise it but have no intention of changing it, this would be something to be avoided.

The benefits of a good SAP R/3 implementation will differ depending on where you are within the organisation and so I have broken this down into different sections.

The CEO or Chairman of the Board.

If I was a CEO I would want a system that turns data into information. That information should be current and accurate. It should be information that adds value to the organisation and it should be verifiable. If sales should show an increase of 5% then this must be a genuine reflection of the business, it should not be caused by corrupt data or by someone misinterpreting the data. This means that the figures should be capable of being broken down to the lowest possible level so that they can be analysed further and verified. So any system that is used should have a full "drill-down" capability that can prove or disprove an interpretation of the data. The source data should be held in a flexible format so that it can be viewed from several different angles to provide the maximum information possible. I call this Return On Information, another interpretation of ROI. SAP R/3 stores the data so well that it can be dissected in whatever way that is required. The power of the integration means that one piece of data is effectively just one link in a massive chain of data and the chain can be followed to either end.

If you decide to implement SAP R/3 and follow the guidelines within this book then you will have the best possible chance of having an edge on your competitors. Your system will be as powerful and as flexible as you could ever hope for.

You will also be able to benefit from the in-built flexibility, SAP have built their system so that it will match the vast majority of businesses. This means that if your business changes, however dramatically, you will probably be able to make the switch as painless as possible and certainly without having to dramatically change the system. I experienced this first-hand in one implementation, I was implementing SAP for a major chemical company and three quarters of the way through the implementation they acquired a company that specialised in magnetic tape products. If we had been implementing a system from scratch instead of SAP then we would have had to throw out large portions of the system we had been building and add in lots of extra functionality to cater for this different business. Because we were implementing SAP we were able to handle the change within the original timescales with the absolute minimum disruption to the project and the business. The flexibility in SAP meant that we could add in a separate company without affecting the design for the original company. This extra company could be configured to match exactly the type of business the new company was involved in and yet it could still use the core design because this was built on "best practice". The end result was a system that suited both businesses, without compromise. The reverse has also happened to me, an organisation selling off part of its business during the project. This can be handled equally well and without problems.

Most organisations change throughout their life and if you have a good SAP R/3 solution then I am convinced that you will have the minimum of disruption should your organisation change, however dramatically.

A more general concern that you may have would be the return on investment (ROI) for an SAP system. As I have pointed out already the ROI depends entirely on the quality of the implementation. Obviously this is true regardless of the system being implemented but never more so than with an SAP R/3 implementation. This is mainly caused by the flexibility of an SAP system. SAP R/3 is so flexible that there are so many options available that it is easy to choose the wrong one. The more standard the SAP system the less risk involved in choosing the wrong option and so this is vital if you want to decrease the risk of a poor ROI. Your SAP contact should be able to provide you with a more detailed ROI projection based on genuine examples.

If you are prepared to put together the right implementation team then the end result should be a pleasant surprise. This includes obtaining the most experienced SAP consultants that are available, this is not an area for economising. With the right team and with this book in hand SAP R/3 can be a major boost to an organisation at all levels.

The Finance Director.

Many organisations decide on an SAP R/3 implementation purely because of its strengths in the Finance area alone. If you have read the rest of this book you will know that I am not in favour of using SAP for just one department in an organisation, but I have seen it used in this way on several occasions and it definitely works. But this would be like buying a car just to use the radio, the benefits of the integration with all of the other modules are huge and the finance department gain tremendously from this aspect of SAP. The integration ensures that the correct ledgers are up-dated by all of the business processes automatically and in real-time. This results in fewer mistakes and better information. The management information reports in the finance department are provided by the CO module in SAP and this gives total flexibility on how the financial data is viewed and controlled. This can be set up to work at the very lowest level of detail if required or it can provide less detail and more simple structures.

The financial benefits from an SAP implementation include the better utilisation of staff throughout the organisation. SAP R/3 is not a system that turns the users into robots, it provides them with the tools they need to enable them to carry out their roles more efficiently and with better information. This results in an organisation that is far more efficient and although I always maintain that SAP is rarely implemented to reduce headcount this can be a spin-off benefit.

Cash flow can be improved due to the excellent AP and AR functionality and the integration between the Sales and finance functions ensure that the risks associated with credit exposure are reduced due to the flexibility and visibility in this area. In all the SAP functionality in the finance area is one of the strengths of the R/3 system and so the finance department should welcome the implementation.

The IS Director.

To be perfectly honest, if I was an I.S. director and I had no direct experience of SAP R/3 then it would be the last thing I would recommend to my board of directors. The horror stories alone would make me feel that I would be risking too much by choosing SAP. The cost is great and so many organisations have poor or no ROI that it would be difficult to justify the risk to the board. But if I was an I.S. director, with the genuine experience of SAP that I have, the only sleepless nights I would have would be caused by the impatience of waiting for the go-live date to see just how big an improvement would be realised and just how popular the resulting system would be.

So unless you are a very trusting person and accept my view then you will have to read this book and form your own opinion. Remember that I get no commission from SAP sales and I don't directly benefit from anyone choosing SAP R/3, my enthusiasm for the system is just caused by me having seen it working as I should. I only hope that I have explained my thoughts and justified my comments well enough for you to be persuaded to choose SAP.

If you do go ahead with the SAP implementation then please do try to get a good SAP consultant with solid experience to work alongside you to ensure that you are fully aware of the dos and don'ts, especially as the early decisions will be the foundation for the rest of the system and these decisions will need to be correct even though you and your fellow colleagues may not yet understand the SAP way of doing this.

There used to be a saying "Nobody ever got fired for choosing IBM" the same cannot be said for SAP, unless you qualify it by saying "nobody got fired for implementing SAP correctly".

Senior Business managers

I will not pull my punches here, you will probably not like SAP R/3 at all, at least not until it has been live for a few months. The change is dramatic, it feels so different to what you have been used to, it will drain your resources during the implementation project, you will feel that you have no control over your processes, you will feel that SAP is too rigid, in fact you will think that it is a mistake for you to be involved in SAP at all. It will be very difficult to feel positive about SAP but it is vitally important for you to commit fully to the project and get as involved as you possibly can. The more negative you are the fewer benefits you will achieve.

The best thing to do is to get to know just what it is that makes an SAP R/3 implementation different from any other system. If you are reading this book then you have definitely made the best possible start. It is important to remember just how many companies have implemented SAP R/3 and just how diverse those companies are. Taking this into account you need to fully buy into the fact that it must at the very least be a competent system. I am sure that you have come across many systems in your career and I would like to bet that the majority of them were less than amazingly good, so it is understandable that you are sceptical of the SAP system. The "horror stories" will do nothing to change this impression but hopefully you have read the section that covers the reason for the horror stories. So if you start from a point where you are prepared to give the SAP system a chance then you may well be very pleasantly surprised (eventually). However, you will need to be prepared for an initial period where the new system will at best be OK and at worst, feel very scary. This initial period feels so bad for many reason, the main one being that it is a new system and however good it is it will take time for you to master it and the "old" system, however bad it happened to be, was familiar and you understood it (including its many problems). Think back to my analogy of a race car and imagine how you would feel stepping into an F1 car for the very first time, it would be very scary and you would probably feel a bit like a fish out of water. But if you enjoy cars and would relish the chance of getting into an F1 car then it will definitely help you to get the most out of the experience, on the other hand if you convince yourself that it is just not for you then it will be all fear and no pleasure. The same applies to the SAP implementation.

If you have to provide some of your people to become part of the project team then please try to give the best people you have, this will ensure that your department will be able to help shape the resulting processes in a way that achieves major benefits. Please do not just send whoever is available, or someone whose absence will not really affect the department. Basically, if the loss of these people will have little or no effect on the running of the department then you might as well not send them. I dislike immensely the saying "no pain, no gain" but it is so absolutely true in this case.

If the impact of their loss is going to be severe then you have probably selected the right people, remember that this is a short term and it can often be overcome by backfilling their positions. This sometimes turns out to be a positive experience in the long term, with replacement staff often "shining" in their new positions and providing a fresh view and new ideas. Another advantage is that they will return as experts in the new system, one that they themselves have helped to mould.

In summary, if you and your department get as involved in the project as you possibly can and be constructive with your input then the project will stand much more chance of being a success, especially for you and your department. If you do not get involved or are negative then even the best implementation is likely to give poor results for you and your department.

Project / implementation managers

If you have been made responsible for the implementation then you are right to be concerned about the outcome, especially if you have heard the horror stories about other SAP implementations. But if you approach this carefully then I am sure that the result will be something that you will be proud of and widely congratulated for. If you are offered this position jump at it, make it work and you will have fun as well as success. Just follow the guidance I have offered in this book and you should not go far wrong.

The most important thing to do is to make sure that you are aware of exactly what it is that is different about SAP and what to watch out for. By reading this book you should be able to avoid all of the major pitfalls that other Implementation managers fall into.

I would also make sure that all of the members in your team get this basic understanding of what this "beast" called SAP R/3 is all about. Get them to read this book (this isn't just to fill my pockets, just pass the book around if you think that), it is vital that they understand the benefits of using as standard an SAP solution as possible. They should also have as positive an attitude towards SAP as is possible, this helps to ensure that they will explore the standard SAP options more fully before they decide to use alternative solutions.

Build a team that has strong business skills, try to get the best possible representatives from the various business departments, don't just accept people who have been offered just because they are available. Fight hard to get the best people from the business, especially if their managers are insisting that their loss will have an impact. This is a clear indication that they are the right people. Do all you can to ensure that their business positions are filled in a way that will have least impact on the business, but do push for the best.

If you are lucky enough to get the full backing of the various business departments then your next challenge is to try to persuade the people from the business to join the project. This is not going to be easy and I would imagine that many of the people you want will turn down the offer to join the project. They will be concerned about several issues and you will have to try to persuade them that their concerns are unfounded (good luck).

One of their main concerns is the fact that they are at the top of their "tree" in the business and yet you are now asking them to join a team of people implementing a computer system. They may feel that the world of computers is a mystery to them and if this is the case then they will be very concerned about the move. Even those people who are quite computer literate will be apprehensive at least. In these situations I always point out that the role they will play will be for them to ensure that the resulting system actually works for their part of the business and more importantly ensuring that their department gets the maximum benefits from the resulting system. If they read this book they should see quite clearly that it is far from technical and their role in the team will be purely functional. One huge advantage for them is that when they return to their position in the business not only will they still have their business expertise but it will now be greatly strengthened by the fact that they not only understand the new system and processes, they actually helped to build them. So anyone worried about being left behind should realise that joining the team will have the opposite affect, it is those people who do not join the team that will be left behind.

Another major concern and perhaps a more tricky one to address, is the uncertainty of what will happen when the project finishes, they will be concerned hat the person who has temporarily replaced them may be so good that it might be difficult to get their own position back after the project. The reason that this is a tricky one to resolve is that there is no clear answer to what will happen after the project. The changes brought about by the system may mean that their old position no longer exists or it may be changed so dramatically that they no longer "fit" the position. This is very rare, even though an SAP R/3 implementation can result in many large changes the basic management structure rarely changes that much. I would ask the person expressing this concern if they would rather stay in their current position and have little affect on what happens, or if they would like to be involved in the process that decides what will change. In addition to this the experience they will gain and the visibility that comes with a high profile project such as this, can only strengthen their position and value to the organisation.

Another concern is the unknown and this is a basic human trait, we are all worried about the unknown. This is where you will be able to address this concern now that you have read this book. They will have no idea of what their day to day tasks will be during the project and if you are new to the SAP world then I am sure that this is a question that you yourself would like answered. In short they will be working with the SAP consultants and the business users to act as a form of Catalyst to ensure that the design that the SAP consultants come up with actually represents what the business really needs. They will be communicating with the business users to answer questions from the consultants and to inform them of the proposals. They will be communicating with the consultants to answer questions from the business and to inform them of business requirements etc. In all they are a bridge between the two different groups. They will speed up the process considerably if they are able to answer questions from the consultants without having to go back to the business all of the time for the answer. At the same time, if they cannot answer the consultant's questions themselves they will be able to direct the consultant to the appropriate person in the business to obtain the information. This in itself results in time savings and more accurate responses.

The consultants will be able to concentrate on the system options and the business team member will be able to concentrate on the business requirements. This forms a very strong team and often lasting friendships, it is in my experience a very enjoyable and rewarding task and the work hard / play hard ethic often surfaces. This is often the first time that the business has played such an influential part in a computer system implementation and it can be very surprising how positive the experience is.

So I would plan for a fight to get the best people and then plan a hard selling campaign to persuade the people to join the team, lose this fight and the end result will be dramatically more negative than if you win it. Implementation managers that have lost this fight or worse still didn't even realise they had to fight are often responsible for yet another SAP R/3 horror story. Please get this right.

If you have managed to get the best team of business people on board you will need the best SAP consultants too. This is also a tricky task especially because there are several options to consider, you could use SAP provided consultants, you could use an SAP implementation partner, you could use independent consultants, you could build a team of permanent SAP staff there are many options. One of the options I prefer involves a mixture of all of these.

If we look at each option and the pros and cons of each then it may help you to decide which is best for you.

Using SAP provided consultants has many benefits; their connection to SAP is obviously a major advantage. In my experience the overall quality of the consultants that SAP use is very high, this does not necessarily mean that you are getting the best available consultants but it does mean that the risk of getting a poor consultant is minimal. SAP prides themselves on their quality throughout their products and throughout their organisation and in my many years of dealing with them I can honestly say that their pride is justified. But you have to pay for quality and you may find that they are more expensive than some other options available. But I would not use this to preclude them from options because a cheaper option could easily result in a much more expensive project in the long run. Remember that I have made the point several times that SAP is a system that the quality of the resulting implementation is inextricably linked to the quality of the consultants you use. Basically if you can afford SAP provided consultants then I would definitely consider using them. There is no need to use them for every position on the team, I would make sure that you get highly experienced consultants from SAP and use them in the more senior roles.

SAP implementation partners are very difficult to measure as far as quality is concerned. No doubts they will be able to furnish you with lots of examples of big name companies where they have successfully implemented SAP R/3. They often have very long lists of previous customers and they may be the best possible implementation partners but you have to be careful. I have tried to point out in earlier sections of this book that after an SAP project goes live it is very difficult for the Company to gauge just how successful it was, it may have been a very poor implementation and yet the company may not realise this, the effects take quite some time to surface and when they do there are often other factors that get the blame. I am not saying for one minute that SAP implementation partners should not be used, all I am saying is that the sales brochures and references should never be taken as a guide to how good the partner will be on your project. The most important thing to check if you are considering an SAP implementation partner is the CVs of the individuals that will be working on your project. In fact whatever option you choose it is the CVs of the individuals that are the most important measure.

In one project I was involved in the company wanted to use an implementation partner that had experience of implementing SAP into a company in the same line of business. The logic was that they would understand the unique aspects of the business and their experience would be valuable. It is difficult to argue with this logic but remember that this experience they had was as a company and it did not follow that the individuals that they would provide would have the relevant experience. I suggested to the IS director that they ask the implementation partner to provide CVs for each of the consultants they would be providing. It was quite surprising to find that none of the consultants that they would be providing had been involved with the project that was for the company in the same line of business as ours.

So if you are considering using an SAP implementation partner then I would support this approach fully, as long as you get to see the CVs of the people they will be sending and as long as you feel they have enough relevant experience to be valuable in your project. I would not commit to using them for every position, I would encourage you to consider using them in addition to other resources on the project. I would not normally suggest that you use them to manage the project or supply the senior consultants unless they clearly have an approach that matches the guidelines I have laid out in this book. I have seen it happen where the company have a good approach to SAP but the senior people from the Implementation partner may not necessarily be fully committed to this approach. It is vital that you retain the power to shape the project in the way you want and with senior consultants from another company you may find that this becomes confrontational. If you are sure that they have the same approach as you then there is no reason not to use them in any position.

I think I just need to make it clear that all I am saying is that you need to look at the individuals and not the company, the strength of the company is a factor and their track record is relevant but it is the actual consultants that will be working on your implementation are more important than any sales pitch. I have seen great implementations by SAP Implementation partners, but I have also seen some that are not so great, so it is no guarantee of quality.

Independent consultants are a genuine option and they offer one major benefit that is often overlooked, you can trawl through the whole market for the best available consultant, whereas using an implementation partner means that you only have there list of available consultants to trawl through and this obviously limits choice. I have heard it said time and time again "If they are a good consultant then they will be working as a contractor to get the maximum financial benefit" this is simply not true. I know many consultants who have chosen the "permanent employment" option who are amongst the best consultants available. It is often a choice based on job security etc. and so do not use this as an indication of the quality of a consultant. Many consultants don't like the uncertainty that is involved in contracting and it is true that all it takes is a small gap in between contracts and the financial benefit can be lost altogether or worse still become negative. One thing is for sure though and that is there are many hundreds of quality contractors on the market and it is possible to get a top quality consultant at a reasonable day rate. But remember that you sometimes get what you pay for and I would strongly recommend that you find the best resource available and then see if you can afford to pay the rate. It may prove to be less costly to spend a bit more on the right contractor and gain benefits throughout the implementation than to spend a little bit less and pay for this later because of a poorer quality implementation.

There are several good agencies in the marketplace and it is worth looking at the resources they have available first. You may be able to man the whole project from the contract market.

Building your own team of permanent consultants at the same time as implementing SAP can be very risky. You will no know just how good they are until it is too late to repair any damage that may have been caused. If you already have competent SAP consultants in your employ then make full use of them on the project, they are likely to have to support it when it goes live, but don't put them into senior positions just because they are your own staff. Having them work alongside the other consultants and possibly being team-leaders is ok, as long as you understand the issues that this may cause. A highly experienced consultant may not be at their best if they are being told what to do by someone with noticeably less experience.

In one project I was working on the company had a strong team of consultants in-house and yet they still used SAP Implementation partners for the projects. The permanent staff wee part of the team but in reality they were left out of many of the decisions and were not all that happy. The next project that came along I persuaded the Company to let them implement it using contractors in the other positions. This worked well and not only was morale boosted but they also gained far more experience. In addition to this the resulting implementation felt more like it was designed for our Company and less like something that had be written externally and applied.

So to sum up, I would use whatever combination of the above that you feel appropriate, I don't think using one option only works in the long run, I am a firm believer in getting the best people for each position regardless of where they come from.

One thing I strongly recommend though is to try to find a very highly skilled SAP consultant that can work alongside you and help ensure that you have full access to someone who can help you with the SAP specific decisions throughout the project. This person can focus on the SAP consultants in the team and you can focus on the business team members.

Consultants

If you are considering a career as an SAP consultant, is this a good move? The answer depends on the current demand for these skills. Long gone are the days where if you could spell S.A.P. then you could get a contract and make money. When I first started back in the late 1980s the demand was so great that you could almost name our own rate, £1000 a day was nothing unusual. Nowadays you can be looking at less than half of this even with as much as 10 years experience. So many people jumped on the SAP bandwagon just prior to the year 2000 that the supply and demand is now not that favourable for a consultant. There are many people out there that are relatively inexperienced and these people will work from £200 a day upwards and many Companies like the value that this appears to offer and so this has driven down the daily rates for SAP consultants. So if you are thinking that SAP is a very lucrative career then think again, it is now very different. Yes, there are still some good rates to be earned if you have the experience but this has to be balanced by the fact that a gap between contracts makes a large hole in your annual earnings. As for a permanent career as a consultant then fine, if you can find a consulting company or SAP partner that is hiring then go for it. Not only will the salary be quite good but the training you are likely to get will help you sustain a career in SAP. But it is not easy to find a company that are recruiting unskilled SAP consultants.

A good way to get an SAP career is to be working in a company that have decided to implement SAP and get involved in the implementation. This can give you a chance to get some real experience on your CV and can be a spring board to a career as an SAP consultant.

So basically, if you can get onto the ladder, even a lower step of the ladder, then I would recommend that you give it a shot. It can be fun as well as rewarding and I always liken a career in SAP as being a bit like being a Rolls Royce salesman, you don't have to worry about the product, it is the best around so if you give it everything you have got then you will find that you have not "put your money on the wrong horse".

Some people try to enter the SAP world by paying to attend SAP run training courses, this is not an option I can recommend, not only are you spending a lot of time and money but few companies accept training as sufficient experience to get you onto that first step. For example, when I was working for SAP UK in their education department I help0ed to set up the BW (Business information Warehouse) academy. I also attended the course to check it for quality purposes and then took the exam. I managed to pass and so I am a certified SAP BW consultant, but this would in no way be sufficient to gain a position as even a junior BW consultant. People want hands-on experience and I cannot blame them. To get experience you have to have worked using those skills, but to get work you need experience and so it is a catch 22 situation. The only way to break this cycle is to be working for a company that are prepared to cross-train you and this is more or less down to being in the right place at the right time.

I have even come across people offering to work for nothing just to get the relevant experience, I have yet to see this work because the company will not have their staff taking time to train you and distract them from their project work even if you are not costing them anything financially.

SAP training

This is a subject I have very strong views on, mainly because I have seen so many different training methods applied and yet so few of them actually work.

If you were to look at a cross section of companies that have implemented SAP then you will find that most of them have entirely different approaches to training and there are varying degrees of success.

Some examples of approaches adopted by other organisations when implementing SAP

Company A

They decided that Computer Based Training was the best way to tackle end user training and they developed an approach that involved little or no classroom training. Instead their users go to an intranet site and select the courses that they require (This is from a list of courses that are pre-selected for them by their manager) and run the courses on their PC in their office environment.

The courses are automatically monitored and there are tests to gauge their competence and also the quality of the training materials. The manager has a list of courses completed by their team and details of their scores etc. The training materials are designed by the project teams and are built by an external supplier (due to the programming required to make them interactive with scores etc.).

The advantages of this approach are that the training is available to everyone on an as and when required basis and users can take the courses as many times as they wish to and they can use the course as help documentation while using the live system.

The disadvantages are that there is no human interaction and so no questions can be asked in real time (there is however, a method of posting a question on-line).

Due to the lack of human interaction, more time and care is spent on designing the course material to allow for this.

Documentation

The only additional documentation required on the project was the standard project documents that deal with the high level design and the low level detailed specifications that describe any non-standard developments of the SAP system (including reports etc.). Basically it was seen that if you have high level process documentation coupled with detailed training documentation and specifications then this is sufficient.

One additional advantage of using the training materials as a main project document was that system changes and fixes would then only need to be reflected in this one document, rather than two, or more. By updating the training documentation the change is immediately visible to the end users and IT team alike and everything is kept in step. Most changes do not affect the high level documentation that describes the processes and so this documentation normally remains relevant.

In general the approach that Company A adopted was seen to be successful.

Company G

This Company had an entirely different approach, mainly because of the volume of end users involved. This meant that the whole of the training development and delivery was subcontracted out to a third party. This meant that training could be managed as a separate project in itself with an associated budget, plan, resources etc.

The training team took examples of the processes from standard project documents, Standard Operating Procedures (SOPs) and transactional specifications, sometimes known as Business Process Procedures (BPPs).

Problems experienced

- Firstly the trainers had to wait until each "BPP" was completely finished and fully signed off before they could even start to produce the training materials (If they had started before the process was signed off then there was a high probability that there would have been changes. In fact, some training materials were started before sign-off and the whole transaction was then dropped making the effort redundant)

- The communication between the training developers and the people who designed the solution was very poor. These people were either too busy developing other areas and had no time and occasionally they were not really able (or willing) to explain, in full, the logic behind the designs (in some cases all three).

- Once they had produced a draft of the training documentation they would have liked to have the project team check their logic and terminology but they were either still too busy, or indicated that they had checked the materials when, in fact, there were errors (some major) that did not surface until the training was actually being delivered.

- They also would have liked to include references to "real world" examples throughout the training materials but they did not have enough knowledge of the business and the project team were again too busy to provide any, especially as these were seen as style rather than content.

- There was nobody who could indicate if there was a full set of training materials for all scenarios etc. The trainers did not know the system well enough to spot any gaps and the project team did not have the benefit of viewing the training materials as a complete block of training, they only focussed on the course material that directly related to their own area of the system.

- When it came to delivering the training courses the trainers were hit with many questions of varying levels that they could not manage. Many questions related to the high level design not covered on the course, or examples of business situations that they could not relate to. They also used a lot of inappropriate examples and used incorrect terminology and this significantly reduced the effectiveness of the course and the trainee's confidence in the trainers.

- Sometimes during the course the trainers would get suggestions for improvements and occasionally have attendees pointing out errors in the design. Not only did they feel unable to comment in detail on these but they also found it difficult to explain these to the project team. In addition to this when they subsequently delivered the same course at a later date they did not really have the confidence to know what to do regarding the errors pointed out on previous courses. If they mentioned them it would trigger a debate that they could not manage and if they didn't mention them then they were hiding errors from them. The stronger trainers "bit the bullet" and discussed the errors but the weaker trainers avoided the subject at all costs.

- After delivering the training several times the trainers were finally becoming comfortable with the content but at the end of the training delivery they had done their job and were no longer required by the company and the knowledge of the training courses was lost.

In general, the approach adopted by Company G was seen as being very unsuccessful, this reduced morale in the business and the benefits of SAP were significantly diluted.

These two examples are extremes, one (Company A) where everything was on-line and produced by the project team and the other (Company G) where the project team were not directly involved at all and everything was developed and delivered by a training team. A third example is more relevant and used an approach that is less extreme.

Company B.

The project teams each had a Business representative/s and these were people who knew the business, its processes and most importantly the users extremely well

The business team member was made responsible for developing the training documentation with the help of the SAP consultants and with the central training department advising on the standards and style of the materials. The business team member and the SAP team delivered the training courses (with the business representative delivering the more complex courses).

Documentation

The training materials were part of the project documentation and as such provided the detailed design documentation as well as the training documentation.

The central training department handled the Training Needs Analysis (TNA) and managed the whole administration of the courses and they also sat in on every course to provide help when specific business questions arose.

In general the approach adopted by Company B was seen to be successful.

Should the project team produce the materials and deliver the training?

The main element that affects who should do this is the number of users to be trained. If there is a huge number of end users to be trained (more than 500 for example), then the option of using the project team to deliver the bulk of the training is not normally feasible and therefore external training resources often handle the training tasks in total. If the numbers are less than this, then the option is feasible and several organisations adopt this with extra resources brought in to fill any gaps (from in-house or external suppliers). In the smaller implementations (less than 100) the project team normally produce the training materials and deliver the training.

Another influencing factor is the complexity of the training, if the functionality is very basic, then the trainer does not really add as much value to the course material as they would if the functionality was quite complex. For example, to train a group of inventory clerks on how to use the stock counting functionality in SAP could be carried out by a trainer with little or no experience in the business. But to train a user in a more complex business process (such as MRP, Plant Maintenance etc.) would need more than just training on the screens and fields to use. The trainer would need to understand how the functionality fits into the existing business and how it relates to current processes and systems. This would be more difficult to teach for someone not currently involved in the business or the project being implemented. The SAP system is quite powerful and so the training is difficult enough without clear, confident and relevant information delivered by someone who has experience. Also the number of "awkward" questions is often linked to the complexity of the functionality and so there is a need for the trainer to understand more than just the subject matter planned for the course.

Therefore, if you needed to train 1000 users on a really basic part of the SAP functionality, it would be clear that it not be efficient to use the project team (even if they had the resources to do it). If you were, on the other hand, to need to teach 2 users a very complicated SAP function then it would also be clear that to would not be sensible to teach a trainer the complex functionality (both business and system) to be used, just to be able to teach the 2 users (especially if the functionality was specific to that implementation and likely to be different in future implementations elsewhere.) Although these are two extreme examples they do provide some basic logic that can be applied to the decision on the approach to be adopted.

Some advantages of using the Project team as a training resource are as follows;

- Their knowledge of the business instils confidence in the users being trained.
- Their knowledge of the thinking behind the design and decisions taken enables them to answer complex questions in full with justifications for the logic.
- Their knowledge of how the system is to be used in that specific project ensures that the training is relevant and can be understood easily.
- The fact that they will most probably return to the business therefore retaining the link to the end users and growing with the system.
- The fact that they already have to produce documentation to describe how to use the system as part of their project tasks and this documentation could be used as the basis for the training materials
- They will have already established some contacts with the people to be trained and as such they will not be a "new face" delivering the training.
- They will be more likely to use the correct terminology and relevant business examples when asked questions during the course.

Some disadvantages of using the project team as training resources are;

- They may not possess adequate training skills
  (In reality the best trainers are the ones that have the in-depth knowledge of the subject coupled with excellent training skills. But this is a very rare "beast" indeed and so we have to try to get the best compromise and in my experience an excellent trainer with little knowledge of the subject is worse than someone with little experience of training and excellent knowledge of the subject, providing that the trainer is able to at least communicate clearly)
- They may be busy with system design changes, unfinished documentation etc.
- (If this occurs then the trainers could not finalise their documentation until such changes had been completed in any case.)
- They may not produce the training documentation to the standards required by the central training team
- (This could be overcome by involving the central training team in the project so that they can influence and monitor the quality)
- They may not be the ideal resource to conduct a full Training Needs Analysis
- (This is true; the central training team would be expected to manage this)
- The time taken to organize the training rooms, schedules and attendance is not a good use of their time.
- (This is also true but the project would have an administration resource that could handle this, or the local training department could manage this also)
- They may not have enough resources to cover all of the training.
  (Any gaps would be filled by resources from the training department (with the relevant skills) or from experienced external resources.)

The approach to training the end-users

I have already said that an SAP implementation is only as good as the training that was carried out and so it is vital to get this right. It is no use implementing a great SAP system if people simply don't know how to use it. It is equally bad if people know enough to use the system but not enough to grow with the system, the more that they use the system the more benefits they should be getting, this will not be the case if they are merely using the system like a robot and pressing the right buttons but not knowing why they are the right ones or not knowing if there are any other options.

The biggest problem of all is the fact that the SAP R/3 system is so powerful and so flexible that it is not that easy to learn it properly. I have even heard of some companies that have had to let some users go after the implementation because they were just not capable of learning the new system. I doubt if this is ever necessary and I wonder if the problem was the training rather than the learning capabilities involved.

The most important thing to do by far is to manage people's expectations. If they think that it is supposed to be an easy system to learn and they have trouble understanding it then you will have problems ever getting these people to learn the system. They will be assuming that wither the system is no good or worse still they may think that it is because they are not capable of learning such a powerful system.

If you remember my comparison of SAP R/3 to a formula one race car then I am sure that you can understand how people will feel when they have to jump behind the wheel for the first time, it is really scary and it will frighten some people so much that they will just not want to go near it. You must let them know that it will feel this way at first and it will be perfectly natural for them to feel uncomfortable at first.

I normally like to get this message across as soon after the announcement that the project will take place, as possible. I like to get all of the users of all levels to attend "road-shows" where the new project team will let them know what is going on, why SAP, what is different about it, the part they will play in the implementation and just how it will feel. This is vital to manage their expectations, if this is not done early enough then the rumour mill will start turning and it will too late to recover their support, especially if they have been discussing the horror stories that some of them will no doubt have heard. These days you are also likely to find that some of the users have already seen and used SAP when working for previous employers. These are the people that need to be talked to as soon as possible, they can become very helpful if their experience was a positive one and if it was not then you need to talk to them to discuss what they felt went wrong and try to make sure that they do not start spreading negative vibes about SAP that are based on poor implementations.

Once you have managed to get the SAP message broadcast to all users the next step relating to training will be the need to train the new business members of the new teams. They will need to be given training on the module or modules that relate to the team they will be working in. If you have the right consultants in the team then you may be lucky enough to be able to get them to present some basic SAP training related to their module. If this is not possible, due to the time available or perhaps the consultants are not good trainers, then you have the option of training courses supplied by SAP themselves. I would suggest that this is a good choice for initial training of the project teams. I would not recommend the role-based training at this point, instead I would send them to the standard SAP training courses that consultants would normally attend. These courses are not technical and only really basic computing skills are needed (Windows, mouse etc.), the fact that they are broad courses that go into all areas of the module rather than just concentrating on the functionality that is thought to be relevant, is a bonus. It will not yet be clear exactly which functionality will be required and so a broad training can be invaluable. This will enable the business members of the project team to know all of the options available rather than just the ones that are to be used, to me it is vital that as broad an SAP knowledge is achieved as is possible, because sometimes a solution can be found using other areas of SAP that were not planned to be used.

After this training I would recommend that the business team members spend some time on a one-to-one basis with the relevant SAP consultant to hone their knowledge and to cover some of the more relevant areas in more detail. This will also help to build the team and help bonding and so is time well spent.

The combination of the training courses and the knowledge transfer from the SAP consultants on the project should give the business members of the project team the right level of training. A much more difficult task is the training of the end-users prior to the go-live date of the project. Getting this right is the most difficult part of the project and yet you have to get it right if the project is a success. People involved in projects where the training did not work often insist that the problem was insufficient training and in a way they are right and yet the users probably could not have coped with more training. Not only would they not have the time to attend but they would be swamped with information. So if too little training does not work and if too much training causes problems then what is the best way to train the end-users? I have personally been involved with both extremes and I have tried various options and I believe that I have found the ideal solution.

Referring back to my analogy of a race car, how would you train people to drive a formula one race car, you certainly wouldn't start by trying to teach them by sitting them in a high powered race car and letting them drive around until they become good enough to take part in a race. This is even more crazy if you try it with someone who has not even driven a car before. One way that would work would be to explain the theory in a classroom situation followed by some practical lessons with a lot of "hand holding" and eventually a few sessions with the instructor driving the car with the student sitting alongside, then the student takes the wheel with the instructor sitting alongside and then finally a few solo laps followed by a few more lessons. Then after some time behind the wheel the student may well then start to feel comfortable. In many ways this matches the situation where users need to be trained on SAP.

Basically you cannot get by with too little training, you have to do everything you can using the time and resources available. So reducing the training really isn't an option, but what you can do is to change the approach and quite radically. My recommended approach is to reduce the classroom training to a minimum, use this time to manage the user's expectations of the new system. Start off by giving them an introduction to SAP R/3, explain what is so different and let them see what it looks like and give them a feel for how integrated and powerful it is. Then demonstrate some of the transactions and functions that they will be using. Do this from a role based viewpoint, try to indicate what they would be doing in a typical day or for a specific task. Draw the process on the whiteboard including the non-system tasks, the previous tasks and the tasks that will follow their involvement. Keep referring to this process throughout the training and make sure that they know how their part fits in with the rest of the system, it is important to let them know how the data that they enter is used and how important it is to get it right first time. They must be able to try the system for themselves and so there must be a range structured exercises. Concentrate on simple examples first, they have to know how to follow the basic process long before they learn how to handle the tricky situations and many variable paths available. If you try to teach every possible combination of events then the training will fail, it is just too much to take in, just stick with the basics in the classroom. Of course the user will need to know how to deal with every situation but this can be learned over time actually on the job. This is the basis of my proposal, give minimal training in the classroom followed by maximum "hand-holding" from day one onwards. As with the race car analogy it is the correct balance of training and practical instruction that makes for successful training.

By reducing the classroom training you can ensure that it is carried out as close as possible to go-live ensuring that it is fresh in the user's minds. The reduction in the time required for training will also result in less disruption to the users and this can only be a good thing, many users will already be quite negative about the new system and anything that helps to reduce this is very welcome. This also removes another problem that more intense classroom training introduces, if the user has been given a lot of training then it is often assumed that this is sufficient for them to work on their own, the user is then left without further training and is only encouraged to contact the team if there are any problems. This often results in the user feeling very nervous at first and can result in them never really feeling comfortable at all, no matter how long they use the system for.

To compensate for the reduced training you have to plan a period of "hand-holding" from the go-live date for 4 weeks or more (depending on the size and complexity of the implementation). During this period the users should not only be told that they can ask for help they must be encouraged to ask for it. Tell them that the first time they use a transaction or the first time they try something different they should ring in and someone will either sit with them or at the very least talk them through it on the phone. Even if they have had good training and they have a decent "how to" document in front of them they will still benefit from being able to say "I do press X now don't I" or "Is it enter or execute now?" This will give them the confidence to try it on there own. Classroom exercises, however good, are difficult for the user to relate too, real examples mean so much more and are much better as training tools. There will be some users that will not want to ask for this help and this is fair enough, they are probably the type that would benefit least from this anyway and they prefer to learn in their own way and at their own pace. The hand-holding will be required for several weeks, because users will only use some transactions occasionally and there will be transactions that are relevant to month-end etc., so plan to have people on-hand for 4 to 6 weeks. The project team members (SAP consultants, business team members and trainers) will be the main hand-holders and they can be supported by other users that have been involved in the project so far. This may well be insufficient to cover all sites and if this is the case I would consider using temporary SAP consultants to fill the gap, they need not be experts but they should at least know the basics of their module well, bring them in during the last few weeks of the project to assist with the development of the training materials etc. and this will allow them to get a feel for the way in which SAP is going to be used by the business.

Using training provided by SAP

The training courses offered by SAP always seem to come in for more criticism than they deserve, many people insist that they are low quality and not worth considering. I would not deny that there are some occasions where the training course fails completely and there are times where the training is merely adequate, but before you dismiss them as an option consider just how many courses they run each week / month / year. It is impossible to guarantee that they will all work as planned and human nature being as it is means that you only have to experience one or two courses that are not up to standard and you soon class the whole thing as a disaster.

Staffing the courses with quality trainers is not easy. In my time at SAP most of the trainers were contractors who had proved that they can deliver the courses, but to make it viable financially they needed a consistent flow of work. A good quality consultant / trainer would not make do with 10 days of work a month. This meant that the training centre manager had to arrange the course schedule so that the trainer was kept busy. This meant that there was a core of contract trainers in addition to the SAP employees. Under most circumstances this approach meant that good quality training could be delivered due to the trainer's familiarity with the course and the required consistency could be maintained. But as soon as one of the core trainers became unavailable due to illness or other commitments this resulted in major problems, the course could not be cancelled or re-scheduled because the attendees had made arrangements to attend and it would not be fair to them to change the timing at such a late stage (the trainer would sometimes phone in sick on the same day as the course was due to start, through no fault of their own). To go ahead with the course, a replacement trainer had to be found and at very short notice, the chances of finding a competent trainer in these circumstances are remote and so the quality would suffer.

To overcome this serious problem it was decided to stop relying on the independent contractors and replace them with teams of trainers from third party suppliers. This at least meant that there should be a pool of trainers to choose from if any became unavailable and so some more consistency was restored. A side effect of this was that the result was quantity instead of quality, the best trainers that had proved time and time again that they deliver high quality training were now removed from the loop. This may have ensured that there were trainers for every course but it did result in an overall lowering of the quality. You only have to attend one or two courses delivered by someone who is ether not a great trainer or one who is but doesn't know the system well enough and you will soon start to feel "sold short". Thankfully SAP has now started to change back to a more skilled training resource (including some excellent permanent staff) and I would suggest that, apart from the odd inevitable occasion, the standard of courses delivered is now more than acceptable. So I would recommend this as a good option when you need broad and comprehensive training, especially for the project team. SAP also offer an excellent range of end-user training and I would recommend contacting them to see if they can help with the training phase of the project.

Recruitment

Agencies

Over the 25 years that I have been contracting I have dealt with some of the worst agencies you can imagine but fortunately I have also dealt with some of the best. There are so many agencies in existence today that I regularly get 5 to 10 telephone calls from them most days. After several years of this it is quite easy to spot the bad ones. They simply have no idea of what SAP is and what each of the modules are and what they do. One of the worst I ever had was when an agency called me and asked if I had any experience of A. B. A. P., they actually spelled it out letter by letter rather than calling it ABAP, I more or less hung up straight away. These agencies are going to be representing you to clients and if they demonstrate zero understanding of SAP what chance have you got of getting the position.

The agencies don't have to be SAP experts but they should be able to demonstrate a basic understanding. Most agencies do this but I still get calls from some agencies saying that they have the perfect position for me, only to go on to say that it is a CO consultant that they need, or some other module not relevant to my experience. They simply don't understand the differences between the modules. This is not only annoying due to the waste of time during the phone call but imagine the standard of CVs that the client is going to receive.

If you are considering using an agency either as a consultant or as a client then please question them on their basic knowledge of SAP. If they struggle with this then put them to the bottom of the pile. I know several good agencies and these are the ones that I contact first when I am looking for a new position. If other agencies contact me and they seem to be of a reasonable standard then I will let them try to place me if they can but only because I would rather be in work than sitting at home and not earning anything. If an agency contact me and display a serious lack of SAP knowledge then I will not deal with them at all.

If I was registering for work for the first time then I would only register with the best agencies but thanks to the internet your CV will soon be reaching hundreds of other agencies, especially if you have registered it with one of the Job Sites and allowed them to broadcast it. So try not to register on too many job sites or you will find that the potential clients will get so many different CVs from you that they will just bin them.

If you are a client looking for consultants then you want an agency that will send you CVs that are relevant and a god match to the job specification. If you constantly get irrelevant CVs then I would suggest that you consider trying other agencies. I know that dealing with agencies can be very painful, with lots of time wasted on poor CVs or many phone calls pestering you for work, but keep trying until you get one or two that have good SAP knowledge and a reasonable "bank" of experienced consultants. I don't want to be accused of blatant advertising but I would recommend that if you are looking in the UK or Europe then you will not go far wrong with Square One of London. I have dealt with this agency for many years, from both sides of the fence and they are a real example of an agency that have solid SAP experience, a good bank of strong consultants and they will not waste your valuable time. I do not get any commission from recommending them and I thought long and hard about whether I should quote any agencies at all but they are worth the risk.

To look at this from a different angle, if you are an SAP recruitment agency then how can you improve your figures and place more candidates?

Firstly I would make sure that you train all of your client and candidate facing staff in the basics of exactly what SAP is all about. It is vital that they understand as much as they can about SAP and not just the terminology. They should at the very least understand why an MM person should not be put forward for an FI position. Even contacting the consultant to discuss a job that is not relevant can mean that the consultant will look elsewhere, after all you are supposed to be representing this consultant and if you cannot tell the difference between MM and FI then you will not last long in this business. Give your staff a basic understanding of the modules, what each one does, where the integration points are and which modules are closely linked together. Ensure that they realise just how much there is in one module and therefore how many years of experience in one module does not necessarily mean that you are an expert in all aspects of the relevant functionality. Get them to read this book, it will give them a good understanding of just what is so different about SAP. (This is not an attempt to sell more copies, pass this copy around if you want to). Get them to identify their main candidates for each of the modules and see if they can persuade these consultants to spend some time with them over a beer or a meal and get as many tips from them as they can.

It is a very competitive market and so there are many ploys that can be used to gain more contacts and grow your client base but do remember that the consultants on your books are relatively intelligent people and they know only too well that you need to use every option you can to grow your client base. Bearing this in mind, asking them for references even before their CV has gone to a client is an obvious ploy to get the names of people who need SAP staff. I would recommend against this action, the consultant is generally able to see why you are asking for this and they often see this as an insult to their intelligence. You are more likely to get some useful names by being honest and asking for them, especially if the agency promise not to mention where they got the name from and promise not to annoy the contact. If your agency is seen as trustworthy and knowledgeable, then the chances are that the consultant will be more than happy to help. If the agency are using desperate tactics to gain contact names then the consultant will be concerned about the way in which the contact will be treated, if the agency are above-board then the consultant will be less concerned that the contact will be pestered.

The client wants CVs that are relevant, do not rely on quantity, the client may well know a lot more than you about SAP and so you have to be very careful, sending too many irrelevant CVs will soon result in the client trying another agency and you may lose the client forever. Get the consultant to comment on how close a fit they feel they are to the position on offer and do not forward any CVs where it is obviously a poor fit. You could even consider using some of your trusted and experienced consultants to assist in these processes. If you have an highly experienced SAP consultant on your books then get them to contribute to the CV selection process to help weed out the poor ones. This can be done anonymously so the consultant cannot take advantage of the details. If you trust the consultant fully you can even let them know the names of the candidates because the chances are that they may have come across the candidates in previous projects.

Whatever happens, you must make sure that your agents sound honest and experienced when talking to clients and consultants. I personally would rather deal with an agent that states that they are unsure of their facts than one who sounds very confident but doesn't know the basics. So please invest a little time and effort in building up your agents knowledge of SAP, once again you could perhaps persuade some of your top consultants to give them a few casual training sessions.

Recruiting SAP staff / contractors

When interviewing people to fill SAP roles, either contractors or permanent staff, there are several things to watch out for.

You need to get the maximum experience that the salary / rate will attract. There is simply no substitute for experience when it comes to SAP. This is mainly because the reality of an SAP implementation is so different to the theory. I have already pointed out how flexible SAP is and how this results in a different implementation every time, so someone who has only experienced one or two implementations many have developed experience of one approach to the use of SAP and this approach may not be relevant or worse still it may be an approach built on lots of non-standard SAP modifications. Someone who has experienced many implementations is more likely to have seen different approaches with varying results. I suppose that you could say that experience is important in any job but with SAP I really believe this to be paramount. I am not saying that inexperienced consultants should not be used, after all everyone has to start somewhere, but I would not use an inexperienced consultant in a position where they set the approach to be adopted without strong guidance from a senior consultant or Project Manager. I am equally not saying that someone with lots of experience is likely to get it right either, it is just a degree of likelihood.

To establish if the person being interviewed has the right experience ask them to describe the differences between the projects they have been involved in, what you are looking for is a demonstration that they have gained knowledge on the "dos and don'ts" in an SAP implementation, along the lines I have outlined in this book. They should mention the benefits of standard SAP and they should mention that it can be implemented in so many different ways. Ask them if they can explain why there are horror stories about SAP implementations, ask them to explain how they will help to ensure that this project will be a success. This applies to any position you are trying to fill, even the most junior posts, it is vital that they are aware of the problems to be avoided and the opportunities to be obtained.

If you feel that they have the right level of experience then you need to somehow find out if they know their relevant module/s well enough. This can be very tricky because you may not have an experienced consultant that can ask these detailed questions. If this is the case then consider contacting one of the many SAP partners and asking them if they can supply a senior consultant that can get involved in the interviews and help out with the detailed questions relating to the modules involved. There is no shortcut for this and the details on the CV should not be taken as an indication of knowledge of a specific area. For example, I had been working as an SAP MM consultant for several years and yet I had not been involved in an implementation that used Vendor Evaluation. My CV was very strong with many years of experience in MM but I knew nothing about Vendor Evaluation. You will also get CVs that cover areas of a module that the interviewee has indicated experience in, but this may be second-hand experience, it may be that the project they worked on had implemented this element of SAP but the interviewee may not have had any involvement. If you are filling a position that requires very specific experience then the chances are that you may not have this experience in-house (or why else would you be interviewing) and so it is not easy to spot any shortcomings, but do make sure that the experience listed on the CV is genuine first-hand experience.

You will receive CVs from people indicating that they have experience of many of the SAP modules and this may well be true, after all SAP is so highly integrated that it is almost impossible to stay within one module during a project. But don't confuse this with genuine experience of a particular module. I personally have first-hand experience of more than 9 modules within SAP but I still class myself as an MM consultant with experience of other modules. I sometimes class myself as an MM/SD consultant because I do have solid SD skills and never as an SD/MM consultant because I do not know all areas of SD well enough to be able to take a positions as an SD consultant. There are consultants who will class themselves as an SD/MM/PP/PM/FI/CO consultant and if you have one of these consultants in for an interview then I would dig deeply to find out what their base module is. You may find out that they know one or possibly two modules really well but a consultant that can genuinely cover three or more modules properly is a very rare beast indeed.

Always try to get the best consultant that you can afford, it is worth extending the interview process to see more people and it is also worth paying that little bit more to get a better consultant because the benefits should result in huge cost savings during and after the implementation and these could easily run into the millions of GBP, USD etc. So advertise the position and have a desired rate in mind but keep your options open.

A career in SAP, is it a good move?

The potential earnings as an SAP consultant are very high and so the answer is basically yes but it is very difficult to get that first position. The potential rewards have resulted in so many people trying to get into the SAP job market that it now quite flooded and there are lots of people still trying to get their first position even after many months if not years of trying. Some people have paid for expensive training courses hoping to recoup the costs from there earnings, many never actually make it and those that do have to take very junior positions to gain the required experience.

Just before the Millennium SAP UK launched various initiatives to increase the number of SAP consultants due to a severe shortage and high demand. This resulted in a high number of new consultants hitting the market just as it started to diminish. The boom due to the fears of Millennium problems changed to a drought just after the start of the year 2000. The SAP job market has never quite recovered from this situation and although there were problems before 2000 with a real shortage of consultants the exact opposite has also resulted in problems of a different kind. Now that there are so many SAP consultants chasing the same positions the salaries and rates have reduced significantly (by around a half in my case). This in itself is not a problem and the current rates are around equal to or slightly lower than they should be, prior to 2000 they were too high and unsustainable. The real problem is that companies looking to fill positions will find consultants willing to accept very low rates just to get into the market and this naturally means that the cost savings are significant and so many organisations are taking on "cheaper" consultants. (and paying for it in the long run). This means that if you are trying to get your first SAP job/contract you will be competing against other consultants that have obtained some hands on experience that are prepared to take less you were hoping for. Some consultants without experience of SAP are even prepared to work for nothing for a short period just to get something on their CV, unless you are prepared to actually pay a client to employ you then you will not be able to compete with these consultants.

I am afraid that there is no formula or tips that I can give you to help you to get into SAP, all I can say is that it will take a lot of luck and hard work to achieve this. In the last 5 years I have had time where I could not find work, on two occasions I was actually "between contracts" for nearly 3 months and I had over 10 years of solid SAP experience. So if you are just about to try to get into SAP be prepared for a lot of disappointments but if you manage to make it then it will have been well worth it.

If you have been lucky enough to be working in a company that has implemented SAP and you have been able to get involved in the project then this is a good way in. You will be able to show genuine experience of SAP on your CV, even though it may have just been as an end user. If this is the case then do all you can to get as involved in the detail of the implementation as possible, ideally as a business representative on the project team itself. This will count as genuine SAP implementation experience and will be a big bonus when applying for your first position.

Find a really good agency, if they tell you that it will be hard and they may not be able to place you then it sounds like they are one of the better ones. If they tell you that it will not take long and it should be easy then look around for another agency. When you find a decent agency listen to their advice, if they think that you need to attend some training and obtain SAP certification then consider this but there are no promises of work and the process can be very expensive. Don't just decide to go for one of the main modules, choose some of the newer functions in SAP, BW, APO, Industry Specific solutions, Workflow, Authorisations etc. etc., these are relatively new SAP areas and so there will not be anyone around with solid experience and so this levels the playing field for you. The agency should be able to give you an idea of which parts of SAP are in demand. If you go for a very new specialist area of SAP the number of positions will be correspondingly low but the biggest benefit of all to you is that there will be fewer people competing for these positions and the length of experience they will have can be no longer that the age of that functionality in SAP. If you choose one of the main SAP modules then there may be more opportunities around but there are also many more consultants and some of them will have 15 years or more experience.

If you are currently working in the SAP area and you are offered any cross training to one of the newer specialist areas then give it serious thought.

Finally all I can say is the very best of luck and if you make it then you are unlikely to look back on it as a mistake.

The SAP certification, is it important?

In a word yes, it is very important to obtain certification in your chosen SAP area, this will not indicate that you are a good SAP consultant but if the client is looking at three CVs of similar experience and one of them is SAP certified then it may be just enough to swing the decision. Any edge that you can get can only help you in your search for an SAP job/contract so contact SAP and ask them about their certification training.

If you are a client looking for a consultant for your project then see the certification as being part of the picture and no more than this, I personally concentrate more on what they know and how much experience they have. If you ask someone why they are not certified then they are likely to say that they have just not had any spare time to take the exam, I don't think anyone is likely to say that the reason is because they failed the exam.

How easy is the exam?

It is not easy and I expect that you will find it very scary at the very least. The exam questions are multi choice (in most cases) and this does not help as much as you would imagine. It is so difficult to write good questions that really do test the consultant without being unfair (I know, I have written many of the SAP MM exam questions myself). However good the questions are there will always be some that appear to be ambiguous or worded in such a way that none of the multi choice answers seem to be correct. This can cause some people to panic and freeze, resulting in a fail. Just remember that there are no deliberate trick questions, the exam is designed in a way that bad consultants fail and reasonable consultants pass, it is not designed to only allow the best consultants to pass.

How to approach the certification exam

I have personally trained hundreds of consultants on the SAP UK academy and to my knowledge only two of these did not eventually pass the exam, a handful failed the first time and had to re-sit later and all bar these two passed at the second attempt. Of the two people that failed twice and did not then re-sit I could see right from the start of the academy that they might have a problem. One of the students just totally lacked confidence and this in itself was the problem, they were in the top half of the class but he just somehow convinced himself that he was not good enough and as it turned out, it was a self-fulfilling prophecy. So please don't talk yourself into failing. The other student that had a problem failed mainly because he was a very experienced non-SAP consultant and he was unable to approach SAP with a clear and open mind. During the academy course he was frequently checking the transactions to see if they were working correctly and to see if they added up correctly. With SAP R/3 you have to take it for granted that the system actually works properly (or else the many thousands of customers might have already spotted any basic errors), you have to concentrate on how to get the most out of it and not keep mistrusting the system. It was just that this person had been developing scratch-built systems for so long that he just could not switch his approach to the "SAP way" of doing things.

Another strange fact was that most of the people that failed the first attempt were those that did particularly well in the classroom, this caused them to "over-answer" the questions. Rather than just answer the question they were reading between the lines and finding different answers that, even though they may have been technically correct, these were not the answers that the examiner was looking for. If I had one sentence that I could give as guidance to someone sitting the exam it would be as follows; Read the question fully and understand it before you even look at the answers, then select the answer or answers that you feel apply without looking for trick questions or complex answers. Many people read the question quickly, trying to ensure that they do not run out of time, then go straight to the answers and pick the one/s that make the most sense. But sometimes the question is written in such a way that it is the least sensible answer that is correct. SAP avoid double negatives where possible, they do not intentionally include questions that say things such as "which of the following statements are untrue" but some can be worded in a way that this is the gist of the question and picking the answer that looks sensible may be the wrong one.

The questions will indicate if one or more answer is appropriate by saying things such as "Which of the following statements are true" and "Which statement is true" a subtle but important difference.

Another reason for failing is caused by finishing the exam too quickly or too slowly.

If you finish too slowly you will leave a number of questions unanswered and this is to be avoided. The time allowed should be more than sufficient to answer all questions. I prefer to answer the easy ones first and come back to the more difficult ones at the end. Why waste a lot of time on one question when you can answer several in the same time. It would be very bad to leave the last few questions unanswered when they may well be easy ones.

As for finishing too quickly, this can be even more dangerous, not only will it mean that you may have rushed some questions but if you have time left over there will be a great temptation to re-read questions that you have already answered, this is fine if you are just re-reading the ones that you were not confident in, but whatever you do, do not go over those that you answered with confidence the first time round, this will increase the risk of you over-answering them and changing answers that were already right. I fell into this trap when I took my first SAP exam, I passed but with much lower marks than I would have expected and this was purely down to changing a whole string of questions that were already correct.

If there is one question that I seemed to be asked over and over again about the exam it was the one about "negative marking" and the basic question most people were asking was, "will I lose marks for answering a question incorrectly". What they actually meant was if, for instance, the time was running out and they had some unanswered questions left, would it be better to leave them unanswered and get 0 marks or should they give their best guess and risk reducing the marks they had already earned from other questions. This is quite a sensible question to ask and it should have been easy to answer but it wasn't. The marking system was more or less kept secret, I can understand why, SAP didn't want people to be using exam strategy to gain better marks, the exam was supposed to measure their SAP skills and not their exam skills. I spoke to several people in SAP and I was given many different answers, not intentionally, it was just that very few people actually knew the answer. I managed to find the few people who knew the answer and even they found it hard to answer the question. I asked if there was any "negative marking" and the answer was "yes" and "no", this was actually a very honest and accurate answer but not the one I wanted. After much more digging I finally managed to get a full answer and I will try to explain it as clearly as I can.

Firstly the negative marking exists within a question and is absolutely necessary when multiple choice answers are used. Basically if there are two answers that are correct and you indicate three of the answers as being correct the extra answer that you have indicated will reduce the number of points you can get for that particular question. If this was not the case then all you would have to do is to mark ALL answers within that question as correct and you would get maximum marks for that question. This cannot be allowed and so negative marking within a question has to be used. So if you mark two of the multiple answers correctly and also mark a further two answers that you shouldn't have you will get 2 points for the correct answers and MINUS 2 points for the two incorrect answers resulting in ZERO points for this question. So negative marking DOES apply. But why then did they also say that it didn't? This is because negative marking does not apply across answers and this occurs because the lowest points you can get for any question is ZERO. For example if you marled 4 potential answers as correct within a question and only one should have been marked as correct, this would be 1 point for the right answer and MINUS 3 points for the wrong answers resulting in -2. But there is no negative marking across questions because you would not be given -2 for any question because the minimum is ZERO.

This means that you should answer as many questions as you can because the worst you can get for a question is zero, but answer each question as accurately as possible to get maximum marks. But the best advice of all is don't leave yourself with insufficient time to answer all questions, get through the "no-brainers" first, then go back to the difficult ones, that way if you don't get time to do them all you may not be damaging your marks because you might have got them wrong anyway and been given no marks for these questions anyway.

As for what to read up on in preparation for the exam there is no golden rule, just try to make sure that you have covered all of the functions in the module to some extent, breadth of knowledge can be more important than depth of knowledge. If you concentrate on depth and get to know certain areas very well by sacrificing others, based on the statement that you will not be able to get to know the full detail of all areas, the there is a real possibility that you may not even get any questions on some areas and therefore you may have been better off at least getting to know all areas reasonably well.

There are also some general questions to watch out for, so don't just concentrate on the module specific functionality, also get to know the basic transactions as well.

So the very best of luck, think positive, read each question fully and answer as many questions as possible and you won't go too far wrong.

Common issues and areas of confusion

Mapping your organisation structure onto SAP

What is the organisation structure?

Basically this is the shape of your business both logically and physically. If you had one physical site and one financial "body" then the major parts of the structure are going to be very easy to set up. But very few organisations are this basic, if you are one of them then congratulations, your SAP organisation structure should be easy to define and will probably not need to be re-worked later in the implementation (unless our actual organisation changes).

The penalties for getting the structure wrong are high indeed and the problem is exacerbated by the fact that you will probably not even know that you have got it wrong. A well designed SAP organisational structure will ensure that you can take full advantage of the flexibility and power of an SAP R/3 system. If you get the organisation structure wrong then this will not be that easy to spot and the problems will not be that visible. All that may happen is that many of the SAP functions will appear to be useless and you will have to use many "work-arounds" to fill the gaps in the functionality. This is where you will find many organisations stating that SAP is a poor system that cannot even do the basic well. If you ever hear anyone stating this then I am pretty sure that you will find that their organisation structure is the cause of their problems and NOT the SAP R/3 system.

So the basic rule is that you MUST do all you can to get the right structure at the earliest possible stage in the design. If you don't do this early enough then when you finalise it later you may find that some of the designed solutions will need to be modified or, in some cases, thrown out and re-designed.

The problem with trying to do it so early in the process is that you may not fully understand the use and effects of setting up such structures such as Company Codes, Plants, Sales Organisations etc., especially if you are new to SAP. But this must not be used as an excuse to delay the design of the structure or to start off with a basic approach that "we can change later", this really would be a recipe for disaster.

The most important thing that you must do is to clearly understand what each of the main elements in the SAP organisation structure are and how SAP *intended* them to be used. Do not make any assumptions here you must fully understand the reason fro each structure and the impact it has on the system. This does not mean that there is a hard and fast rule to follow for each element, many of them can be used in several different ways and you can set them as high level or low level elements, but you MUST understand what the restrictions are if you place them at too high or too low a level.

For example let's take an imaginary element of the organisation, you may decide to have only one of these imaginary organisation elements or you may decide to have hundreds of them (one per physical site you have for instance). If you decide to have only one of them then you will be able to view the total of all data at this level and therefore see a full picture across the whole organisation, but will you be able to break this data down to individual site level? Not easily, because you have only the one element. If you therefore decide to have one of these elements at each of your sites then you can get the data by site, but can you easily get the data totalled for the whole organisation? The answer is probably yes but not without some extra reports etc. So of the two extremes, which is worse? It obviously depends on several factors but in my experience it is far easier to assemble data from several elements together to produce a total than it is to try to break down a total and get the individual elements of that data.

If you have read the earlier sections in this book then you may remember that I pointed out that one of the strengths of an SAP R/3 system is the fact that you can drill down the data in SAP to get to the lower levels. But this is only possible if the data is stored at the lower levels already and so you have to get the organisation structure correct so that the data is stored at the lowest level required.

The correct organisation structure is not only critical for the ability to access the data, it is also a major element that affects the day to day transactions and the master data that they need to have access to. I have detailed a specific example in the following section "Plant or Storage location?", but you have to remember that SAP have designed the system to be used in a specific manner and this will be based on a reasonably flexible organisation structure, but if you wander too far from the basic design then this will definitely result in less functionality being available. Get the structure right and all of the SAP flexibility is available, get it wrong and you will "block off" options, the system will still be as complex but you will not be able to take advantage of the flexibility and power that causes this complexity.

How to get it right.

This is one of the first steps in the implementation and it can be thought of as the foundation upon which the SAP R/3 system will be constructed. As with any foundation it has to be right or it will have a major impact on the finished product.

One of the biggest problems is that you have to get the structure correct long before you actually know what structure is absolutely correct for your organisation

There is no simple formula to follow but there are some guidelines that I can give that will give you the best possible chance of getting it right first time.

The first and perhaps most important rule is to try to produce an organisation structure that matches reality as close as possible, do not under any circumstances try to produce an artificially simple structure to make things "easier".

Many people will suggest a simpler structure because this will reduce the amount of master data to be maintained and I can see why they suggest it, it sounds sensible. But if you decide on a simpler structure then it will have an impact on how well the system operates and how flexible it is. So ask yourself this question, "How many times do you update master data and how many people are involved in this process?" Then ask yourself "How many times each and every day will we be using the SAP functionality, how many orders will be placed, how many receipts, issues, transfers, write-offs, invoices, etc. etc.?" I think that you can see which impacts the most people and how often. So if having the correct structure allows the full functionality to be used properly but involves a higher requirement for master data maintenance, then surely this should be one less long drawn out discussion. If your organisation is actually very complex then there is no way that you should try to achieve a basic simple organisation structure, it will not reflect reality and it will definitely result in a less optimal implementation. Bite the bullet and accept the extra load on the master data, it really will be worth it. Those organisations that have decided to try to reduce their master data in favour of a simpler organisation structure are often the same ones that contribute to the many horror stories about failed or poor SAP R/3 implementations. They are right, their SAP system is not all that powerful, it is not all that flexible and it certainly appears to be a very badly designed system, but remember that this is true simply because it is THEIR SAP system and they have implemented it in such a way that the genuine SAP functionality cannot be used in full.

Designing your organisation structure

If your organisation has several physical sites throughout your country and nowhere else and you have one financial body, then this is likely to be what I would class as a *relatively* simple SAP organisation structure. The main area for discussion will revolve around how many Plants (using SAP terminology) you will need and how many storage locations. It is vital to get this right from a logistical viewpoint but it also has a major effect on the other modules you are using, including the FI module.

If you have physical locations in several places, are they all classed as part of the one financial body (Company code, to use SAP terminology)? This question has to be considered properly and the answer you give will affect the shape of the design and configuration of the SAP R/3 system.

There are some guidelines I can suggest that may help you with your structure but these are far from hard and fast rules and some levels of the organisation are easier to decide on than others.

The "Client".

Starting at the very top, you have what SAP call the Client level. It is very difficult to summarise exactly what a Client is but you can think of it as the SAP system itself. If you have two clients then you have basically got two SAP systems that can be set up differently and use different data. There are some tables that will be shared across clients but these are quite rare and do not normally affect any data.

I am aware of some SAP customers who have decided to use more than one "Live" Client but this is something that I would avoid at (almost) all costs. As with anything there are bound to be exceptions but in the vast majority of cases you would only have one "live" client that you use for your actual business system.

Typical uses of multiple Clients are for testing, training and development.

Many organisations will have one Client that is the real live system that everyone uses for actual processing of live data etc. I have heard of some SAP customers who have multiple live Clients but this is exceptional and I have never come across any genuine reason for doing this. If you have all of the elements of your business on one Client then you have access to all of the data and this can be shared and accumulated wherever necessary. If this is spread across several Clients then this summary and access to data is difficult to achieve and in some cases not feasible. If you are considering having multiple live Clients then please only do this if there is absolutely no alternative. The integration of an SAP system is a huge strength and you will not gain the full benefits.

There is also a Development client where the Analysts and programmers can work on the configuration and coding in a development system that will have no impact on the live system. This is often on another "box" (separate hardware) not connected at all to the live system.

There will also be a client for system testing and this is normally as close a copy of the live system as possible, so that changes can be tested in as real an environment as possible.

Frequently there is also a training client that can be kept isolated and therefore stable during training (changes can be applied in bulk at selected points rather than as they happen.

There is often a regression testing client that has a full set of "live" data from a very recent copy of the live system and this client is used to carry out a final test on near live data before the changes are applied to the live system. This takes a lot of maintenance to keep the data up to date and takes a long time to continually refresh it with current data but the effort and cost involved pays dividends when it prevents corruption of the live system. Only a few organisations actually manage to have a fully maintained current copy of the live system as a regression test Client.

There are sometimes additional Clients for things like ABAP development etc. and I am sure that no two SAP customers have an identical number of Clients and an identical strategy.

The "Company Code"

It is normally not that difficult to decide on how many company codes you need in SAP, this is normally driven by the legal structure of your business.

The basic rule (not unbreakable but a good firm guideline) is that if your organisation submits statutory reporting for a part of your business then this should ideally be set up as a Company Code. Therefore if you only ever report one set of figures for the whole of your organisation then having one Company Code is a great starting point for the design.

As with any rule there are exceptions but if you can keep it to this basic approach then you will not go far wrong.

In a recent project I was working on the organisation was effectively one big business with lots of divisions. Each of these divisions did not report separately for tax and legal matters. The basic recommendation was therefore to have one Company Code and this was implemented. However, when I joined the project (some time after going live) there were many concerns that SAP was just not capable of providing basic reporting. The reason for this was that the senior management wanted to be able to report and manage each of the separate parts of the business individually. The Managing Director wanted any transfers of stock between the different parts of the organisation to be treated as Sales and Purchases rather than simple transfers of stock. Standard SAP prevented this from happening and so special processes were developed to handle this. Firstly the question should have been asked "Why does SAP not allow you to buy and sell items across separate parts of your business? It is supposed to be flexible !!!!). This is a very good question and as I have mentioned in other sections of this book, SAP is not a stupid system. SO why wouldn't it do this basic process? Well firstly, it could be modified to do this and this is where the problems start, many customers change their SAP systems to allow them to break the basic rules within SAP.

But why was SAP not capable of handling a sale and purchase between two parts of the organisation? The main reason was the organisation structure, it had been set up as one Company Code, which was quite correct and there are basic accounting and/or legal reasons why an organisation cannot make a profit or loss by selling or buying between parts of the same Company. So in effect, it was not a shortcoming of the SAP system, it was a sensible and appropriate blocking of an invalid process.

Standard SAP does not have a simple transfer process that involves a profit and/or loss between two parts of the same Company. So by modifying the system to do this you are actually opening up a whole string of potential problems. Instead of modifying the system it would be better to look inwards at the business and try to determine what is actually going on. The business wanted to have this "feel" of a sale and purchase between two parts of the Company to ensure that the benefits of the transaction could be passed onto the correct part of the business. For example, if one part of the business manufactures an item and then another part of the business uses this item as part of another transaction and makes a profit on the deal, where should the profits be attached? If you merely transfer the item from one part of the company to the other then this is done at cost and so the manufacturing part of the business sees no benefit from the transfer. The part of the business that actually closes the deal sees a nice profit on the item because the obtained it at cost. This is a common problem in most businesses and one apparent solution is to sell the item to the other part of the business, but this is only a theoretical sale and the accounting has to be done in such a way that no rules are broken. A better way is to merely transfer the items at cost using the standard SAP transfer functions (there are many alternatives available to choose from). Then at regular intervals these transfers can be summed and valued and a value can therefore be assigned to the relevant parts of the organisation again using standard SAP.

The project I was involved in had decided to use a sales order and purchase order for this process instead of a transfer and as a result of this they could set a price and profit margin for the item when it was "transferred". The users were complaining that the process was unwieldy and complex and many man days were lost in managing the process. The reason for the high cost involved to manage the process was that they had to have a Customer for the part for the business that received the items and a Vendor for the part of the business that supplied the items. These were treated as genuine customers and vendors and so they have credit limit functionality, invoice matching etc., etc. There was a sales order, invoice and sales ledger involved as well as a purchase order, invoice and purchase ledger. Each "transfer" had to have a payment from the customer matched against the invoice in the sales ledger and another matched against the invoice in the purchase ledger. There were lots of small discrepancies due to the nature of the item (Bulk deliveries that were not always exactly what was ordered) and so invoice matching became a nightmare. The end result was a team of people checking that payments cancelled each other out and that invoices were matched to the payments and yet this was two parts of the same company transferring stock.

If they really wanted to act like separate companies then they had two options.

One option was to use the standard SAP functions for transfers and then have a regular report that listed the transactions involved and suggested a figure for the extra value that they wanted to apply.

The other option (the one that they finally adopted) was to set up each of the parts of the company as separate Company Codes in SAP. This allowed them to act as separate companies and yet use the standard functionality in SAP to accumulate the financial reports into a higher level "company" for legal and reporting purposes.

My preference was for the former solution because of my golden rule of "stay as close as you can to reality", if they are legally one company then set them up in SAP as one company and find ways of managing any unusual requirements from the business.

If your organisation is a collection of companies then setting up one SAP Company Code for each is a good starting point.

Plants and Storage locations

Firstly, as with any other part of the organisation structure it is vital to understand what SAP intended these elements to be used for. This doesn't mean that you have to stay with the SAP approach to these structures but at least you will understand the consequences of varying from them if you should decide that you need to.

There is a large amount of functionality built around Plants and Storage Locations and SAP have built this functionality to use these levels in a particular way. They have built in a fair degree of flexibility but the basic use of Plants and Storage locations is quite firm.

The Plant is meant to represent a part of your organisation that is physically situated at a specific address. It is very much a physical plant such as a building or a site. The basic rule that I apply is that if you have more than one physical site in your organisation and they have different addresses and if an item was to be moved from one to another it would have to leave your premises and travel to the other site, then I would give set them up as different Plants. The SAP functionality has been built around the basic premise that the Plant has an address and movements within the plant do not necessarily have to go via any kind of transport.

A Storage location on the other hand, is seen to be a physical area within a Plant, such as a warehouse or physical area. It is assumed that movements from one Storage location to another are done either logically or without the need to transport the items externally.

Some points to consider when deciding if Plants or Storage locations are appropriate.

Firstly there are many "intangible" reasons for using Plants but the most important thing to consider is that by using Storage Locations for physically separate sites / addresses there will be many options in SAP that will be no longer available. Using Plants for these elements will keep all options open. The one thing that you need to try to avoid in SAP is blocking off options, even if you do not intend making use of those options. Keeping these option open not only allows you to handle major changes in the business in the future but it also indicates that you are using the organisational units in the way they were designed.

In my own involvement in many SAP implementations no SAP customer has ever said that they regret using Plants instead of Storage locations, whereas several clients that have used storage locations where they should have used Plants often use phrases such as "Surely SAP should be able to do something as basic as .....,", "Why can't it do xxxxxx?" only to be told that it <u>can</u> do it, but not if you use storage locations where Plants should have been used.

One of the problems is that you can make an SAP system operate even if the organisation structure is not correctly set and quite often with no apparent disadvantages and so it is very difficult to argue the case for using Plants correctly but I have listed several areas below that are directly affected by the option chosen and these should be considered before a final decision is made.

Lead times

The lead times for a material are held at the Plant level and so it is not possible to indicate that a material will need to be shipped x days before it is required if Storage Locations are used. For example you may buy an item for your plant in London from a vendor also based in London. You may also buy the same item for your Plant in Scotland from the same Vendor. If you have used Storage locations for Scotland and London instead of Plants then you cannot store a lead time for each site you can only store one value because this data is held at the Plant level in SAP. Projects that have this problem will be very disappointed in the SAP functionality and may not realise that this is simply caused by a less than ideal organisation structure. By using a separate Plant for each site you can now store a relevant lead time for each (along with a huge amount of other useful data)

Stock valuation

The stock value and price control (Standard Price or Moving Average Price) is held on the Plant level in SAP and so if you use Storage locations instead of Plants then you cannot have a different value at each site. Using the previous example of Scotland and London the vendor may charge more to deliver the items to Scotland because it is several hundred miles from his warehouse and so transport charges will apply. This means that stock in Scotland has cost more than the same item in London, yet you cannot have a different stock value for each storage location you can only have this set by Plant (disregarding split-valuation functionality covered elsewhere). You may even want to have a different stock account for each site and again this is not standard at Storage location level, but it is at Plant level.

Stock transfers

The options available for this are greatly reduced if Storage Locations are used, yet the options for storage location to storage location transfers are still available if Plants are used (you can still use two step transfers from Plant to Plant without using Stick Transfer Orders). So using storage locations instead of Plants will block off options that you may need later.

MRP

There is functionality within SAP known as "Storage Location MRP" but the functionality is greatly reduced and all that is available is a basic form of Re-order point planning. This may be enough for simple MRP but there are many useful functions available in MRP that cannot be used for Storage Locations. If you really want to make full use of the powerful MRP functionality then you are likely to need more Plants not fewer.

Physical location of stock

Storage Locations are designed to be used to denote the physical location of the stock within the Plant. This means that if a site is designated as a storage location you lose the ability to break it down any further to indicate the location of the stock (Unless you use the complex warehouse management functionality in SAP, this is really only applicable to structured warehouses with shelving etc.)

Stock Availability

In general the automatic stock availability checks operate at the plant level and so if you wanted to repair a piece of equipment on a site and wanted to see if the materials were available, the system may well indicate that the job can go ahead today when in fact the materials are available but stored at a different address.

If the site was set up as a Plant then the material could indicate a lead time of X days (the time needed to get the stock from the Warehouse). This would mean that the user would be correctly informed that the job could not start for X days. If the stock was already on the site then the system would know this (From the Plant availability check) and the user would be informed that the job could start today.

So it is important to ensure that you are aware of the above issues and the consequences before you finalise the design of the Plant and Storage Location structure.

Purchasing Organisation

This is one of the elements that relates to the MM functionality and although it can be used in many different ways it is important to understand what SAP intended this element to be used for.

It is actually quite difficult to summarise exactly what a Purchasing Organisation is meant to be in SAP and so I will rely on a few examples to help explain.

Many companies can actually get by very nicely with just one Purchasing Organisation, even some of the larger companies do not need more than one and unlike my recommendations for aiming to have more plants than you may have expected I would actually recommend that you have as few Purchasing Organisations as possible.

They are mainly used when raising Purchase Orders and contracts etc., they are a mandatory field in these transactions and that is because much of the purchasing master data is keyed by Purchasing organisation There are not that many reports that are broken down by Purchasing org and so there are normally no major benefits of having too many of them. There are however certain circumstances that will dictate the need to have multiple Purchasing orgs. One example is as follows;

One part of your organisation buys from a vendor and the same vendor is used by another part of your organisation but in a very different way. An example of this might be a vendor that supplies you with a raw material that you buy regularly over time and yet another part of your organisation may just purchase small amounts of the same product very occasionally. The vendor might charge a different price depending on the part of the organisation that is placing the order, or they may have different payment terms or use a different currency. By having a separate purchasing org for each you can have different data, such as prices, lead times, currency, payment terms etc. All the person ordering has to do is to use the right purchasing org and the data will be defaulted correctly.

The purchasing organisation should not be seen as a purchasing department as such. There is no link between purchasing groups and purchasing orgs for instance. There is no reason why several purchasing departments can't all use the same purchasing org. If the price is different according to the Plant that the items are to be delivered to then this is handled by the info records which can be different depending on the plant being used.

So if you have a situation where the same material is provided by the same vendor to the same Plant but with different default data such as price, lead times and payment terms then you will probably have to have more than one Purchasing org.

Importantly there are very few reports that can break information down by purchasing org. and so this should not be a main reason for using multiple Purchasing orgs.

Try to see if you can use one or two and only add others where you have to. It can be useful to have one central purchasing organisation that can be used for all sites and one or two local purchasing orgs if necessary.

Purchasing Group

As I have already pointed out in the previous section there is no direct connection between Purchasing groups and purchasing orgs so do not try to artificially group together these two elements, they have no relationship.

In essence a purchasing group is a buyer or a group of buyers that are responsible for the procurement of certain materials or services. The description of the purchasing group is often the name of the buyer.

One if the main uses of purchasing group is to "steer" the requirements to the appropriate person for action. So when a requisition or a purchase order is raised it will appear on searches by purchasing group, so that the appropriate buyer will see these requirements on their lists. The purchasing group is normally stored on the material master record so that when an order is placed the appropriate buyer is linked to that order.

If workflow is used to electronically send the requisition or order to a user for authorisation then this will normally use the purchasing group to determine the individual user that should receive the notification.

So ideally you would set up a purchasing group for each buyer, if you want to use groups of people instead of individuals then be aware that the system will still operate but you will be losing one of the levels designed to help allocate a requirement to a buyer.

A further benefit of the purchasing group is that a printer can be assigned to a purchasing group so that any printouts can be directed to the printer nearby the buyer automatically.

Sales Areas

The Sales area I SAP is actually a combination of Sales Organisation, Distribution channel and division.

The approach for this is the same as the approach for Purchasing Organisations, the main consideration is the master data and order control. The Sales Area is also useful for reporting purposes (more so that the Purchasing org) but again, the main consideration is the complexity of the master data.

Cost centres

I am constantly surprised at the number of projects that I have worked on that appear to have misunderstood or at best, under-utilised Cost centres.

I am not an accountant and I have no formal accountancy training but I have worked alongside many very experienced financial consultants and I have developed a basic but sound grasp of the main areas of integration between the logistics modules and the FI/CO modules. I am convinced that a major benefit is being missed in many implementations.

To put it into really basic terms, Cost Centres are a method of breaking down financial postings into groups so that costs can be interrogated and analysed.

For example, if an invoice for the restaurant facilities is received and posted onto the system this will result in the whole of that charge being posted to a General ledger account and yet some of that charge relates to the factory staff, some to the office staff and some to the warehouse staff. So how can we really know how much it costs us to make something or how much it costs us to store the materials? The payment for the restaurant should be broken down into the respective amounts for each department, but this is not always possible, the restaurant charges are not specific to who uses the facility.

This is where cost centres bring major benefits. Formulas can be used to break down the charge, by number of employees for instance. These formulas can be used automatically to allocate the cost to separate cost centres. The when other items are purchased these too can be linked to cost centres. For instance, if new kitchen equipment is purchased this too can have the cost centre specified on the purchase order (this can even be spread across several cost centres if required). When the Purchase order is received the costs are automatically allocated to the correct cost centre and so the data is both contained in the single posting to the appropriate General Ledger in addition to an equal value posting to a cost centre (or spread across several cost centres). But in most of the implementations I have seen, the cost centre has been set as equal to the Plant and this just doesn't make sense. If it is set to be equal to the Plant then how can the costs within that Plant be broken down. A Plant could have a production area, a warehouse, office facilities etc. and yet the lowest level has been set at the Plant. So how can anyone calculate exactly what the production costs are if the warehouse and office costs are included in the same posting.

So I would recommend that the cost centres are used, as the name suggests, as collectors of costs for the various departments etc. involved in the organisation and not merely mapped one to one against the Plants.

Material Master management and control

In many implementations the design, approach and controls that will affect the material master data are tackled at the very beginning of a project. In larger implementations this is often planned and staffed separately to the main project, but even when this correctly planned and staffed the work involved often takes longer to complete than the actual project being implemented, so it must be given the correct priority and focus. It is easy to underestimate the effort involved in a central material master database shared by all of the various departments and sites in the organisation. In many cases the switch to SAP involves far more integration than expected and this often results in having to produce a completely new (to the business) approach to the structure and management of the material master data.

To gain full advantage from a central material master database some kind of catalogue is normally required. There is no sense in investing the time and effort to maintain the material master data if users cannot find the record that they are looking for. There needs to be a form of cataloguing that will enable the users to easily find the appropriate record. The catalogue function to be used must be decided upon before any work can take place on the actual data load so that the data will be catalogued as it is loaded. Just how complex the cataloguing needs to be depends on the type of organisation and the level of complexity involved in the material master data. Some organisations can just use the match code function that is available as standard within SAP other organisations, this allows the user to enter partial information such as description etc. and the system will then propose a list of materials that contain this partial data. However in a more technical environment the user may need to be able to specify complex characteristics of a material to find the correct one, this may include things like temperature range, tolerances, chemical properties etc. Organisations that have this level of complexity will need to consider the extra workload involved in developing a more complex cataloguing approach, but the most important point to consider is that the catalogue design will need to be agreed right at the beginning of the project so that it does not hamper the development of the overall material master approach.

When the approach to the catalogue has been agreed and the structure of the characteristics designed, the rest of the process can continue.

The main stages of the process include

> Defining the Catalogue approach
> Defining the Catalogue structure
> Defining the Processes involved in maintaining a Global Material Master file
> Defining the data load approach
> Data cleansing of the "legacy" data
> Specification of incomplete/missing data/materials
> Data Load
> Data verification
> Ongoing maintenance (add, delete, change, extend)

Defining the Catalogue approach

The following questions need to be understood and resolved before an approach can be finalised,

- What are the benefits of a Global Material Master database and which of these benefits are seen to be the main requirements of the organisation?

  The benefits of a central Material Master record are well known but you will need to identify the elements of this that are important to the organisation.

  The reduction of redundant Material Master records and the prevention of duplicate records are important issues that need to be controlled, so that the correct materials are used in all processes so accurate reporting can be used to determine precisely what is being purchased, used, scrapped etc.

  You will also need to encourage users to specify a Material Master record on all Purchase Orders, PM orders, Requisitions, etc. so that this data can be analysed fully. If Material Master records cannot be found easily there is always a temptation to use free text instead and this destroys the accuracy of reports and prevents the ability to "slice and dice" the historical data.

- Do you need to have one Global Catalogue or can some elements of this be local or specific to the type of business?

  There may well be areas of the business that need to have a different structure to the Catalogue due to the nature of their use of Materials. For instance, the maintenance of an oil Rig requires a certain type of catalogue, very different to the requirements of a buying department responsible for the purchase of Computing equipment or services etc. It is possible to have a central catalogue that can cater for all parts of the organisation, but if their use is dramatically different then it is possible to have multiple catalogues without decentralising the data.

- Do you want to have a central department that solely maintains the materials and the catalogue or can some of this be maintained locally?

  Although many organisations start off with an approach that uses a central material master department that results in all changes and additions to material masters and the catalogue being handled centrally, this often changes after several months when they are inundated with requests to change fields that have no central affect. The local departments then become frustrated as the lead times involved changing what they see as "their" data, start to grow. So many organisations switch to a compromise solution where the main data is controlled centrally and "local" data is maintained locally. The major problem with this is that it makes the "line" between local and central very vague and the important control of the data is diluted. This often leads to a further change in approach that results in changes being made locally but authorised centrally. The local users maintain their own data and these changes are monitored centrally with some changes being rejected or at least investigated further before being applied. The creation of new materials is handled centrally and the main data that is purely central is blocked via authorisation to prevent local amendments.

- Do you need multiple methods of cataloguing materials to match the many requirements for reporting, searching and maintaining this data?

    Within SAP there are many different types of cataloguing.

    Classification is the most powerful with the ability to create classes and characteristics and link the objects (in this case material master records) to them. This enables very complex searches and is the best option to use, especially as the resulting catalogue could be as basic or as complex as required. You can even create simple classes without any characteristics and link the materials directly to these.

    Product Hierarchies are not as flexible as classification but they are very useful where a simple hierarchical structure is required. The structure can have many levels and reports and transactions can use this structure.

    Material groups are a third option but this is not a very powerful option and many implementations use this as a main search option and are often disappointed with the results. This option should be seen as mainly a method of reporting and even then there are many reports that do not contain material group as a selection option. In many of the implementations I have seen the material groups have been set at the wrong level with too much detail, for instance instead of having a material group for Inks, they have set up Red Ink, Black Ink, etc. this results in no capability to break down the simple reports into a total by Inks. So my recommendation is to aim to have fewer material groups and have them set at a higher level. If you need to break down you groups to a lower level then use the product hierarchy field or better still use the classification functionality.

There is a final option but it is not one that I would recommend and that is to use structured descriptions. That is to use the description on the material master record to hold a structured text that can also be used in searches. This is very limited, difficult to "police" and removes the ability to store a full and proper description. However there may well be certain kinds of materials that would benefit from a structured material description. For instance bolts, screws and fasteners, if there is no set structure to the description then it would be possible to have one material master for a 3mm roundhead bolt with a description of "3mm roundhead bolt" and when a user is searching for a "Roundhead bolt 3mm" this material would not be found and the danger is that a duplicate record may be created. So structured descriptions do have a place in the control of material master records but I would not recommend them as a cataloguing function.

- Have we identified all of the business functions (and therefore departments) that will use this catalogue function (Sales, Purchasing, Maintenance, Planning, Reporting etc.)?

  The catalogue should be suitable for all departments that use material Masters, it is easy to overlook a department in the early stages of the implementation only to find out later that it is either too late to accommodate their requirements or that it results in significant rework or redesign. The main departments are the Production, Plant Maintenance, Sales and Procurement departments, but Management reporting needs to have the catalogue function for reporting. Other departments, such as Finance, benefit from a catalogue but in varying degrees.

- Will the methods used be flexible enough if business/requirements change?

If the standard functionality available in SAP is used then this should ensure that it is flexible enough to be able to react to changes in the business or business processes.

- As material numbers and catalogues will probably change are there any hidden impacts such as part numbers etc. that are currently printed/affixed on site etc. (Warehouse or end-use)?

  In some cases the material number and or catalogue structure is used in printed labels, signs and serial number plates in and around the warehouse/site. This needs to be managed early enough to enable the changes to be made in time. The alternative is to use manually generated material numbers in SAP rather than automatically generated numbers but manually generated material numbers do mean more problems managing available numbers that can be used. One option is to migrate the materials from the legacy systems retaining their numbers but then switching off the ability to create any new materials with manually generated numbers and switch on the automatic option.

- Are there any gaps or shortcomings of the current catalogue approaches that must be addressed by a new approach?

  If an existing catalogue is used as a base it would be worth investigating to see if there are any gaps or problems with this currently. These gaps and problems can then be resolved in the new Global catalogue.

Defining the Catalogue structure

There would need to be significant analysis to determine the basic structure of the catalogue. Should it be simple or complex? If simple will it be powerful enough for all uses? If complex will it be too complex to update and therefore be poorly maintained?

The SAP option is flexible enough to have complexity where it is need-ed (certain kinds of items are more complex than others and can therefore be given a different class with more levels and more characteristics) and less complexity where required..

The structure can be changed, added to and adapted during its lifetime and so it is often best to start with as basic a structure that fulfils the main needs and then build on this over time.

Defining the Processes involved in maintaining a Global Material Master file

It is important to decide the basic process as early as possible, including how new materials will be created and by whom, and how materials will be changed and by whom.

This is best achieved with a combination of central and local control. With the obvious fields relating to central information being only maintained centrally, new materials being maintained centrally and local fields being maintained locally. This needs to be analysed thoroughly to ensure the correct balance between control and ease of maintenance. Too much central control will hamper the business without sufficient benefit, too little control will result in changes being made incorrectly and bad data being used, resulting in inaccurate information.

Defining the data load approach

This is to be decided by the project teams implementing the system but this must follow the basic approach of the central catalogue, i.e. it must include the creation and maintenance of the classification structure and the correct cataloguing of the materials as well as the creation of the materials using the global standards.

The actual data load should be as automatic as possible with one option being an extract from the legacy system/s to a spreadsheet with the ability to add, change and delete entries and then have this file uploaded to SAP (Including the classification and the Info records)

Data cleansing of the "legacy" data and specification of incomplete/missing data/materials

It is vital that the data extracted from the legacy system/s is cleansed and sense-checked to the highest quality possible with the available resources.

In previous implementations I have been a part of Contract Engineers were used to cleanse the data and manage the spreadsheets involved. This was done by site visits where each item was located, identified and checked (starting in the warehouse).

In one example this process took 4+ months for 4 contract engineers on one site (a Cement Plant – The largest and most modern in Europe with approximately 30,000 items). The result was a high standard of accuracy and a good base to build on for the Material Master database and catalogue.

Data Load and data verification

The data load needs to be carried out as late as possible to ensure that last minute changes have been captured although one alternative is to do the initial data load early and have the users maintain the new materials and changes in SAP before the project goes live. This enables the users to become accustomed to the processes involved. The preference is marginally for the latter option.

Once loaded, the data can be validated by random checks and by using basic SAP reporting to ensure that all is well.

Ongoing maintenance (Add, delete, change, extend)

There will need to be a clear business process for the ongoing maintenance of the data and this can be achieved via the use of paper forms for requests for additions and changes or by a more complex use of electronic forms management (complex to build but easier for general use).

This process should be such that it will maintain the integrity of the data without resulting in long lead times for the business.

Invoice Verification

Typical problems with the Invoice Verification functional design

It amazes me just how many implementations I have seen that just don't seem to have understood this process. The result is a growing list of blocked invoices and a long list of unhappy suppliers due to the fact that they are just not being paid on time, if at all.

The invoice verification process in SAP is not the problem, it is normally the interpretation of exactly what is involved in the use of the settings and transactions available.

One of the factors that contribute to the problems with the use of this functionality is the fact that the Materials Management team will assume that this is a Finance function and so it is not their responsibility. The trouble is that it is seen by SAP as being the responsibility of the MM team and the Finance team will not know enough of the detail to be able to configure it and develop the processes correctly. This results in the process and configuration not getting the correct focus. The MM team must manage the design of this process with the help of the Finance team. This is not that unusual when you actually understand the invoice verification process, you will see that it is merely checking the invoice value against the PO price and the quantity received and two of those elements are firmly within the MM area.

It is vital to take several steps back and just look at what the basic process of invoice verification is. The first thing to note is the role of the person inputting the invoice into the system. Few organisations comprehend that this position could be completed by a very junior person, they assume that due to the involvement of an invoice and clearing this for payment this must be carried out by a more senior clerk. To clarify this we need to realise just what the Invoice Verification transaction does. Quite simply the transaction is not an authorisation to pay, it merely checks the values to see if the invoice should be blocked from payment or not. The validation to pay is determined by the check to see if we actually committed to pay the vendor anything and if the vendor has fulfilled their requirements. The term three-way matching is used and this helps to explain what happens,

The quantity of the material we have received is checked against the goods receipts posted on the system.

This quantity is multiplied by the price that is stored on the relevant Purchase Order.

The total is then checked against the invoice total and if it matches, the payment will be pass to the payment program as accepted, if it does not match then the payment is still passed to the payment program but with a blocking flag that ensures that no payment will be made until the flag is removed.

The process, no matter what the invoice verification clerk does, will not pass a payment to the payment program for a value more than the amount owed to the vendor.

The basic process

In reality the Invoice matching transaction could be carried out by a robot!

There needs to be no decision process or authorisation concerns (in general) In effect the transaction could be carried out in full by using a scanner and several organisations actually do use scanners and third party software to input their invoices.

ALL that the system needs to know is

- Which PO the invoice relates to
- What is the Date and Reference number on the invoice
- What is the value of the invoice (including tax)

It needs NOTHING else.

If the Invoice matches correctly

- The invoice is posted as an outstanding debt to the vendor account
- The amount is paid to the vendor at the appropriate date. (If we get 30 days to pay, it will wait for 30 days before paying the vendor)
- The GR/IR clearing account is balanced out and cleared for this entry

If the invoice does not match correctly

- The invoice is still posted as an outstanding debt to the vendor account but blocked for payment
- The payment will be blocked until the discrepancies are either resolved or accepted
- The GR/IR clearing account is balanced out and cleared for this entry if the discrepancy is on value only. If the discrepancy is related to qty then the GR/IR account will remain unbalanced until the situation is resolved.

There are two main checks that Invoice verification carries out and both are VERY different even though they are both checking that the invoice balances.

The first check is a purely mathematical check.

The total value from the invoice MUST equal the sum of all of the line items included. (Even if SAP has suggested these item values itself, based on GRs etc.) If it does not balance mathematically the invoice CANNOT be posted. (There is a tolerance for exchange rate / VAT rounding if the difference is due to rounding)

As long as the sum of the line items equals the invoice total manually entered (copied from the Invoice "bottom line") the invoice CAN be posted, <u>even if the value of the invoice bears NO RESEMBLANCE to the amount due to the vendor.</u>

The second check is the 3 way matching and providing the amount on the invoice is matched to PO lines due (qty and value) then the invoice is posted and made available for payment.

If it does not three-way match then the invoice is still posted but the payment is blocked.

If the invoice does not balance mathematically then extra detail will have to be managed. The system will propose the item quantities and values based on the GRs and PO details. Therefore if the vendor is invoicing for more, or less, than the amount expected, the total entered will not match the sum of the lines proposed.

For example, if an invoice arrives for £1000 and the system has found GRs for 100 items for a PO price of £20 each, the invoice will not mathematically balance. The total invoice value (from the document) will be £1000 but the system will "fill in" the line item qty of 100 items multiplied by £20 (from the PO price>, this totals £2000 and so does not mathematically balance. This does not mean that the invoice should be parked, it merely means that the detail from the invoice will have to be checked/corrected. On the paper invoice there will be a breakdown of the quantities and values involved. In this example it could be that the vendor is only invoicing for 50 items at £20 or for 100 items at £10. As long as the invoice details (on the screen) are changed to match the paper invoice, then it will balance mathematically and can be posted. The invoice will then be blocked for payment if the differences are outside set tolerances.

If the vendor has not quoted a PO or Scheduling Agreement number on the invoice then the Invoice should be rejected but this may lead to the vendor putting the account on "stop" due to non-payment.

If the PO/SA number is not known but we still would like to match the invoice then this is possible. There is a search facility built into the invoice matching transaction. A search can be carried out by Vendor number, Material number, Plant, Document date etc. etc. The system will then display items that match the criteria that have not yet been invoiced and relevant items can be flagged and brought into the invoice verification transaction very easily.

This process could be used to clear some of the unmatched invoices without too much manual effort. This would also reduce the entries remaining in the GR/IR clearing account.

If an invoice has been blocked for payment then it will remain blocked until the blocking flag/s have been removed. There are two ways to remove these blocks, manually or automatically.

If there is a mismatch on qty (qty on GR < qty on Invoice) then a subsequent receipt may result in the invoice being released automatically (A std SAP transaction is run daily to release Invoices that are no longer mismatched)

If there is a mismatch on value (PO price < Invoice price) then the same applies, except that the invoice will only clear when the PO price has been corrected.

Manual releasing is possible but this can release invoices that still do not match and so its use should be tightly controlled

Invoices blocked for payment can be released via the Workflow functionality in standard SAP, but this is merely a "front-end" for releasing invoices in the standard way.

The workflow message indicates the problem (No GR or price error) and the user can then (from within the workflow message) change the PO price or post the GR (subject to authorisation controls) This then balances the invoice and the automatic release can then remove the block as appropriate.

Parking an invoice.

Parking an invoice has a specific function and it is vital that this is understood.

Parking is designed to be used where the invoice needs to be saved but not posted / matched on the system. This is ideal where a large invoice has arrived and the clerk entering it onto the system has to leave the process before it has been completed. (i.e. to go home etc.) It is NOT designed to be used as part of the basic process of invoice verification. An invoice should NOT be parked just because it does not match. Invoices that do not match should still be posted fully, this ensures that they are handled correctly and are completely visible.

Parked invoices do not get released if they become matched (i.e. after a receipt). They do not trigger workflow messages to instigate corrections. They are merely seen as Invoices awaiting posting.

Goods Received / Invoice Received clearing account

Basically the account gives details of the situation regarding un-invoiced receipts and/or invoices received for items not yet received.

The total value in the account can indicate the amount of cash we need to have available to pay for the items we have received but not yet paid for.

It is designed to handle qty discrepancies not value discrepancies, so mismatches related to prices will not affect the clearing account.

If there are entries in the account that have not cleared automatically then this indicates that we have either had invoices for items we have not yet received or we have items that we have received that have not yet been invoiced.

Invoices matched against incorrect receipts effectively double the errors.

An example

We send a PO to the Vendor for 100 items @ £1 each

The vendor sends a partial delivery of 50 pieces

Upon receipt, a posting is made of £50- for 50 pieces to the GR/IR clearing account. (With the opposing £50+ posted to the Stock a/c) We can therefore see from the GR/IR clearing account that we need to keep £50 available to pay for an invoice we are about to receive

The vendor then sends an invoice for £50 for 50 pieces for this first delivery

When we post the invoice it will post a balancing entry of 50 pieces at the GR value (regardless of the invoice value) (£50+ with the opposing £50- being posted to the Vendor a/c as a debt to be paid).

The end result is a zero balance on the GR/IR account, £50 in the stock a/c and £50- in the vendor a/c

Another example

We send a PO to the Vendor for 100 items @ £1 each

The vendor sends 50 pieces

Upon receipt a posting is made of £50- for 50 pieces to the GR/IR clearing account. We can therefore see that we need to keep £50 available to pay for an invoice we are about to receive

The vendor sends an invoice for £100 for 100 pieces (the full amount even though we have only received half of the order)

When we post the invoice it will post a balancing entry of 100 pieces at the GR value (regardless of the invoice value) of £100+ to the clearing account and the invoice will be blocked for payment

The end result is a balance of £50+ for 50 items on the GR/IR clearing account and this will remain there until we receive the remaining 50 pieces (or via a clearing entry)

Another example

We send a PO to the Vendor for 100 items @ £1 each

The vendor sends 50 pieces

Upon receipt a posting is made of £50- for 50 pieces to the GR/IR clearing account. We can therefore see that we need to keep £50 available to pay for an invoice we are about to receive

The vendor sends an invoice for £25 for 25 pieces (this is less than the delivered amount)

When we post the invoice it will post a balancing entry of 25 pieces at the GR value (regardless of the invoice value) of £25+ and the invoice will be cleared for payment

The end result is a balance of £25- for 25 items on the GR/IR account and this will remain there until we receive an invoice for the remaining 25 pieces

A final example

We send a PO to the Vendor for 100 items @ £1 each

The vendor sends 50 pieces

Upon receipt a posting is made of £50- for 50 pieces to the GR/IR clearing account.

The vendor sends an invoice for £75 for 50 pieces

When we post the invoice it will post a balancing entry of 50 pieces at the GR value (regardless of the invoice value) of £50+ the invoice will be blocked due to the price difference

The end result is a zero balance on the GR/IR account even though the vendor has charged more than we expected. This is because we were expecting an invoice for 50 pieces and we now have an invoice for 50 pieces so there is no balance to account for.

Invoice Verification and the GR/IV flag (Goods Receipt based Invoice Verification)

This flag is the cause of many problems in many of the implementations I have seen and this is merely because people misunderstand its use. If you simply look at the name of the flag you could be forgiven for thinking that it does what it says and most organisations want Invoices to be checked against goods receipts and so they insist that it is switched on for every PO. But the flag title is misleading and should be called the Delivery note based Invoice Verification flag, because that is what the flag is designed to do. Instead of matching against the total received against the PO line the match is carried out against specific deliveries. This is ideal if the vendor forces you to accept invoices against specific deliveries, but completely unnecessary and only causes only problems if used for "normal" situations.

It surprises me how many times I have to try to convince people that they are misusing this flag. On three separate occasions I have had to arrange for a detailed presentation of how the flag is used and have many side discussions before they are prepared to even consider changing the way that the flag is used.

The biggest problem of all is that if the flag is switched on then you cannot post an invoice unless the goods receipt has taken place, you simply cannot post it even with the payment blocked. The only option is to park the invoice and this only adds more complexity and less control to the process.

There are some basic principals involved in invoice matching and the process needs to be as lean as possible, when considering the use of the GR based Invoice Verification flag please consider the whole process.

1. The term Three Way Matching refers to the check of the qty received so far, multiplied by the price from the Purchase order, compared to the invoice details. So the GR, PO and Invoice are the three elements that are checked. (These are all checked whether the GR/IV flag is set on or off.)
2. An invoice should not be paid if the vendor is asking for a payment for which they are not entitled. In other words if one of the three elements do not match then the invoice should be blocked for payment
3. There are tolerances that can be set as to what deviances are allowed. For instance it is not sensible to block an invoice if the

vendor is requesting too little money (although if the difference is too great then the invoice should be blocked because it may be a complete mismatch rather than a small error). There are other tolerances for other purposes not relevant to this document (Rounding errors and errors due to foreign currency conversions etc.)

4. The invoice matching process should be as simple and a quick as possible so that the many thousands of transactions can be processed efficiently.

5. If we agree that we owe a Vendor a certain amount of money and the vendor is asking for no more than this then it would not be good business to withhold payment for so long that we are put on "stop" with that vendor.

6. The system should automatically prevent a vendor from being paid more than they are entitled to.

7. Any invoices that are blocked for reasons of a mismatch should be able to be cleared in as uncomplicated manner as possible (automatically when the mismatch has resolved itself)

8. If the vendor insists that they want to send us invoices that detail deliveries line by line then we must be able to match those invoices delivery by delivery.

9. If the vendor does not wish to (or could be persuaded not to) invoice us delivery by delivery then this should be possible without any loss of control.

10. Any process that increases the matching rate and reduces effort both in the Invoice entry process and the process of releasing mismatched invoices that now match, without involving any increased risk should be considered.

Setting the GR/IV flag off where appropriate will reduce complexity and obtain the required benefits without losing any of the necessary controls. Excessive use of the GR/IV flag will, in many instances, add unnecessary complexity to the process with additional risks and no benefit.

There are two basic rules that should be followed with regard to setting this flag and they are simple and easy to implement.

Rule number one – If the Vendor INSISTS on sending in invoices that have a line for every delivery and they want us to match each delivery against that invoice, then the GR/IV flag MUST be switched on for that Vendor.

Rule number two – if the Vendor does NOT send in invoices that have a line for each delivery being invoiced then the GR/IV flag has only negative effects and should NOT be set for that Vendor.

Benefits of GR/IV flag in rule 1.

The benefits of having the GR/IV switched ON are obvious, this gives the required detail during invoice entry to enable us to match deliveries against the invoice Any missing receipts can be identified at that stage and handled.

Problems are not postponed until later invoices arrive.

The problems are as follows,

- No Invoice can be posted if a receipt is missing or if the invoice is for a qty greater than the received qty on that delivery. It may well be our fault that we cannot make the match but the Vendor will still not get paid (Even if in total we owe the Vendor far more than he is claiming).
- Because the invoice cannot be posted we lose the benefits of Workflow and the remaining functionality that deals with Invoice Releasing.
- The document has to be Parked (or not keyed at all). This removes the document from the lists of reports relating to posted invoices. They can be included in some reports but only as a separate column, but many reports will not include them.
- The document is classed as not being posted financially and therefore some benefits (VAT) are lost.
- When the receipt has been posted (if it was missing or unidentifiable) nothing will happen to the Invoice automatically, someone will have to try to post the invoice again so that it can be matched.

MRP – Material Requirements Planning

This is the functionality that helps to manage your stock levels automatically, it fulfils two main objectives (amongst others) and they are as follows

MRP will suggest quantities of stock that are required to maintain sensible stock levels (those stock levels that the organisation have deemed to be sensible).

MRP will highlight any stock that is or is about to become below the acceptable levels, it will issue warning messages that can be monitored by the stock controller enabling measures to be taken to either obtain stock from alternative sources or quicker than usual, or to change the production plan so that the problem materials cause minimal disruption.

In short, if you only have one or two warehouses and each of them only contain a handful of stock materials then you may find that MRP will not do a tremendous amount to help, but this would be a very rare situation. On the other hand if you have many different warehouses containing many thousands of materials then how could you manage to monitor every item and ensure that the stock over time will always be at the correct level, not too high (causing unnecessary storage costs) and not too low (causing problems matching Sales orders etc.).

To me, the most surprising thing about the SAP MRP functionality is that so many people I meet say that they use SAP but not the MRP functionality because "it does not do what we need it to do". This comment always disappointed me, to think that some organisations are using SAP but missing out on the excellent MRP functionality seemed strange. After asking these people exactly what it was that they believed that SAP's MRP functionality could not do, it was quite clear that in each case the reality was that it was a case of them not knowing how to make it do it rather than it not being capable of doing it. To get MRP to perform at its best you must get to know its process and in particular the configuration settings and the options that this offers. My normal response to these people was "MRP within SAP can almost make you a cup of tea while it is controlling your stock for you, it is that flexible". So please do ensure that you fully exhaust all available options within SAP before you decide to use any alternatives which would hugely reduce the overall benefits of a fully integrated SAP implementation.

MRP in more detail

Who is involved in the MRP process when it is used in an organization?

- EVERYONE is in one form or another
- The actions of all personnel in the organization can influence the success of MRP
- From the Cleaners to the Managing Director
- The closer you are to Production / stock, the more influence you will have, but everyone can influence the results to some extent
- In Particular anyone who is involved in :-

  - Sales
  - Production
  - Procurement
  - Stock
  - Master data
  - Finance
  - Shipping
  - Maintenance
  - Etc.

So what is MRP?

Basically, MRP manages stock levels, in reality it does far more than this but effectively this is the main function of MRP.

Sales Stock – MRP tries to ensure that the correct products have been made in time so that Orders can be taken, and delivered to the Customer as and when required.

Raw materials / components – MRP tries to ensure that all of the required materials are available in time for the production process

Consumption stock – This is the stock that you wish to keep available for your own use or for those materials that are used in other processes that need to be available as and when required.

However, to do this MRP needs to be told a LOT of information;

- How many do we plan to sell, when and where from?

- How many can we make in any given period?
- Where should we make them and when?
- What raw materials / components do we need to obtain and when do we need them?
- What lead times are involved?
- Are there any minimum and/or maximum stock limits?
- How many should we keep in stock regardless of known requirements?

Why do we need MRP?

This is probably easier to explain by asking who wouldn't need MRP. MRP wouldn't be needed if you have -

- Unlimited production capacity
- AND "Bottomless" warehouse space,
- AND Sales forecasts that were 100% accurate (every time),
- AND one sales product with one colour/design,
- AND stock that would not go out of date or degrade over time,
- AND one site that produced everything for the whole of the organisation,
- AND no "Seasons", slumps, booms, competitors etc. etc.

So this indicates that most organisations would benefit from MRP
Different people have different views on what MRP is and what it does and this is confused further by the terminology that is used, you will hear of the terms MRP and MRP II sometimes used in completely different contexts and sometimes even used to describe the same thing. |So we need to clarify the difference between them (and what happened to MRP I if there is an MRP II?)

What is the difference between the two terms?

- MRP II is more of a *concept* than a system,
- The MRP in MRP II stands for Manufacturing Resource Planning
- It is a MEASURABLE process of Planning

- MRP II is basically common sense (but planned common sense!)
- By following the principals of MRP II you are likely to get things RIGHT!

But WHAT things will you get right?

- You should be able to minimise inventory without causing supply problems and delays
- You should be able to maximise Customer Service by being seen as being a flexible and reliable supplier
- You should be able to maintain a realistic and feasible Production Schedule

MRPII will help you to achieve the following

- Customer satisfaction – By ensuring the correct quantity/quality of the ordered product, is delivered at the requested time and by making sure that those items that are sold from stock have constant availability.
- Appropriate utilisation of the resources (people and machines/ equipment etc.), this will ensure that the resources are not over utilised one moment and then under-utilised the next. The utilisation can be smoothed so that sensible levels of use are maintained.
- Correct stock levels (in the correct location), keeping the stock between the minimum and maximum stock levels and ensuring that storage costs are kept to a minimum safe level.
- Minimum wastage, because of the management of sensible stocks, thereby reducing obsolescence through age, or at the end of the life of a product.
- Early visibility of stock problems, thanks to the total visibility of requirements and stock.
- Ability to react quickly to changes in demand, the impact of those changes can be seen and managed with precise control

If that describes MRPII then what is MRP then?

- MRP is part of the MRP II process and the initials stand for Materials Requirements Planning
- MRP concentrates on the planning of the materials required for the manufacturing process.
- It tries to make sure that we have the individual materials in the right place at the right time for the production run or sales orders etc.

MRP II in more detail

MRP II really is just common sense but most importantly it is <u>planned</u> common sense

"But planning? I really do <u>hate</u> Planning! I can't predict the future and when I try to, I get it wrong, so there is no point in wasting time. it is easier to live day by day and handle problems as they arise".

"However, because of this I am <u>always</u> overdrawn at the bank, I often miss important meetings, I am frequently late and I get lots of unpleasant surprises.

Basically I am always worried about things that might happen"

"I wish I was more organised!"

So planning is something that we should all do but we need something that will help us plan. As far as business is concerned that something is MRP II.

In effect because it is common sense we actually follow MRP II principles in every day life anyway.

For example, when your child wants a party what do you have to do to make sure that it is properly organised? (Apart from pay someone to do it all?)

You have to PLAN it !

Get the plan right and everyone will be happy!

What are the steps involved in planning the party?

- You first of all have to decide that you want to have a party and basically what type of party, so at the highest level you are starting the planning process with a basic idea of what you want to achieve, without the detail.

- You discuss this with your child to see how many friends she thinks will be coming, just a rough idea so that we can make the decision as to what type facilities we will need, the front room of the house or a hired function room. She decides that she wants to invite 50 friends and it must be on the Saturday evening. So we now have a clearer idea of what is required and so we can now start the detailed planning.
- Is there a venue available in the area?
- Are helpers available?
- Is the equipment available?

This now tells us that the idea is feasible and so we can book the facilities and start the detail of the basics.

- We need to order the cake in advance, make the jellies the night before and then buy the fresh cream on the day.
- Then we need to have the party (followed closely be the nervous breakdown after managing the 50 screaming children)

This process that we have just followed is exactly the process involved in MRPII. The only difference is the terminology used and, of course, the applications that the process is applied to.

The typical steps in an MRP II are as follows

Business Planning

This is where the members of the Board agree the long term strategy for the business, over the coming years, setting the high level targets and plans. They may set a target increase in revenue or profit etc.

In our party plan this was the decision to have the party and basically what type of party it was going to be.

Sales and Operations Planning (SOP)

- The sales people meet with the production people and look at the options available, looking at previous years figures they decide which materials have capacity for increased sales.
- They then inflate the figures by the required amounts and check to see the effect on production (how much would we have to make to match the required sales), is it basically feasible? The

figures can be changed and checked and then a high level plan is produced.

- This plan is normally set at the monthly level and used to feed into the next step of the MRP II process.

In our party plan this is where we talked to our child to decide what type of party we were going to have and how many children we could expect. This enabled us to plan the search for the appropriate premises and set the type of party we would have.

Master Production Scheduling (MPS)

This identifies what will need to be made in the coming <u>weeks</u> and so the level of detail is increased. The SOP plan is taken down a level to the planning of the individual materials.

The result of this process is what we would call the Production Plan showing exactly what we want to make and when. The available capacity is checked in detail at this level and the SOP plan is normally smoothed across the duration of the plan removing the peaks and troughs and ensuring the correct utilisation of resources.

This process is cyclic and may need several attempts to get the best options. This results in scheduled production orders and these orders are fed into the next step in the process.

The MPS plan feeds into Materials Requirement Planning. The bits needed and when!

In our party plan this was where we decided on the venue, the date and how many children we would actually cater for (this may have been affected by the size of the hall we were able to find. We also checked to find out how many people could help at the party.

Detailed Material / Capacity Planning

This step is effectively an MRP run (Materials Requirements Planning).

Now that we have specific orders for the production of specific products on set dates we can check the stock of the components and the availability of resources (Work centres, equipment, people etc.). Shortages can then be managed by placing orders against vendors or transferring stock from other sites etc. considering lead times, minimum quantities etc.

MRP will look as far into the future as we want, or it can just focus on the next X Days. It looks at each material at each site and checks to see if any action is required, if there is, then it will propose actions or generate warning messages as appropriate.

It takes into account basic rules that we set regarding re-order quantities and methods and suggests sensible order quantities and dates. It can also handle DRP (Distribution Requirements Planning), i.e. making sure that existing stocks are transferred to the appropriate locations as and when required.

MRP will generate "Planned Orders"

These are "suggested" Production Orders

They can be checked, changed, converted into Orders or even cancelled.

They can be handled individually or in total.

If MRP data has been maintained correctly the planned orders are normally converted with minimum intervention.

The output from the MRP run (Planned Orders and/or Production Orders) can be used in the next step

In our party plan this is where we are doing the MRP process manually and we are looking at how many jellies, cakes, plates, tables, chairs we need

Plant and Supplier Scheduling

The output from MRP (requests for procurement / transfer) is used to indicate exactly what is required, how many and when.

Stock is checked first of all to see if sufficient stock exists before any order suggestions are created.

Orders can be accumulated so that larger quantities are ordered, reducing overheads and often obtaining better prices. This should ensure that when the production is started ALL of the required materials and resources will be available.

Lead times are used throughout the process to ensure that materials are ordered at the latest sensible point in time.

There are several lead times to consider, all affect when action should be taken.

Vendors lead time

Goods Received Processing Time

Purchasing Department lead time

If these lead times are set correctly then stock remains low and changes to plans have the least affect.

In our party plan this is where we decided that we had enough plates, but we needed to order (hire) some tables and chairs. We also had to order the birthday cake in time for it to be made and buy the jellies and small cakes etc. the day before the party so that they are nice and fresh.

Execution

The finished products are made and placed in stock ready for orders. It is vital to capture what happened in as full a level of detail as is sensible, e.g. if the process took more raw materials than normal, or took longer, then capturing this information will help with the planning of future production runs.

Accurate cost information is also important and this will be derived from the data entered during execution.

This step also releases the capacity for further production.

This is the equivalent to having the party and we should try to use the experience gained to help us in the future, if we had lots of food left over then next time we might buy a bit less, did we have extra people turn up and leave us short of anything, next time we might need to order more for contingency purposes.

As you can see, even though MRP II is full of terminology that at first appears difficult to grasp, the process is simple everyday common sense, but PLANNED.

If we look at each of the steps involved in an MRPII process in SAP;

Sales and Operations Planning (SOP)

This is not normally carried out Material by Material (Product by Product). "Product Groups" are often used – Blocks, Beams, Tiles etc. It is often too much effort to plan individual materials at this level but it depends on your business, it may be possible to plan at the lower level, if so, then this saves time and effort later in the process but the higher level is normally fine for most large organisations.

The SOP plan gives us a rough idea of what we need to produce over the next 12 to 18 months. This is then "Disaggregated" into specific products at specific sites.

The SOP function within SAP is basically a spreadsheet with simple formulas and tools.

Enter the stock you want and the sales you expect and it will suggest the amount you need to make. Enter the sales you expect and the production we are planning to do and it will suggest the stock levels you will have. There are many options available to spread, inflate and adapt the figures involved.

The MRP process steps

There are several kinds of MRP process

- Full MRP (Plan Deterministic PD)
- Re-order point Planning
- Others

Full MRP looks at ALL requirements and is the most powerful and most complete option. In fact it is so powerful and complete that it is a bit of overkill for some basic materials and so the other options can be used and this will reduce the processing involved.

Re-order point Planning looks at current stock level and acts on this and so it uses much less processing power but it is more than sufficient for many of the less complex materials.

Others include Consumption based forecast and stock optimisation.

MRP can be broken down into separate stages and there are three main stages involved

- Net Requirements Calculation
- Lot sizing
- Scheduling

Net requirements calculation looks at the known requirements that will reduce stock, the current stock and known incoming stock and the stock levels required. This will indicate precisely what quantity of stock is required. But this quantity may not be a sensible quantity to order. The suggested quantity may be for two pieces of an item that is normally bought by the thousand. But this is the base figure that the system will use in its calculations.

Lot sizing will then use this figure to determine a sensible order quantity. There may be a minimum order quantity and so the lot size may result in the order being placed for the minimum quantity. It could be that we have set up this item to be ordered in sufficient quantities to cover a set period (two months for instance). In any case the lot size takes the requirement quantity and ensures that it is a sensible order quantity. The system now knows how many to suggest to be ordered.

Other settings will indicate if this item should be ordered from an external source or made, transferred etc).

Scheduling will then take this quantity and look at the dates required and add the order date to the suggestion.

In effect the system will now have a suggested order for the MRP controller to view, adopt or place as an actual order or transfer.

Some of the terminology that is used in the MRP functionality

Make To Stock (MTS) – Make to Order (MTO)

This is exactly what is says it is, but the confusion is normally due to the interpretation of the words "Stock" and "Order".

Basically MTS is saying that we will make something and place it in stock EVEN IF WE DON'T HAVE ANY ORDERS. In Effect we are making against PLAN, rather than Orders.

MTO is something that we will ONLY do when we have a specific Order for the product. No sales, means no production.

So which one is appropriate?

If you have a product that you know that you can probably sell within a reasonable period of time regardless of the current orders, then Make To Stock is normally best. With this option you are more likely to be able to fulfil last minute orders because you are likely to have the items in stock.

If you have products that are very specific and made to a customers specification then Make To Order is normally best because if the items are to be kept in stock then you may have to stock too many different versions with a real possibility of obsolescence.

You may decide to take a risk if something is reasonably specific but you can probably sell it eventually, you could use MTS, this would have benefits regarding lead times but a cost relating to long term storage and the benefits may outweigh the costs of storage and/or scrapping

"Assemble to order" or "engineer to order" may also be used. This is where components of a product are MTS but you then assemble them or machine them into the finished product ONLY when an order is taken.

This is effectively a combination of MTO and MTS, you have the ability to quickly assemble the individual parts to match the customer requirements but you do not have to hold the assembled product in stock and so the risk of obsolescence is reduced yet the stock availability can be high.

Independent Requirements

This terminology is used within MRP to indicate a requirement for an item where there is no direct link to an order or other requirement. They can be used to indicate a forecast requirement for instance or a manually entered requirement that does not relate to any specific requirement. These must to be consumed as orders are taken and this requires a decision to be made as to how they are consumed so that they are not "double counted".

For example

If there is an Independent Requirement in the system for May of 1000 and another in June for 1500 then you would have to decide what to do with these when we have had some genuine sales orders.

If we take orders for only 500 in May – what happens? Should we just reduce the IR to 500 or is this an additional requirement and therefore we should leave the IR for 1000 as it is.

In another example if we take orders for 1200 in May (200 more than the IR of 1000) – what happens? Should it consume the entire 1000 (it cannot consume more than this) and then consume the remainder from the IR in June, or should it just consume the 1000 and leave the June figure untouched.

Decisions like this are managed by the consumption settings in SAP. You can have forward consumption (in other words consume any balance from the future IRs), you can have backward consumption (in other words consume any balance from previous months). You can even decide to not consume any IRs at all. All of this has to be decided during the project but it does indicate the flexibility available in SAP's MRP functionality.

Distribution Requirements Planning (DRP)

DRP is a very useful tool for making sure that you have the right product in the right place at the right time.

You may have one production facility supplying multiple sites throughout your organisation and you may also have certain products that are manufactured at more than one site. When this happens you need to be able to look at all sites together and plan and distribute accordingly.

DRP will look at the requirements of each site and suggest transfers etc. to "level out" the stock and production.

Lead times

These are <u>extremely</u> important.

If you enter lead times that are too short then you will run out of stock and delay production etc. If you enter lead times that are too long then you will be ordering things too early and when plans change there will be a cost involved in changing the orders etc. (not least the effort involved). You will also be carrying more stock than you need and this too has a cost associated.

So ideally you should order (or plan to produce) things at the latest SENSIBLE point in time

There are several lead times to consider

- GRP – Goods receipt processing time
- Vendors lead times
- Production lead times
- Purchasing department lead times
- "Floats" – extending lead times forwards and backwards

GRP – Goods Receipt Processing time

This is meant to be the time taken from the point at which you receive the goods to the point at which they can be used.

- Many materials would have no GRP, especially if they are simply off-loaded from the vehicle and placed directly into storage.
- Some materials would have a true GRP time entered (e.g. the number of days that it takes for the Quality check)
- GRP can be used for other purposes but care has to be exercised to ensure that it does not result in extra stock being held.
- It can be used to ensure that materials arrive slightly earlier than they are actually required, but only if this is essential.

- The GR processing time is used by MRP to calculate the delivery date that should be requested.

Vendors lead times (for externally procured items)

These are normally expressed in "calendar" days (we are not likely to know full details of the vendor's workdays). These should be true lead times without "buffers" or we may find that we have added a buffer with GRP and added it again here. This should be the number of days that the Vendor quotes as being the true lead times (product by product and site by site). This indicates to MRP the latest possible date that the PO must be sent to the Vendor.

Production lead times (for internally procured items)

These are normally expressed in "Calendar" days because we are aware of the days that the production facility operates. These should be true lead times without "buffers" or we may find that we have added a buffer with GRP and added it again here. This should be the number of days that the production team quotes as being the true lead times (product by product and site by site). This lead time is only used if we are NOT using detailed production scheduling. This indicates to MRP the latest possible date that the Production Order should be released (enabling production to start).

Purchasing department lead times

This is basically the number of work days that the purchasing department take to convert Requisitions into Purchase Orders. If this is set correctly it will reduce the number of requisitions that a buyer has to examine, because MRP will create requisitions at the latest possible point in time. Then if plans change, the effect is minor. This indicates to MRP the latest possible date that a Requisition should be created.

"Floats"

If MRP uses all of these dates exactly as planned and a buyer does not check for a day or two, or goes on holiday for a few days, then the items will not get ordered in time.

There are floats available that can ensure that requirements are made visible earlier to allow for these situations.

The purchase order creation date and delivery dates etc. are not affected by this, but the requisitions are merely created X days earlier (where X is the number of days specified in the "float")

Lot sizes

These are used to ensure that quantities proposed by MRP are sensible.

For instance if we were 1 kilo short of sand we wouldn't want MRP to suggest that we order 1 kilo! We might want a fixed lot size of one truck to be suggested, or we might prefer to order in enough for X days, weeks or months, or we might order enough to fill a silo or bay etc, etc.

There are even dynamic lot sizes that can compare the costs involved in ordering stock with the costs involved in storing the stock and suggest sensible quantities.

We "tell" MRP how we handle order quantities by using "Lot sizes"

To summarize MRP, it is a tool that can help manage stocks but to get the most benefit you have to manage the configuration settings correctly and ensure that the material master records have the correct data so that each material is handled correctly.

One word of warning, one implementation I was involved in had a reduction of stock levels as one of the main reasons for switching to SAP. Within days of going "live" with SAP the MRP functionality had increased stock so dramatically that there were serious storage problems caused by the warehouses being over filled. There were two reasons for this, during the project it was discovered that there were many materials that were causing delays to the production process because they were constantly running out of stock. The new settings meant that more of these items were now being held in stock and so this took up more space in the warehouse and this was a benefit because of the fewer stock-outs involved. But it did take up a lot of storage space. This in itself was manageable and would not have caused a major problem.

The real problems were caused, not by the system but by the people managing the stock. This is not such a surprise when you look at what is happening, you have a stock controller who is responsible for maintaining the stock of a selection of materials. If the stock of a vital material runs out, then this stock controller will be held responsible for the huge cost of delaying production and losing customer orders. So even though the system is supposed to reduce stock, you will often find that not only has the stock controller suggested a slightly higher level of stock holding but they have also asked for longer lead times and longer GR processing periods. If the stock is too high in the warehouse it is far less obvious than if one item has run out of stock and held up the whole process. So the stock controllers set the stock levels too high. Multiply this by the number of stock controllers and the number of materials involved and the warehouse is quickly overfilled.

So if you are expecting a decrease in stock then prepare for the opposite at first while people become more confident in the system and start to reduce the levels required. In this case a few months later the stock was down to an all-time low and with significantly fewer stock-outs and this trend continued over time and stock was reduced further. But it does take time.

"Inter-company" Transfers.

Overview

Many organisations want to have the ability to transfer stock from one part of the organisation to another. Some organisations want to merely transfer the stock at cost and others want to transfer the stock with an associated profit or loss. SAP can handle this using several options but there is one main restriction. In standard SAP you should not try to show an artificial profit and or loss on a stock transfer between two Plants that belong to the same Company Code. This is not merely an SAP restriction, it is not good accounting to make a profit or loss by moving materials from one area to another within the same financial area.

I can fully understand the business needs to do such a thing and many organisations will see this as a standard business practice. But this is only possible in standard SAP functions if the two Plants belong to different Company Codes and you may find that your Organisation Structure has been set up incorrectly, or at least in a way that prevents the accounting processes required.

So if you do need to show some kind of profit or loss on transfers between Plants within the same Company Code then you have two main options, one is to change the organisation structure to ensure that these are contained in separate Company Codes. If this is not possible then you have to find a workaround that will at least give the appearance of a Sale and Purchase instead of a mere transfer.

Thanks to the flexibility of SAP there are several ways to manage the workaround but there are some options to avoid.

Firstly one popular work around is to use a Vendor master record and a customer master record and use a Sales Order and a Purchase Order just as if the transaction was between two separate entities. This does work to some extent and you do have full control over the price and therefore Profit and/or Loss involved. On the face of it you will also get the accounts postings that you would expect. But think this through before you choose this option, in effect you are moving a material from one part of your company at one price and then receiving the same material in another part of your company at another price and yet the difference is posted to the account used for Profit / Loss caused by a sale. This is not only incorrect but I wonder how the Auditors will view this? In addition to this you will now have the extra processes of Invoice matching and clearing of the A/R and A/P accounts, which is extra work that adds no value and can cause delays in the management of true Vendors / Customer payments.

So I would strongly suggest finding an alternative workaround, even though, on the face of it, this one seems to be appropriate.

So how can you find a suitable workaround if the organisation structure is not going to be changed? I would refer back to several earlier sections where I constantly suggest staying within standard SAP for the solutions to business scenarios that appear to be unavailable in SAP. If you really want there to be an uplift or reduction in value for certain materials when they are transferred then do just that. Transfer the items using standard SAP but then calculate an uplift or discount separately on a regular basis, perhaps monthly. That way the transfer takes place correctly and with full and proper accounting, the functionality ensures that it is carried out with the minimum of effort and you can still cater for the financial postings of any theoretical profits by running a scratch built ABAP that totals the quantities of items transferred and applies a "price" to the move and posts the total value to s specified account. The end result is that the prices can be managed and the stock movements take place using the minimum involvement. There are no Invoices to match, no A/P or A/R postings to clear and yet the benefits of the move can be attributed to the desired Plant.

A possible solution in detail

The transfer of stock uses the standard SAP movement types available for this use and can use the Purchase Order functionality known as Stock

Transport Orders if required or simple inventory management movements (one-step or two-step).

This will cause a simple transfer of the qty and value from the issuing plant to the receiving plant at the value from the accounting view of the material at the issuing Plant. Any difference caused by this movement (if the receiving Plant value differs from the issuing Plant value) will be posted to the standard G/L account for "Stock value increase/decrease due to transfer". For example if the material is priced at £10 in the issuing Plant and £15 in the receiving Plant, the transfer will reduce the issuing stock account by £10 (x quantity moved) and increase the stock account of the receiving Plant by £15 (x quantity moved). The difference in Value (£5 x quantity moved) will be posted to an account that SAP normally calls "Stock value increase/decrease due to transfer" but we can use a different account if we want to.

This would be the complete process if we did not wish to show a "profit" on the movement and is therefore completely standard SAP. However we need to now manage this "profit".

The proposed method of managing the "uplift" in price is to capture this information from the movements that have taken place from Plant to Plant by running a program that will collect together all of the movements and post a summarised value to the appropriate accounts etc. (This program can be run daily/weekly/monthly). This program will need to know what "uplifted" price to use for the transfer and so a new table will need to be created within SAP to hold this data. This will mean a manual input and maintenance of this data but this will replace the requirement to maintain the prices and other data in the form of Info records.

This table will contain the material number, the "From" Plant and the "To" Plant and a "Price" (if the price is the same for all Plants then the plant field can be left blank).The key to this table (i.e. the way in which entries can be selected) can be quite flexible, it can be keyed by Plant (from and/or to) and Material. We may also include a price date field so that new prices can be entered in advance and become valid at the appropriate date. The table will be in a format similar to a spreadsheet, in that the data will be held in columns and so should be easy and quick to maintain.

It would be possible to add fields to the table for other purposes if required.

Moving Average Price versus Standard Price

Firstly, these are not to be thought of as Sales prices **or** purchasing prices, they are actually stock valuation prices and in fact, if the material is not a stock material, they are not even required. If you multiply the quantity of stock by this price you will find that the result is the value held in the stock account. So the price can be used to value the stock holding or any movements to and from stock. They do not necessarily represent the true value of the material, although they should give a reasonably accurate representation.

The prices cannot be changed on the Material Master record directly, future prices can be entered but the price cannot be changed with immediate effect, this rule cannot be broken, even if the stock quantity is zero.

To change the price you have to use a special transaction, (The menu path is

Materials management > Valuation > Valuation > Change price). This transaction does not just change the price, it also re-values the stock and posts the difference to a special account (with full audit trail).

There are other ways to change the prices including the Balance Sheet Valuation function. This can revalue the stock based on First In - First Out (FIFO), Last In – Last Out (LIFO) or Lowest Value principles. (These functions revalue the stock based on standard accounting practises).

In most implementations you will find that the financial department will have a preference for which valuation method to use. Some prefer to use Standard Prices on all materials, some prefer Moving Average Prices and some organisations prefer to use a combination of the two, one valuation method for certain material types and the other for the rest. If they have a preference then it is probably going to be very difficult to change their approach, if no decision has been made then it is best to understand the differences between the two so that maximum benefit can be achieved.

Both valuation methods act very differently. Moving Average Prices (MAP) change ("move") automatically, Standard prices remain unmoved by the system, unless you want to revalue them manually (individually with the 'Change Price' transaction, or in bulk with the 'Balance Sheet Valuation' transaction.)

MAPs are an average of the material values, e.g. if you receive a quantity of 1 (of a new material) at £20 and then the second piece of the same material at £30, the MAP changes automatically to £25. (The MAP is always the total value of the stock divided by the quantity). The main advantage of this is that the MAP really is an average of the value of the material and therefore an issues and usage will be at a reasonable value.

Standard prices do not move automatically, this means that if you have a material with a Standard price of £10 and you receive an additional one valued at £50, not only does the Standard price remain at £10, but the value written to the stock account is £10 (even though the actual price paid was £50). The £40 difference is posted to a price variance account, so that the total value of the posting is correctly accounted for. The fact that standard prices do not move can be a huge advantage. All movements, receipts, transfers, issues etc are valued at the fixed standard price, so this helps departments with their budgeting. It can also be a 'fairer' method, because anyone withdrawing stock will know the value will not vary (until it is manually changed, normally year-end). If MAP is used, one withdrawal of a material can be at a completely different value when compared to another withdrawal of the same material (even within minutes of each other) because more of that material may have been received at a different value.

With Standard prices, the Accounts department and the Purchasing department can decide sensible levels for the costs of materials and set the Standard price accordingly. This can then be used to monitor any deviance in the price because every deviance causes a posting to the price variance account (the £40 in the above example). These postings can 'capture' details such as Material number, Purchase Order number etc; this enables detailed breakdowns of such deviance from the agreed standard price. Standard SAP transactions can be used to interrogate the postings or a simple report could be written listing the deviance sorted in value order. This could be produced regularly, highlighting individual purchases of materials that have increased or decreased in cost when compared to the Standard Price. These purchases can then be investigated to find out why the item cost more or less in this situation, it may be due to the item being required urgently and so an extra charge was made by the supplier and so changes to the lead times stored in SAP may be able to remove the need to do this again in future.

With some materials however, these advantages turn into disadvantages. Materials such as Gold, Oil and other materials that have volatile prices can vary almost minute by minute. This would mean that virtually every movement would cause a price variance.

Another disadvantage with using Standard price is that it is a manual entry and therefore may never reflect the true value of the material. With MAP at least the price reflects the true average value.

An advantage of the MAP is that you do not get price variances (except in special circumstances) and therefore you do not have to reconcile the price variance account.

One of the biggest advantages of MAP is that all costs are posted directly to the stock account, including delivery costs etc. With Standard price, only the Standard price is posted to the stock account and any balances (negative or positive) are posted to other accounts.

A disadvantage of MAP is that, because there are no price variances, it is more difficult to spot price variances.

If MAP is used, you have to be very careful with Invoice Verification, as Invoice price discrepancies affect the stock account and MAP. The following example demonstrates this.

A Material is ordered at £1 and it is received into stock. At this point £1 is posted to the stock account. If an Invoice is entered for £10 for this purchase order (perhaps the Invoice clerk or Vendor made a mistake with the decimal place), it will be blocked for payment, <u>but</u>, the additional £9 will be posted to the stock account and the MAP will change (to £10 in this case). Any issues or stock consumptions that occur until the correction is made will be at the inflated price and will not be automatically corrected. when the credit note is received or the Invoice is reversed/cancelled. (It is because of this problem that you occasionally get the warning messages in Invoice Verification and POs stating that the MAP will change by more than X percent. It is warning you that you may be corrupting the MAP.)

To summarise

- MAPs change automatically, Standard prices do not.
- Standard prices store price variances separately, MAPs do not (there are some exceptions).
- The true cost of the receipt is posted to the stock account with MAP, with Standard price only the Standard price is posted to the stock account.
- The MAP is maintained by the system even if you use Standard price (for information only).
- You can change from MAP to Standard and vice versa at any time just by changing the price control on the Accounting view of the

material master. The price **must** stay the same and you can do it even if stock exists (as the value is not changing).

N.B.

To use very low prices you can enter a quantity that is greater then 1 in the quantity field, in other words, to set a price at 0.005 for 1, you would have to enter a price of 0.05 and a quantity of 10. The price that you see is rounded up to 2 decimal places, but the system stores it to more decimal places. Thus if you issue 100 pieces of a material that is showing a price of 66.67, it may value the issue at 6666.67.

Automatic Account Assignment

This is probably the least understood of all of the functions within the MM Module. This is hardly surprising when you look at the terminology used. Most of the terms start with the word "Valuation" and their real meaning is not always apparent from the names used.

This area of the system is one of the few that cannot really be self-taught and so many consultants with in-depth knowledge of MM still don't really know how it works. However, if you break it down to the basics, it is not as complicated as it appears.

The most important thing to realise is that you are not configuring the way that the system carries out the accounting, you are merely con-figuring the > of the G/L accounts that the system should use in different circumstances. (You <i>can</i> change the way that the system carries out the accounting, but this is rarely required). The system has standard accounting practices built in and if you change these, you are effectively changing accounting rules, this is not normally required or necessary. and it is certainly NOT recommended. This leaves us with the task of deciding which general ledger accounts should be used when values are affected by MM transactions.

Firstly we need to cover some basic principles.

Every time the value of a material is affected upwards OR downwards, a value is posted to the General Ledger accounts. When this happens, an Accounting Document is always created, this is the "audit trail" and lists the values and account numbers used.

Values are affected by many MM functions, but the most common ones are receipts, issues and transfers (others include Invoice Verification, Stock revaluation and GR/IR reconciliation.).

Many people expect the configuration of Automatic Account Assignment (AAA) to be the responsibility of FI. (This is normally the MM consultant hoping that the FI consultants will do it!). It does appear to be a financial responsibility, but only a MM

Consultant can be expected to know the range of transactions and Movement types involved. In fact it is one of the few areas that is very much a joint responsibility. The MM consultant needs to be able to understand the MM functions involved and the FI consultant needs to be able to understand what G/L accounts need to be updated in various circumstances. So to succeed, it really must be configured jointly, it is not a function to be tackled in isolation.

To understand the functionality of AAA, we need to break it down to a very high level overview first, then once we understand the basics we can then concentrate on how to get the most out of the flexibility offered by this function (It is the flexibility that causes most of the confusion).

So first, the high level explanation.

To determine which account to post to, the system needs to know three basic things:

- What is happening?
- Where is it happening?
- What is it happening to?

This is because you can use a different account for each combination of the above.

For example:

- The "What is happening" could be a posting to the stock account following a 101 Movement type receipt or a 201 goods issue, both update the stock account but one increases it the other reduces it.
- The "Where is it happening" gives you the ability to use different stock account numbers for each Plant used (or each type of Plant of you want to group Plants together).

- The "What is it happening to" gives you the ability to use different stock account numbers for different materials.

The more technical terms used for these are:

- "What is happening" is controlled by the "Transaction/Event Key".
- "Where is it happening" is controlled by the Valuation Area.
- What is it happening to is controlled by the Valuation Class.

The Transaction/Event Key is derived from the SAP transaction (and Movement type, where appropriate).

The Valuation Area is normally equal to the Plant (or group of Plants) especially in any organisation that holds stock. It can be set at the company code level but this only suits (very rare) businesses that have no stock.

The Valuation Classis derived from the Material Master record (Accounting View) and this can best be thought of as the accounting material group (it contains all materials that are to be treated exactly the same way as afar as finance is concerned..

The Transaction/Event Key, presents the biggest challenge when trying to understand the functionality. The best way to treat this, is to accept that the system "knows" which ones are to be used and in which circumstances. This is not strictly true, but few people ever need to change this area and it is far easier to understand the whole process, if you accept that it is almost hard-coded. (There will be more than one Transaction Event Key for each SAP transaction. We will explain how it really works in a separate section). Typical examples are BSX, PRD, WRX, GBB.

"BSX" is the transaction event key for the Inventory Posting, in other words the stock account posting. It is the most common key that is used, it is posted to for every receipt, issue or transfer, to and from stock of any material that has a stock value.

"PRD" is the Cost price Differences Posting, in other words the Price Variance accounts postings. It is used to post the differences between the actual price and the standard price, or any differences in transfer values (e.g. £10 in one Plant £15 in another).

"WRX" is the GR/IR Clearing Posting. It is used to post the value due to the Vendor upon receipt of the Goods or Invoice. (Goods receipt will post a negative value to this account, Invoice Verification will post a positive value to this account. (Therefore, if the values match, the account is self-clearing).

"GBB" is one of the trickiest to set-up, it is the Offsetting Entry For Inventory Posting. It sounds very strange, but it is exactly what it says. It is the account used whenever you post directly to or from the Stock account (without a P.O). It includes movement types 501, 561, 201, 261, etc., etc. You need this account because every posting has to have an equal and opposite posting. So if you scrap some stock, the system will reduce the Stock account by the correct value and then post this value to the account indicated in the GBB posting (The offsetting posting). This is normally made more complex because it uses something called the Account Modifier (also known as the Account Grouping Code. Both will be explained in later sections and should only be considered when the basics have been understood)

There are many other Transaction Event Keys but the ones mentioned here are the most common, we can cover the others later.

The Valuation Area can also be called the Valuation Area Group. It is most common for the grouping option to be used. It groups together Plants or Company codes if (unusually) the Valuation Level has been set to Company code. All Plants in the group must belong to the same Chart of Accounts, but they can belong to different Company codes. You should group together all Plants that are treated the same way. The FI consultant should be able to decide how many groups are required by asking the users in the financial department. It is then easy to setup the groups in Config. Some examples may be a group of Warehouses, a group of Production Plants and a group for Plants that are merely offices, another example might be a group of Plants in one country and a separate group of Plants for another country.

The Valuation Class is also a type of grouping, as it groups together Materials that are treated in the same way, as far as accounting is concerned. Again, the FI consultant should be able to decide how many Valuation Classes are required, by asking the Financial department "How many different Materials are there, as far as the accounting department is concerned?". This may well relate directly to material types, but it does not have to. For example, you could group together some of the Raw Materials with some of the Finished Materials by giving each of the materials the same Valuation Class. The Valuation Classes are linked to the Material Types, via the Account Category Reference. This link is quite a strange one, there can only be one Account Category Reference for each Valuation

Class, there can only be one Account Category Reference for each Material Type. However, you can have more than one Valuation Class linked to an Account Category Reference and you can have more than one Material Type linked to an Account Category Reference. This leads to the relationship between Material Type and Valuation Class being a "many to many" relationship. What is also strange is that in effect, the Account Category Reference and the Material Type do not directly affect Automatic Account assignment. The main use of the Account Category Reference is

Purely for validation of the Valuation Class during Material Master maintenance and nothing else. (In fact you could allocate a Valuation Class to a material then change the link of that Valuation class to the A/c Cat. Ref. and this will NOT affect the AAA. The Valuation Class determines which accounts are updated and this has not changed.

It is these three rules that determine which account number will be posted to. Now we have established this, how do we proceed?

The hardest task of all is to set up the AAA from scratch, so this should be avoided at all costs. If you are lucky, you can actually save a great deal of time, by using one of the standard chart of accounts provided with the system instead of creating a new one. (This depends on the co-operation of the FI team, even then it may not be possible). This is quite often possible when setting up the prototype, test or "play" Clients. (INT is a Chart of Accounts to consider).

If you have to start with a new Chart of Accounts, then the task can be very challenging. One possible plan would be to continue as follows;

Check with the FI team/Users to see how many different groups of Plants you will need. Set them up in the configuration menu (Activate the Valuation Grouping and then just allocate a group Id to each of the valuation areas). This sets up the Valuation Area Groups.

Then Check with the FI team/Users to see how many different groups of materials you will need. Set these up in configuration menu by creating new Valuation Classes and Account Category References and link them to the correct Material Types (this last step, the link to Material Type can either be done in the same area where you create the Valuation Classes or in the configuration of Material Types).

You now have the total number of possible combinations of the two, you can now configure the AAA table. Use the configuration path to get to the AAA configuration table (with all of the Transaction Event keys listed). You now have to make sure that you have a valid entry for EVERY possible combination of Transaction/Event Key, Valuation Area and Valuation Class. If a combination is not possible, you don't have to configure it (For instance, if you don't keep stock in one of the Valuation Area Groups, you don't have to have any entries in the BSX Tran/Event key for this combination. The system only checks the entries when it attempts to make a posting).

The major problem here is that there are so many combinations, where do you start?

The important thing to remember is that this task MUST be done by an MM and an FI together, not one after the other. The MM person will be able to determine which events will take place and the FI person will be able to determine which Accounts must be updated for each of these circumstances.

There is no function within the system that can help in this task, but there is one option that is almost hidden. If you use the "SIMULATION" function within AAA (any valid combination), when the results are displayed, click on the leftmost menu option and you will see an option to produce a report. When you run this report you can leave some of the settings blank or use ranges, this will produce a very large report, so be careful. But within this report will be all of the possible combinations of Movement Type, Valuation Area Group and Valuation Class. The Financial users are normally very busy and cannot devote time to sit with the MM Consultant while AAA is configured, so by printing off this report, they can read through it and write the correct numbers against the appropriate entries.

Once you have configured all possible combinations, the task is complete (Remember that the configuration is within the Chart of Accounts and you will need to do this for each COA) (there may well be only one).

The thing that makes the maintenance of AAA a lot easier than it would appear, is that (unless you are doing something very radical) you only have two areas to consider, "Where is it happening" (the Valuation Grouping Code) and "What is it happening to" (the Valuation Class). So if you have a new Plant that needs special accounting (A "bonded" warehouse for instance), you need to place it in a separate Valuation Area Group and configure the AAA table with all possible combinations of Transaction Event Key and Valuation Class. If you have a special material that needs special accounts (Precious metals etc.,) you need to consider creating a new Valuation Class for them. (and configure the AAA tables for all possible combinations of Transaction Event Key and Valuation Area Group).

If you are having problems with error messages that indicate that the AAA is not set up for this combination. (The message will include references to something similar to INT BSX 0001 3000), then this is really easy to solve. Just click on the message itself and the full message will tell you the Chart of Accounts, Trans Event Key, Valuation Area Group and Valuation Class involved. Just note these down or remember them and go to the second page of the message and you can click on the proceed button and you will be taken to the correct place in the configuration menu. Use the information given to make the entry that is missing (You will need to find out which account should be posted to). Also remember that even when you have corrected the entry for this transaction Event Key, it may then just stop at another one. This function is so easy to use that I have seen some consultants use it to configure the whole of the AAA. They do not configure the AAA table, instead they try various movements, receipts and issues for a combination of Plants and Materials. When the system gives the error message, they use the above approach to solve the problem. I am certainly NOT recommending this as an option, but you can perhaps understand why it is tempting. A better option when starting from scratch, is to configure the most common Trans Event Keys first BSX, PRD, WRX and GBB. This should enable many standard transactions to function, you can then configure the rest as they occur.

Some other items that you need to know about: Rules and the Account Modifier (also known as the Account Grouping Code).

Firstly the Rules On the screen where you enter the Account Numbers in AAA, you will see a function box marked "RULES". It is important to not "play with" they rules to see what they do, because if you change them you will lose the entries in any of the rules that you have switched off. To see an example of the effect that the rules have, compare the number of columns that you have to maintain on BSX, WRX and GBB. In the standard system WRX has *no* Valuation Class column (It has been switched off in the rules.) and GBB has an extra column that we have not yet discussed (The Account Modifier).

Why do we have the option of switching columns off? If you take the example of WRX (The GR/IR Clearing account). The reason that the Valuation Class column is switched off is that this type of posting is not affected by the material causing the posting. Without the ability to switch the column off, you would have to enter all of the valuation classes with the same account number. Switching it off is the same as telling the system to ignore the entry.

Now the tricky one! What is the Account Modifier (also known as the Account Grouping Code or account group) column used for. (Switched on in GBB in the standard system). Firstly let's have a look at what GBB is. It is the "Offsetting entry for Inventory Posting" and it is the account used to post the value to when the stock account is updated in most movements other than those related to a PO. If there is no PO, then you cannot use the WRX (GR/IR Clearing Account) to offset the value posted to or from the stock account and so it has to be posted somewhere, the GBB posting. One example is the 201 movement type, it removes stock to go to a Cost Centre, so one posting will be a reduction to stock (BSX), the other is the offsetting posting (GBB). Another example is the "scrapping" movement type, this also reduces stock (BSX) and posts an offsetting entry (GBB). How then can we ensure that the two use different accounts for the offsetting entry? It is the Account Modifier that solves this problem. The best way to think of the Account modifier is to imagine it as a grouping function for Movements (Movement Types). To find out which Account Modifier is used on each movement type, you can either look at the config of movement types or look at the "Account Grouping for movement types" configuration path in AAA. It is not as obvious as you would expect

as you will find many Account Modifiers for each Movement type. This is because the to the entry includes things like the QTY and Value flags, Consumption Indicator, Special Stock type etc. Each different combination of these can be linked to a different account Modifier (Also you will see which Transaction Event Key is listed).

Another area that contains the Account Modifier is the Account Assignment Category, used on the PO item line. Each A/C Ass Cat can have a different Account modifier, this is how the system is able to suggest the account to be used when entering the PO. It does not know what movement type will be used in the receipt until the receipt has been posted (If there is a receipt), so it picks up the A/C Modifier from the A/C Ass Cat. (You can create new A/C Ass Cats if you want to, you can therefore get the system to post to different accounts depending on the AAC).

For example, you could have 2 or more Account Assignment Categories for Cost Centre purchases instead of just the one (normally "K". The user therefore does not have to choose the specific account from a huge unfriendly list, instead the entry is filled in automatically based on the AAC used.

Split Valuation

This really is a hidden gem in SAP. Many people know of its existence, but not everyone knows what it really is or what it can do.

One of the biggest problems is that users will rarely ask for it by name and so when they need the functionality, they normally get alternative options that don't really suit.

Most companies would benefit from the use of Split Valuation, but to explain this, it would be clearer to use an example:

Company X make their own Widgets at a cost of £1, but sometimes their production line is so busy that it cannot make enough. When this happens they buy some Widgets from their supplier at £2 each. They are exactly the same apart from the cost. Company X wants to monitor costs closely and so they want to keep track of the materials they use.

The problem is that they want to store the two values and cost the issues according to which material was used, the manufactured one, or the bought one.

There are two common solutions used for this problem, both of which are far from ideal.

The first and most common solution selected is to create a duplicate material master record, one for the manufactured material and one for the bought material. This means that you now have the ability to value one at £1 and the other at £2, using the A/C view of each material. The biggest problem here is that you now have two material numbers for the same material. This causes many problems, especially with MRP, Purchase Orders and stock reports and enquiries.

The second solution is to create a dummy Plant, this also allows the use of different prices, one on each accounting view of each Plant. This does not require two material numbers, but there are similar problems with MRP, Purchase Orders and stock reports and enquiries, as you have to consider both Plants when calculating stock etc..

So in basic terms, the real problem here is that there is only one accounting view for each material / plant combination. If this rule could be broken, then the above problem could be solved quite easily.

This is exactly what Split Valuation does! It enables you to have as many accounting views as you need for the one Material / Plant combination.

The above example is just one of many. Other examples include the following situations:

- You have a material that is sometimes imported and sometimes bought from within your own country, it is the same material, but when imported you incur customs costs etc. You buy the material from several countries, each charging different costs, or the same costs but you want to keep the values in separate stock accounts.
- You have a Batch controlled material and each Batch has a different value (due to gold content, or chemical potency, for example).
- You have a material that has different grades, each with a different value.

In each of the above situations, the problem is the same, you need one material master but with multiple accounting views at the same Plant.

Setting up Split Valuation.

To use Split Valuation, you need to configure the system correctly. You have to indicate that split valuation should be activated it and then build the structure you require and indicate how it will be used locally (i.e. at each Plant).

There are two new terms to understand here: Valuation Category and Valuation Type

The Valuation Category is a single character code, entered on the accounting view to indicate that this material is subject to Split Valuation. The character that is entered, indicates the kind of Split Valuation being used (Internal / External, Country of Origin, Batch, Duty paid? etc., etc.). The Valuation Category is used to control which Valuation Types can be used.

Valuation Types are used as the "Key" to the additional accounting views so that you can indicate which accounting view should be used to determine the cost and account postings. (Typical Valuation Types would be "Europe", "USA", "Japan" etc. if the Valuation Category was Country of Origin or "Duty paid" or "Duty not paid" to control imports, etc. etc.)

The extra effort and complexity involved in Split Valuation is that on every transaction that has a potential affect on stock value, you will have to indicate which Valuation Type is to be used. (In some cases this can be automated). This includes transactions such as Stock Counting, Receipts, issues, transfers, etc. This extra effort is not normally a problem because to gain the benefits, you would expect to have to identify the type of stock specifically.

Stock of a split valuated material is clearly identified. In fact you get two levels. The qty of the material for MRP, or availability purposes is the total stock of all Valuation Types in the Plant, but the stock overviews will list the individual Valuation Types separately, under the storage location level.

To use the functionality when configured, you have to firstly create the accounting view of the Material as normal (although at this level it must be use the Moving Average Price option) but you must enter a Valuation Category on the accounting view to indicate that this material is to use split valuation at this Plant. When this has been created, you need to create extra accounting views for the same material in exactly the same manner, except that you enter a valid Valuation Type on the Organization Levels screen at the start of the MM01 transaction. This gives you the ability to have different Price Controls (Std or MAP), Different Prices and use different accounts (by using different Valuation Classes) on each Valuation Type.

In all it is excellent functionality with few drawbacks. It is certainly worth experimenting with to see just how much it can help.

A brief overview of each of the main modules in R/3

The following sections just give the briefest high level overview of the basics of each of the main modules in R/3.

What is FI?

The FI refers to the first two characters of the word Finance

In simple terms FI functionality covers the accounting processes that MUST take place, in order to satisfy local legal requirements, of course it does far more than this, but its focus is statutory reporting.

It has the flexibility to cover all of the complex accounting requirements of any country.

Many people are given the impression that SAP is essentially a financial system. This is simply not true! However, many organisations choose SAP because of the strengths of FI, particularly it's integration with other modules.

Some of the functionality includes;

General Ledger
Accounts Payable and vendor payments
Accounts Receivable and cash allocation
Credit management and debt collection
Statutory Reporting
Money Management
Bank Reconciliation and Cash position
Fixed assets register – purchase, transfer and retirement of assets
Travel and Expenses management
Vat reporting
Legal Consolidations
Strategic Enterprise Management
Real Estate Management

What is CO?

The CO refers to the first two characters of the word Controlling

Or in other terminology this is referred to as Management accounting

In simple terms, CO allows for flexible enquiries, reports and updates based on the FI data stored in SAP. The FI data cannot be modified or "massaged" because it is statutory data but a copy of this data for management reporting purposes can be extremely useful.

It can produce information that can help to make the business more efficient and more effective.

Amongst other things it allows the use of Cost Centre controls and reporting and Profitability Analysis.

It is not a "must have" module, but only very few organisations would not wish to use the CO functionality.

Some of the functionality includes

Management reporting
Cost and Profit Centre accounting
Other Cost collectors – Internal Orders
Activity Based Costing
Product Costing
Profitability Analysis
Project Systems
Budgeting and Planning
Commitment Management

What is SD?

The SD refers to the first characters of the words Sales and Distribution

In simple terms, SD covers all of the functions of Sales, Shipping and Billing.

Of course it does far more than this, but its focus is the Sales department.

It uses many aids to streamline the processes involved in entering Sales Orders, despatching goods and invoicing Customers.

Amongst other things it has the ability to handle complex pricing, Picking/Packing, Route determination and Service Management.

It is a popular module. Most, if not all, organisations "sell" and SD has a full coverage of the required functionality.

Some of the functionality includes

Product proposals
Alternative products
Complex Pricing
Rebates
Promotions
Packaging
Route Determination/Drop sequencing
Shipments (Multi order / multi customer)
Complex Pricing structure
Scheduling (Part loads, full load)

ATP (Available to Promise)
Contacts database
Credit stops, delivery block etc.
Availability check at Order entry and delivery (Safety stocks)
Consignment stocks
Profitability by Material, sales area, region, etc. etc.
Sales Information system

What is MM?

The MM refers to the first characters of the words Materials Management

In simple terms, MM covers all of the functions of the management of products, items, components and their procurement.

Of course it does far more than this, but its focus is the Purchasing and warehouse departments.

It is used to procure (internally or externally) items required for resale, consumption, plant maintenance, production, projects, etc. Its main focus is external procurement, but it also covers internal procurement requests that are passed on from the PP dept.

Amongst other things it includes functionality for stock (Inventory Management referred to IM) MRP, External Service Management and Invoice verification.

It is also a popular module. Most, if not all, organisations "buy" and MM has a full coverage of the required functionality.

Some of the functionality includes

Stock visibility (Current and future)
Visibility of requirements / requirements planning
Automatic Vendor selection (where required)
Consignment stock
Electronic authorisation controls (Requisitions / POs)
Stock transfer options
Cycle counting
Shelf life management
Automatic account determination
Info Records
Source lists

Quota Arrangements
Material Master
Purchasing Information / Inventory Information systems

What is PM?

The PM refers to the first characters of the words Plant Maintenance

In simple terms, PM covers all of the functions required to maintain plant and equipment.

Of course it does far more than this, but its focus is the Maintenance department.

The level of detail controlled is very flexible, you can manage complete production facilities as one item of plant or you can maintain each part of that facility separately but still retain the connection to the production facility (hierarchical structures can be used).

Amongst other things it includes functionality for Preventative and scheduled maintenance, breakdowns, etc. and triggers can be set such as number of hours used, throughput etc..

It is a module that is growing in popularity. The functionality is now far more comprehensive and many organisations are switching to PM from their own Maintenance systems.

Management of breakdown and malfunction reports
Management of Work Permits
Work Order Management
Organisation of Preventative Maintenance
Tracking of key measurements
Maintenance resource levelling using work centres
Key Performance Indicator Reporting
Cost of Ownership Reporting
Full Integration with Stores, Procurement and Finance

What is PP?

The PP refers to the first characters of the words Production Planning

In simple terms, PP covers all of the functions of the Production of goods for sale or consumption.

Of course it does far more than this, but its focus is the Production department.

It is used to plan and control the production facilities within an organisation. It can ensure that the available capacity is used to the maximum required.

Amongst other things it includes functionality for, SOP, Costing, Scheduling, MRP, routings and Bills Of Materials (BOMs).

The functionality is comprehensive and many organisations are switching to PP from their own Planning systems.

Some of the functionality includes

Capacity management
Scheduling
Operations / stages
Work Centres / Shift patterns
Production Resources and tools
Backflushing
Pipeline materials
Bill of Materials / Recipes
Production Versions
MPS
MRP
Forecasting
Long term planning and "What ifs"
Production costing
Process planning
PP Information system

What is LIS?

The LIS refers to the first characters of the words Logistics Information systems

These are standard SAP functions requiring little or no configuration.

They provide powerful and comprehensive reporting.
Extremely quick response times considering the amount of data.
Cover most major areas.
They include graphics.
They have long drill down paths (with considerable flexibility).

Layout and format can be changed by the user (and saved for future use).

There are many fields of data to select from.

Output can be viewed, printed, emailed, faxed etc.

There are many comparisons available (plan/actual, this period/last period etc.). They also include exceptions reporting and event triggered reporting.

Basically the LIS reports are another hidden gem and any organisation not currently using them would be well advised to at least investigate the functionality they provide.

Contracts or Scheduling agreements

Within the procurement process there are documents that SAP have described as "Outline Agreements", effectively these are contracts or long-term agreements and they are processed in quite different ways. They differ from Purchase Orders in that they relate to a long period rather than specified deliveries and there is a need to "call-off" from the agreement for each subsequent delivery.

As I have said in previous sections of this book it is important to understand exactly what SAP has intended them to be used for before they are used for other purposes. SAP intended them to be used when there is an agreement between your organisation and the vendor to purchase a specified quantity of certain items at a set price over an agreed period. The price is fixed at the beginning of the agreement period but this can change over time. When items are required from the contract a call-off takes place and the delivery is valued at the price from the agreement and any other specific terms quoted on the agreement are applied to the call-off. So if SAP has provided two different types of document then how do you decide which is appropriate? In short there are big differences in the processes involved and they both have specific uses, if you use the wrong type then the process still works but will have unnecessary overheads or worse still will result in a problem that builds up over time and is often not realised until it is too late.

Firstly the Vendor Scheduling Agreement, SAP have designed this to be used for the kind of agreement that results in large numbers of deliveries over time. It is very easy to call-off from a VSA and no other documents are required, in fact one of the strengths of the VSA is how easy they are to operate and how changes can be made without too much effort. They are ideal for deliveries of bulk materials although they can be successfully used for non-bulk items too. One main advantage is that the call-offs can be created automatically by MRP with no need for any extra input.

The Contract on the other hand is a more rigid and controlled document and call-offs are made using Purchase Orders linked to the contract. This results in a more complicated process with changes being more difficult to achieve. The main benefit is the control and extra historical data that can be achieved.

Many organisations select VSAs because they are easy to use and very flexible and it is easy to understand why. But there are reasons why they are not ideal for all situations and often problems can surface many months after they are used.

One example is the under and over delivery tolerances, because the VSA is designed to handle a series of deliveries an over delivery will not trigger a warning message if there are future deliveries scheduled, the system will assume that the over delivery is merely part of a future delivery. This is not a major problem unless you really do want to impose limits on the delivered quantities, but if it continues to happen the extra will constantly consume future deliveries until there is no more to consume and the problem is then apparent. Invoice matching can also have problems matching individual deliveries and using the GR/IV flag will help but this often results in invoices not being paid due to the inability to link the invoice line to the correct delivery on the schedule.

I favour contracts because of the full control that they offer, this is provided by the way that call-offs are handled. Each call-off has to be carried out using a Purchase Order linked to the contract, the benefit of this is that each call-off can now use the full functionality available in the SAP Purchase Order. This includes the use of the under and over delivery tolerances and a full audit trail via the Purchase Order history function. The disadvantage of Contracts is that MRP can only create a requisition for the call-off, a further step is then required to convert the MRP generated Requisitions into call-off Purchase Orders. This fact alone often causes organisation to decide to use VSAs instead and they frequently regret the decision later. If you are considering using VSAs just because of this reason then please use contracts instead and use the standard SAP functionality to convert the MRP generated requisitions into call-off Pos instead.

So to summarise, I would recommend the use of Contracts for all outline agreements apart from any materials that you buy in very large quantities and/or in bulk. I have personally seen several organisations with data accuracy and other problems solely caused by a decision to use VSAs just because they are easier to use.

External Services Management

This is functionality that SAP has provided to assist in the processing of services. Services have always been difficult to manage in any system because the services are often difficult to pre-order due to the often unknown type and duration of the services required. For example, there is a leak on a pipe, you want to bring in a plumber and so you need to raise a Purchase Order, but how many hours will you put on the order and will it be for one plumber or two and will they need to use a plumbers mate, in all, a very difficult situation to convert into a Purchase Order. SAP like most other systems does not really help with this situation but simply because the problem is not system related it is just being caused by uncertainty of the end result. The normal way that this is handled is to raise the PO after the event when all of the detail is known, this way the PO is merely being used as a mechanism to enable the invoice to be matched and paid. Until release 3 of SAP R/3 there was no special process for services (apart from the use of services via material masters and / or account assignment categories), so in release 3 SAP launched new functionality entitled External Services Management. Many consultants understandably assumed that this would solve the problems associated with examples such as the above. The problem is that ESM does nothing for this kind of service, it is designed to handle complex services, especially those associated with large projects or building construction etc. The main difference is that a two-stage "receipt" process is involved allowing for a confirmation of completion followed by an authorisation to pay. This functionality does not help with "normal" services and in fact, it adds extra complexity.

So if you are looking for a solution to services such as general engineers, plumbers, mechanics etc. then I would recommend that you use material masters and/or account assignment categories and raise the POs after the event. If you are dealing with complex services especially if hierarchies are involved and want two stage receiving, then ESM is ideal.

About the Author

Stephen Birchall is 52 years old and has been involved in the design and implementation of integrated business system solutions for over 25 years. He has assisted many major organisations in their use of computer systems to give them that all important "edge" over their competitors. Initially this was designing systems from scratch and then using SAP systems for the last 15 years.

He has also taught several hundred consultants how to implement SAP at SAP's premises in the UK and throughout Europe. Stephen was also asked to write some of the consultant certification exam questions for SAP AG and identify and correct any existing questions that were in error.

Stephen has implemented systems in many industries including chemical, utilities, home electronics, car manufacturers, pharmaceutical, FMCG, heavy building materials, food producers, computer manufacturers, confectionery producers, kitchen and bedroom furniture producers, personal hygiene products, Fork lift truck manufacturers, Aerospace, etc. etc.

Stephen is known for his common-sense approach mixed with the ability to use radical methods that result in simple solutions. He is also know for his sense of humour and many of his colleagues will remember just how bad the jokes were. He is also remembered for his love of unusual vehicles including his 8.2 litre V8 London Taxi that was often seen outside the SAP UK training centre while he was teaching there.

In all Stephen is highly respected by the clients he has served and his fellow colleagues and many of his engagements are as a result of him being known by someone at the client.

He is a member of Mensa with an IQ of 158.